ArtScroll Series®

Rabbi Nosson Scherman / Rabbi Meir Zlotowitz

General Editors

LIVE!

REMEMBER!

Published by

Mesorah Publications, ltd

TELL THE WORLD!

The Story of a Hidden Child Survivor of Transnistria

As told by Leah Kaufman, M.A. (Judaic Studies)
Written by Sheina Medwed

FIRST EDITION
First Impression … January 2005
SECOND EDITION
First Impression … February 2011
Second Impression … February 2018

Published and Distributed by
MESORAH PUBLICATIONS, Ltd.
4401 Second Avenue
Brooklyn, New York 11232

Distributed in Europe by
LEHMANNS
Unit E, Viking Business Park
Rolling Mill Road
Jarrow, Tyne & Wear NE32 3DP
England

Distributed in Australia & New Zealand by
GOLDS WORLD OF JUDAICA
3-13 William Street
Balaclava, Melbourne 3183
Victoria Australia

Distributed in Israel by
SIFRIATI / A. GITLER — BOOKS
POB 2351
Bnei Brak 51122

Distributed in South Africa by
KOLLEL BOOKSHOP
Northfield centre, 17 Northfield Avenue
Glenhazel 2192, Johannesburg, South Africa

ARTSCROLL HISTORY SERIES®
LIVE! REMEMBER! TELL THE WORLD!
© Copyright 2005, by MESORAH PUBLICATIONS, Ltd.
4401 Second Avenue / Brooklyn, N.Y. 11232 / (718) 921-9000 / www.artscroll.com

---

ISBN 10: 1-57819-671-X / ISBN 13: 978-1-57819-671-5 (hard cover)

Typography by CompuScribe at ArtScroll Studios, Ltd.
Printed in the United States of America by Noble Book Press Corp.
Bound by Sefercraft, Quality Bookbinders, Ltd., Brooklyn N.Y. 11232

"שמע בני מוסר אביך ואל תטש תורת אמך" (משלי א:ח)

"Listen my son to the voice of your father,
and do not forsake the teachings of your mother."

(Proverbs 1:8)

As children we have watched you
"live and remember."
We thank Hashem
for enabling us to see you "tell."
May you continue to inspire others
until 120 years.

Love,

Lisa and Seth Kaufman
Jonah, Talia, Elaina and Ariana

Baruch and Rachel Kaufman
Rivka Yocheved, Yehudis Bracha, Ruchama, Tehila,
Moshe Benzion, Elisheva Liba, Avraham Abe, Yosef,
Aaron Leib and Yaakov

Yossi Shalom and Chaviva Kaufman
Shmuel Dovid, Zivia Malka, Yechiel Menachem,
Bracha, Michael Dov, Devora Chana,
Levi Yitzchak and Tehila

FOUNDER & PRESIDENT
Rabbi Noah Weinberg

WORLD CENTER
Jerusalem, Israel

BRANCHES
Boston, MA
Boca Raton, FL
Cleveland, OH
Denver, CO
Detroit, MI
Herzliya, Israel
Johannesburg, S. Africa
Kiev, Ukraine
Las Vegas, NV
Los Angeles, CA
London, England
Melbourne, Australia
Miami, FL
Minsk, Belarussia
Moscow, Russia
New York, NY
Philadelphia, PA
Ramat Gan, Israel
Santiago, Chile
Seattle, WA
St. Louis, MO
St. Petersburg, Russia
Toronto, Canada
Washington, D.C.
Winnipeg, Canada

JERUSALEM FUND
Los Angeles, CA
Miami, FL
Toronto, Canada
New York, NY

DISCOVERY
Jerusalem, Israel
Brooklyn, NY

JERUSALEM FELLOWSHIPS
Jerusalem, Israel
Brooklyn, NY

JERUSALEM FELLOWSHIPS
Jerusalem, Israel
New York, NY

Mrs. Kaufman has for years, shared her experiences by communicating them in person to thousands of young people.   A natural educator, she knows how to touch the soul of all and never ceases to inspire with her unswerving trust in "Netzach Yisrael lo yeshaker". Future generations are fortunate in that her keen sense of historic responsibility has lead her to commit her unique story to print.

Mrs. Kaufman lived through and bears testimony to levels of human depravation on the Death Marches of the wastes of Transnistria that are unique even amidst the hell of the Holocaust.

Mrs. Kaufman survived committed to "uvacharta bachayim" She has Chosen Life and embraced her Heritage and People in a most profound way. She has never given up hope in the ultimate good and that much as men can sink to the lowest, they can too soar to the greatest heights.

We are grateful for this legacy of commitment to life.

Rabbi Noah Weinberg

One Western Wall Plaza 1 רחבת הכותל המערבי
POB 14149, Old City, Jerusalem, Israel   ת.ד. 14149, הרובע היהודי, העיר העתיקה, ירושלים
Tel: (972-2) 628-5666 • Fax: (972-2) 627-3172 • Email: Jerusalem@aish.com • http://www.aish.com

TABLE OF CONTENTS

Acknowledgments

Blessed are You, Hashem our G-d, King of the Universe,
Who has kept us alive, sustained us,
and brought us to this season.

You have changed for me my mourning into dancing,
You undid my sackcloth and girded me with joy. So that
my soul might sing to You and not be silent, Hashem,
my G-d, forever will I thank You. [Psalm 30: 12, 13]

To Hashem, for allowing me to Live, Remember, and Tell. I hope that my words will in some small way inspire others to help make this world a better place.

לזכר נשמת הורי אחי ואחיותיי וכל יהודי רומניה שנהרגו בדרך הליכות המוות ובטרנסניסטריה בלי קבר בישראל

To my parents, brothers, and sisters, and all the Jews who perished during the Holocaust in Romania and on the Death March to Transnistria.

To the Righteous Gentiles without whose courage I and countless others would not be here today.

To Pinchas and Chaya Hubberman, my foster parents, who, along with the Canadian Jewish Congress, the Canadian government, the people of Calgary, Alberta, and the Canadian citizens, who welcomed us, the destitute, Jewish orphans of the Holocaust. Your humanitarian act empowered us to create a better tomorrow for ourselves and for the country we love.

To Dr. Seth and Lisa Kaufman, for underwriting this book, for encouragement and for constant support by urging me to write for the sake of future generations. For blessing us with Jonah, Talia, Elaina, and Ariana.

To Rabbi Baruch David and Rachelle Kaufman, "our first *olim*," for their love and devotion, and for always understanding our needs. For blessing us with Rivka, her husband Menachem Eisenbach, and their daughter Goldie; Bracha, her husband Chaim Weiss, and their daughters Malka and Miriam; Ruchama, her husband Avraham Mose Schwarts, and their daughter Raizel; Tehilla and her husband Avigdor Weiss; Moishe and his wife Batya (nee Mesner); Elisheva, Avraham Abbe, Yosef, Aaron Leib, and Yaakov.

To Joseph Shalom and Chaviva Kaufman, for always being there for us, for making our *aliyah* to Israel easier, for opening important doors for us, and for introducing us to the Beitar community who became our friends. For blessing us with Shmuel Dovid, Zivia Malka, Yechiel Menachem, Bracha, Michael Dov, Devora Chana, and Levi Yitzchak, and Tehilla.

To Aaron and Helen Yermus of Toronto, for their friendship, love, and hospitality; who nurtured me during my most difficult times as well as during our times of joy. They will always be our children's aunt and uncle.

To my beloved late brother and sister-in-law, Avraham and Betty Buimaz, and our beloved nieces and nephews: Shmuel and Tzila Etzion and family of Netanya, Israel; Dov and Yehudit Gofer and family of Kiryat Gat, Israel; Yuval and Sara Lampel and family of Hod Hasharon, Israel; Yehudit and Shmuel Hiley and family London, England; James and Sarah Bell and family, Toronto, Canada; Eleanor and Jeremy Zeid and family, London, England.

To Rabbi Naftali Shiff, Director of Aish HaTorah, UK and his devoted staff, who made it possible for me to speak to the thousands of students across England in schools and universities.

To Brian and Fiona Rabinovitch, our hosts for my first Aish HaTorah sponsored speaking tour in England. To Rael and Lorne Gordon and their children, for the incredible warmth and love received during my second and third Aish HaTorah Universities and Schools speaking tour of England, and for sponsoring the Hebrew translation of this book.

To Rabbi Nechemiah Coopersmith, of Aish HaTorah, Jerusalem, for his encouragement and support, and for publicizing my message.

To Mina and Yechiel Glustein, our wonderful neighbors and loyal friends, who made us part of their family. Within their home I learned how to celebrate life even while mourning. Their *ahavat Yisrael* knows no bounds.

To all the students of the international community who heard me speak at Yad Vashem, Michalalot, Yeshivot, Aish, Discovery, Fellowships, universities, and synagogues in Israel, England, USA, and Canada.

To Dr. Joshua and Gelle Fishman, Riverdale, NY, for their friendship, love and support at all times. They provided a home away from home for Seth, Baruch, and Yossi, while they studied at Yeshiva University in New York.

To all my hidden child survivors, adopted siblings, especially to Renata Zajdman, Prof. Yehudi and Francoise Lindeman, my sibling of the Shoah, Marcel and Marilyn Tannenbaum, Bela and Herschl Teichman.

To all my wonderful friends who helped me reach this point in my life, my students, parents, and co-workers; Beth Zion Ladies Torah Class; Eleanor Birenbaum; Mr. and Mrs. Fred Bettman; our beloved machutonim, Prof. and Mrs. Cyril Domb; and Dr. Larry and Diane Wruble; Rita Bosin; the late Dr. and Mrs Lou Boxer; Dr. Claudio Feler; Mr. and Mrs Zvi Feldman, for our friendship of 56 years; the late Mr. Myer Fenig; Mrs. Bina Fenig; Dr. and Mrs. Quentin Fisher; Rabbi Pincus Kantrowitz; Dr. Bella Kisselman; Dr. Irene Kuphersmidt; Ben and Chana Marmor; Mr. and Mrs. David Saxe; Rabbi and Mrs. Sydney Shoham; Mr. and Mrs. Neil Tryanski; and the late Mrs.Toby Verblunski.

אחרון אחרון חביב – The last is the most precious.

To my husband Mark, ע"ה, my beloved companion of 57 years, my best friend who was a constant source of encouragement and support. Mark meticulously recorded all of my presentations. Without his help I couldn't have gotten this far.

Leah Kaufman
January 2010

Note: To contact Leah Kaufman or schedule a speaking engagement, visit liveremembertell.com.

Blessed is Hashem, who does kindness with the undeserving, and who has given me the privilege to meet, learn from, and write about Leah Kaufman, who emerged from the death fires of Transnistria, with her faith in G-d, her commitment to Judaism, and her belief in humanity intact.

Mark Kaufman, Leah's husband, was a loyal and meticulous assistant. Mark recorded and catalogued Leah's speeches and documents, updated her resume, and collected the thousands of response letters from the audiences at her speaking engagements. Mark contributed constructive criticism to each chapter. A devoted husband, proud father, grandfather, and great-grandfather, Mark accompanied Leah and attended to the technical requirements of her presentations.

I am grateful to Dr. Seth and Lisa Kaufman, who generously sponsored this project. Rabbi Baruch and Rachel Kaufman, and Rabbi Yossi and Chaviva Kaufman have provided support and encouragement along the way.

Hashem has blessed this project with two creative collaborators who have been on call, day and night. Arline Chase has been available to encourage, critique, research, answer questions, provide professional guidance, and emotional support. Professor Richard Alan White, historian, Fulbright scholar, and author of *Breaking Silence, the Case that Changed the Face of Human Rights* (Georgetown University Press, 2004), has been a teacher and creative guide for me. Leah and I were honored and grateful that he agreed to check the historical data in the chapters. However, Professor White has gone far beyond the verification of information. Often working with Arline against the clock, in the midst of the final preparations of his own book, Professor White has given his complete and wholehearted devotion to this project because of his own dedication to human rights issues. He has been a wellspring of relentless constructive criticism, and has given me both intellectual and emotional support.

I am grateful to the many people and institutions who helped me with different aspects of this book: Professor Martin Kempner, National Director of The Bard College Clemente

Program; Dr. David Williamson, chairman of the Sociology Department at The University of North Texas; Reb Shmuel Blitz, of Artscroll, Jerusalem; Rabbi Pincus Kantrovitch; Avraham Scheinman, Aish HaTorah in England, New York, and Jerusalem; Rabbi and Rebbetzin Heyman; Ahuvah Gray, Ellen Lawson, Loretta Sherman, Mrs. Aviva Rapapport, of Jerusalem Publications; Aviva Zweig; Debbie Goldberg; Lisa Aurel; Ruth Pepperman; Esther Leah Lewin; Kim Benjamin; Tzvia Ben Chaim; Bathsheva Gefen; Rebbetzin Horowitz; and Shulamit Tilles.

I am deeply grateful to Gele Fishman, Leah's lifetime friend, who received me in her Riverdale home — in New York — and spent hours speaking with me about the Hebrew Yiddish Teachers seminary in Montreal. Her penetrating insight into Leah's development helped me with the middle chapters of the book.

It was a privilege to speak with Gisela Tamler, author of *Before and After, Surviving the Romanian Holocaust in Transnistria*, and the persistent force behind Leah's decision to speak out.

Many thanks to the staff at the Yad Vashem library and archives: Dr. Bella Gutterman of the Yad Vashem Publications department, Nava Weiss, and to Professor Jean Ancel, who spent eighteen years compiling research on the Holocaust in Romania.

There is an infrastructure to this book. It is made of prayer. My mother, Mrs. Rose Kempner, may she live and be well, prayed day and night for the successful completion of this project. Her midnight phone calls and inevitable inquiries of "Nu, what did you do today for the book?" were a source of vitality and rejuvenation. One of my best critics, she has given me advice as both a person with a reservoir of life wisdom and as an educated reader.

My husband, Zalman Medwed, and my son, Yitzchak, have taken devoted care of their "writer in residence." I am deeply grateful to my husband for reading parts of this manuscript and helping me to clarify and express certain difficult concepts.

Primary source documentation for this book includes oral and written interviews with Leah Kaufman, audiotapes and transcripts of her presentations from 1995 to the present, and her extensive annotations in books and articles. Each chapter was reviewed many times by Leah and Mark Kaufman to check for accuracy.

Leah, you trusted me with your life, and we journeyed together. May the wandering of the Divine Presence cease. May our people all return. May we see the "House of Prayer for all People," the rebuilding of Jerusalem, and the coming of the Redeemer speedily in our days, Amen.

Sheina Medwed
Har Nof, Jerusalem

INTRODUCTION

"FACING IT"

by Sheina Medwed

I t was late afternoon on a crisp winter day in Jerusalem. My seven-year-old son and his friends were in the backyard digging for earthworms. My husband's chiropractic patients were sitting in the waiting area of our living room office. The strains of the Vivaldi concerto coming from the stereo lifted my heart as I watched the sky, colored with purple, magenta, and pale blue-pink, turn to dark blue. It was almost time to call in the boys and make the transition to evening.

Sitting at the kitchen table, I looked at the pile of papers in front of me, my third batch of stories almost finished and ready to be a book. *I'll give it just a few more minutes*, I thought. *Just one more page.*

As I reached for my pen, a familiar voice greeted me, "Hi, Sheina, what are you doing?"

I looked up. "Yossie Kaufman!" I greeted him. "How are you?"

"*Baruch Hashem*. My back needs an adjustment. My brother Baruch recommended that I see your husband. What are you doing, Sheina? What are all these papers?"

"I'm writing a book."

"Really! *B'hatzlachah*. About what?"

"About Jewish women."

"Sheina, if you're writing a book about Jewish women, you have to meet my mother. She's amazing. She's a hidden child survivor from Transnistria and her story is one miracle after another."

"Trans- what?"

"Transnistria."

"I've never heard of such a place. Where was that?"

"Transnistria was an area in the southwest Ukraine that was bordered by the Dniester River, the Bug River, and the Black Sea. It was a German-occupied territory, but at the beginning of the war when Hitler and the Romanian dictator, Ion Antonescu, were allies, Hitler 'rewarded' Romania with governmental control over that area. Marshal Antonescu set up a military government modeled on German principles, with the specific intention of making it a mass graveyard for Romanian Jews.[1] Recently, Transnistria has come to be known as the 'Romanian Auschwitz.'"[2]

"But I thought Romania was good to the Jews during the war. I thought they fought against Hitler."

"That was only at the very end, when it became clear that Hitler was going to be defeated. Then they modified their policies and presented a different face to the world. Before the war, Romania had the third-largest Jewish population in Europe, about 850,000. A lot of people think that it was a haven for the Jews during the war. But the truth is that half of our people, some 400,000 souls, were massacred. The Romanians often were more brutal than the Germans! Before the Nazis even set up the gas chambers, Romania set about 'cleansing' the country of Jews. The military dictator, Marshal Antonescu, was proud to be known as the 'Romanian Fuhrer.'

"After the war, he was brought to justice and executed for his crimes. But in the last ten years or so, Antonescu has been rehabilitated. Streets have been named after him, and plaques

---

1. Ancel, Jean, *Transnistria, The Rumanian Mass Murder Campaigns, Volume One, History and Document Summaries*, p.17.

2. Carmelly, Felicia, *Shattered! 50 Years of Silence, History and Voices of the Tragedy in Rumania and Transnistria*, p. 72.

and busts of him have been put into government buildings. At the monument dedicated to his memory, a moment of silence is even observed on the anniversary of Antonescu's execution!"

"Why is so little known about this place?"

"That's a good question. Historically, it's partly because of geography, unstable borders, political policies, and the fact that after the war, that area was taken over by the Red Army. Information about the other European concentration camps was documented by the Allied forces, but information about Transnistria was hidden.[3] As a matter of fact, until about fifteen years ago, you couldn't even find it on a Holocaust map.

"The other reason Transnistria was shrouded in mystery was because so many of the people who did survive were children who were so traumatized by the horror that they couldn't speak about it until much later in their lives. My mother was one of those children and, like I said, her story is one miracle after another."

"What do you mean by 'miracles'?"

"Let me give you a short example: She was hiding with her parents and six siblings in an abandoned home when the Romanian *gendarmes* burst in, searched the house, and lined up the whole family to be shot. Suddenly the commander recognized that my Bubbie, my mother's mother, had been his midwife and family doctor. He ordered, 'Put down your guns! I can't kill this lady. She brought me into the world and saved my life many times. I can't kill her and I can't kill her children. Let's go.'

"But that was before the Death March. Many months later, when they finally reached Transnistria, my mother was the only surviving member of her family. She was nine years old."

I sat there stunned. Of course I wanted to hear that story and include it in my book, but I felt apprehensive about meeting Yossie's mother. I couldn't bear to hear about all the tragedies she'd experienced. I couldn't even begin to imagine the constant pain she carried with her as an adult. I was afraid to write about a hid-

---

3. Carmelly, *The Nizkor Project.* www.nizkor.org.

den child Holocaust survivor. I didn't want to face that part of my people's history and that part of my personal identity as a Jew.

Suddenly, I remembered the first time I had ever seen evidence of the death camps. It was when I was eighteen years old, a freshman at Rutgers, and overwhelmed with term papers to write. The student center on campus was located not far from the library. In the student center was a small candy store. One day, on my way to the library, I stopped in to buy some chocolate. As I took a bite I froze. To the left of the candy vendor, at the entrance to the student center, was a life-size photograph of an Auschwitz survivor. It was part of a month-long exhibit of the concentration camps.

I could barely swallow. I closed the bag of chocolates and made my way slowly through the aisles of photographs, my stomach knotted and throat tightened. I wanted to run out of there, to escape, far, far away to a world where evil did not exist. There were pictures of Auschwitz, Bergen-Belsen, Treblinka, and other concentration camps, but I didn't remember seeing anything about Transnistria.

I was a Jew. What did this mean to me? The juxtaposition of the skeletal survivors in their striped prison rags standing behind the barbed wire, and the bag of chocolates in my hand, also told a story. I, too, was in a picture frame and this stance was my portrait. I stood in that frame, an eighteen-year-old blond, green-eyed college student who knew next to nothing about her heritage, her culture, and her people.

The emaciated prisoner with the star on his shirt seemed to stare at me. What did that Yellow Star mean to me? Did it touch my daily life? Did it affect my future? On the surface, not at all. But it touched my core. It touched me in a place so deep that I didn't yet know it existed. It bound me to an ancestral past that coursed through my blood with an imprint that went beyond my personal life. It called out to me with a voice echoing from the blood-soaked earth of a 3,500-year history: "You are also a Jew! Had you been born at a different time, in a dif-

ferent country, you might also have worn this star. Face me. Face yourself. Face your link in the chain of Jewish destiny."

"Maidele (little girl)," the prisoner seemed to whisper in a cracked, dry voice, "Hitler didn't care about religion. All one needed was one drop of Jewish blood. And look what happened! Do you know who did this to us? It wasn't just the uneducated peasants. It was the elite of the society, the cultured people, the intellectuals. They became the worst executioners."

I stood there, shaken and silent. And a part of me wanted to scream in response, "Leave me alone and let me eat my chocolate." Shocked, horrified, and confused, I forced myself to continue on my way to the library, haunted by the fact that someday I would have to face all this.

I tried to shake off the horrible images that had surfaced in my mind, and to pay attention to what Yossie was saying about his mother. How could anyone live through something like that? How could a nine-year-old child survive? How could a person rebuild a life from such a shattered place? How could a person emerge from such a hell and maintain her faith?

I looked up at Yossie, who had just given me a gift from his personal history, and I asked, "How can I meet your mother? Where does she live? Do you think she'll talk to me?"

One year later, in that same kitchen, I met Leah.

Sitting at the kitchen table with the tape recorder on, I studied the face of this petite, blue-eyed, blond lady. There was an aliveness and openness in her expression. In a soft, low voice, Leah spoke for two and a half hours about her life. Over and over, through my tears, I marveled at the fact that Leah wasn't bitter. Leah hated no one. Leah was full of love — love for life, for G-d, for the Jewish people, and for humanity.

But for almost half a century, she had been silent about her past.

"I wanted to raise my children as normal Canadian kids," Leah told me. "I did not want to inflict the anguish and terror of my past on their childhoods. But when the Holocaust deniers came to the fore in Canada, I resolved to break my silence. I realized that by remaining silent, I was an accomplice of the enemy. I decided that no matter what inner hell I had to go through, I would begin educating the world about Transnistria."

"Leah," I said, as I turned off the recorder, "you did more than survive. You rebuilt your life and transformed yourself. You could have chosen to remain silent. Yet for the sake of future generations, you continually force yourself to tell your story and to relive your pain."

I knew I was in the presence of a rare and dignified person — someone who had been thrown into the personal and historical furnace of suffering, and who had emerged with a wholeness and faith that had transformed her very being. Now she was sharing this tragic part of her life with the world, but it wasn't for the sake of revenge; it was for education, Jewish continuity, and noble ideals. It was for the sake of helping the world reach a higher level of humanity.

How did she do it?

How was it possible for Leah to pick up the fragments of her identity and move forward to forge a new life? How could I face the prospect of going along with her into her memory to record that part of her personal and collective history that was branded into her soul in letters of blood? For the sake of those who were forever silenced, Leah forced herself to remember. For the sake of those who will carry our history into the future, we must record, we must listen.

Here is Leah's story.

Let her speak for herself.

CHAPTER 1

LEAH, YOU MUST SPEAK FOR US

I t was a late November afternoon in 1993, and I was on my way home from teaching at the Peretz School. My fourth graders were excited about their learning. The Sukkos party in my garden had been a great success. Parents were still calling to thank me for helping their children develop a love of Hebrew and Yiddish, along with strong feelings of Jewish pride. My heart was always with my students. I carried their names and faces with me wherever I went.

As I walked along Montreal's Leger Avenue towards my home, I noticed that the maple trees in our Côte St.-Luc neighborhood arched their autumn branches in a red-golden hue above my head. The Montreal sky was turning blue-gray, an indication of the coming winter. As I looked up, a familiar feeling of foreboding and uneasiness gripped me as the haunted past that I carried daily bore witness to my silent, inner life.

I looked down at my feet, warm in new fur-lined winter boots, but the feet that I saw were bare, red, bruised, and frozen from the cold. It was right around this time of the year, when I was a little girl of nine, that the Romanian soldiers had forced me, along with my family, out of our home to begin the Death March. We left together with the remnants of the Jewish community from our town of Herta, in the Dorohoi county, in the Moldova region of Romania. We were brutally driven, in sub-freezing temperatures, on the Death March to Transnistria, that forgotten cemetery, that piece of land designated for the purpose of making Romania *Judenrein* (free of Jews).[1] Most people were ignorant of Romania's support of Hitler. Romania joined the allies only in the summer of 1944, when it was clear that Hitler was losing the war.

I turned my key and heard the familiar sound of the lock clicking open. As I walked into the entranceway of my home, I noticed the red message light flashing on the answering machine. I pressed the button and listened to the recording. "Hello, Mrs. Kaufman, this is Gisela Tamler. I'm putting together a group of people to help publicize and memorialize what happened in Transnistria, and I need you to help me."

I stood there immobile, with a deep chill spreading throughout my body. *No,* I thought, *I can't get involved in this. I'll call her right away and refuse.* I dialed her number with trembling fingers. "Mrs. Tamler, this is Leah Kaufman. Yes, I am a survivor, but please — I don't want to talk about it. I don't even want to think about it. The pain is always in my heart, and I will never forget it, but I don't want anybody to know. My husband doesn't know the full extent of my pain, and my children don't know either. I'm a teacher here, I'm known in the community, and I don't want to go public."

The next call came the following week. It turned out that Gisela Tamler had known my parents. Our families had lived opposite each other on Peacock Street in the town of Herta.

---

1. Hilberg, Raul, *Destruction of the European Jews*, p. 495.

The year that I was born, Gisela got married and moved to the home of her husband's parents in Czernowitz, a neighboring town. During the beginning of her marriage, Gisela recalled, she used to come by bus to visit her parents and she would often see a little blue-eyed girl with long blond braids playing outside. "I thought," Gisela confided, "that since your brothers and sisters were all dark-haired, you must be a servant's child! One day, I finally asked my mother, 'Mameh, who is that little *shikse* (non-Jewish girl) who is always playing in front of the Buimaz house?'

"'That's Lea'le. She's their seventh child.'

"'Mameh, she's so fair-skinned.' I just couldn't believe that you were actually your parents' child."

Gisela had recently heard my name mentioned by a child survivor in Toronto, who somehow knew that I had lived through Transnistria. Still, despite this close connection between us, I repeated my staunch refusal. "Gisela, I've managed to build a normal life and I don't want to go public." I knew that as a survivor, Gisela had the quality of persistence, but I was totally unprepared for her response:

"Leah, there is no way that you will escape me! I'll call you day and night until you give in!"

Gisela Tamler was true to her word. But after that, I didn't return her calls. I didn't want to speak to her, to be convinced to go through hell again. Although I felt harassed, I was awestruck by her perseverance. Morning, noon, and night, day in and day out, she left me messages. "Leah, I will not let you rest. You cannot allow those martyrs to be forgotten. You are a person with an education; only you can help me." Gisela repeated my name, her voice becoming almost shrill: "Leah, you must speak for us!"

For one entire year, I refused her requests and I ignored her incessant messages. Yet her pleas now haunted me. How could I possibly relive the torture and death of that horrendous time of my life and share my experiences with the public? I knew that I was living with a monster inside of me, pretending that it didn't exist. I chose to live in a different kind of hiding, to become Canadian and pretend that things hadn't happened. I wanted to give my children the best Jewish education, and to raise them to have a normal life. I wanted to shield them from the trauma of knowing about my pain.

It took almost fifty years of silence before Gisela managed to make me realize the urgency of testifying as a witness who had experienced the hell called Transnistria.

Transnistria literally means the other side of the Dniester River. It bordered a 24,840-square mile piece of fertile land in the southwestern Ukraine. In August 1941, as a reward for the "splendid military operations and the extraordinary spirit of sacrifice demonstrated by the Romanian armies" against the Soviet Union, Hitler gave the Romanian dictator, Ion Antonescu, governmental control over this piece of land.[2]

Structured according to the *Fuhrerprinzip* (Fuhrer principle), Transnistria's civilian governor was Professor Gheorghe Alexianu, whose reputation as an extreme nationalist descended from a family of anti-Semitic jurists was well known. Prior to leaving his province in Romania, Alexianu met with a German delegation sent by Heinrich Himmler to discuss the structure of the government and to request that Germany be granted permission to "handle" Romania's Jews. But Romanian Marshal Antonescu didn't want to hand over "his" Jews to Nazi Germany. He preferred to capitalize on the ancestral anti-Semitism that simmered in the hearts of the local populations. From uncouth peasant to cultured elite, everyone joined the brutal persecution and murder of the Jews.

Centuries before the German gas chambers, "Anti-Semitism, as a form of social expression ... always existed in the life of Romanian society."[3] Romania was a country whose vile and

2. Ancel, p. 17.

3. Butnaru, I. C., *The Silent Holocaust: Romania and Its Jews (Contributions to the Study of World History)*, Forward by Eli Wiesel, p.1.

bitter anti-Semitic history created a national furnace of hatred towards the resident Jewish "aliens." The construction of this furnace spanned the centuries. Its smoldering layers were composed of religious, legal, economic, intellectual, social, political, and cultural coals, which ignited the ancient flames of Jew-hatred in the hearts of Romanians in every single stratum of the society.

Romanian children were born and bred in the cradle of hatred. This feeling was fed to babies with their mother's milk, to children in the public schools that banned Jews, and to the students in universities that allowed only 15% of the Jewish applicants to pass the entrance exams, and then to enter at exorbitant fees and to study under abusive, oppressive, and often physically dangerous conditions. With rare exception, Jews were legally prohibited from entering the legal, medical, and tobacco industries. Most were forced to earn a living as workers such as merchants, tailors, shoemakers, blacksmiths, water carriers, and other occupations.

Romanian soil had often borne witness to spontaneous pogroms and blood libels. In the late 1800s, the coals of this furnace were stoked by King Carol in his "Law of Aliens." Fueled by the fierce opposition to the Berlin Laws mandating Jewish citizenship, and by the anti-Jewish propaganda that the Romanian government circulated at home and abroad,[4] the Antonescu regime needed only to "strike a match" for the entire country to ignite into raging flames of Jew-hatred that resulted in brutality and violence that equaled and at times surpassed that of the Nazi beast.

Romania was unique among the European countries. She had been in secret alliances with Germany since 1883[5]. With Hitler's rise to power, Romania began to formulate its own structured plan to exterminate the Jews.

---

4. Butnaru, p. 28.
5. Butnaru, p. 30.

POLIȚIA ORAȘULUI BACAU

ANUNȚ

In 48 ore, orice evreu și evreică, vor purta pe piept în partea stângă, steaua evreiască (două triunghiuri suprapuse) din postav galben, a căror laturi vor fi de 6 cm. fiecare, afară de cei imbrăcați militari în serviciul armatei.

Cei ce nu se vor conforma, după această dată, vor fi arestați și predați organelor polițienești și comandaturii militare.

4 IULIE 1941

Șeful Poliției,
Subinspector I. CUPTOR

An edict by police in the Romanian city of Bacau ordering every Jew to wear a Yellow Star

Initially, Romania embraced Hitler and did its best to duplicate his barbarism, with less sophisticated means. Romania was a country primed for Hitler. *Romania was not invaded by the Germans, but invited them in!* The Nazis were welcomed into Romania to help make Romania *Judenrein.*

Transnistria is not found on a regular map, only on a Holocaust map. Transnistria was created for the sole purpose of having a place to torture and to exterminate the Romanian Jews of the provinces of Bessarabia (Basarabia), Bukovina, and Moldova. Each one of Transnistria's villages became either a death camp or a labor camp. Shrouded in silent mystery, very little was known and less was recorded about these mass burial grounds.

Gisela was asking not only for my historical testimony, but for much, much more. I shuddered to think that I would have to recount the death and brutality that my nine-year-old eyes had witnessed. Although I had nightmares every night, I had never been compelled to speak about the horrors I had experienced, or the images that haunted me. How could I live through the torture of both remembering and speaking about my past?

Yet a voice within me presented an opposing argument. I had survived in such miraculous ways. Did G-d keep me alive so that I could hide behind a nice, quiet personal life?

Or did my moral imperative to confront my past place me in a framework of collective history? I had given my children a strong Jewish education, religious training, and a deep sense of Jewish pride. Perhaps now I was being given another task: to contribute to world memory a firsthand account of man's capacity for evil, and to testify to the ability of the human soul to transcend it.

One night, during Pesach (Passover) of the year of Gisela's incessant phone calls, unable to fall asleep, I had a particularly vivid recollection of my first anti-Semitic experience. It was not unusual for me to be tormented by the images of my past before I fell asleep, but this time, the force of this memory shook my conscience. It was as though my memory itself were pleading for a voice.

Although I was allowed to play outside my home, I learned at age four-and-a-half that the Romanian children, some of whom were my friends, reflected their parents' deep historical hatred towards the Jews. This is what happened:

My mother had finished braiding my hair, as she or one of my sisters did every morning. "Lea'le," my mother whispered, as she tied the pink ribbons on the ends of my braids, "today, you must stay home." It was the beginning of springtime, when the days were getting warmer and the new blades of green grass were just starting to push their way up through the last remaining patches of snow.

I stamped my foot near the wood-burning stove in the middle of our kitchen.

"But Mameh," I whined as I pulled on the pockets of her blue wool dress, "I want to play with Vera."

"Vera has a holiday today, and she can't play with you."

I stood in the warm kitchen, looking out the window. The shaft of sunlight shining in seemed like an inviting hand to the world of the large yard that surrounded our house. As I looked outside, I wished I could run off to school as usual, to my kindergarten, where I was already learning the Hebrew and Romanian letters. My teacher said that I would learn to read quickly, and then I could help the other children.

"I know, Mameh, she told me that she has a big party. I won't stay a long time."

"Listen to me, Lea'le; stay home."

Undaunted by the firm edge in my mother's voice but outwardly obedient, I reached for my school bag under the table and took out the pages with the capital letters. As the day progressed, my mother, a midwife and healer, became busy preparing herbal tinctures. I waited for an unsupervised moment, and quickly sneaked out the door to our front yard. The frozen winter earth was beginning to thaw, and the bare branches bore tiny buds that were coiled tight with the promise of new life. I looked up and down the street, and then I saw them.

"Vera!" I called, as I ran towards my friend and her brothers. Dressed in holiday clothing, they were walking down Peacock Street towards their neighboring house. After my exuberant greeting, Vera and her brothers pounced on me like wildcats, beating me, pounding my head and feet against the cold earth. "Killer! You killer!" they screamed over and over. I do not know what finally made them stop.

Somehow, gathering my strength, I managed to stand up. Bleeding, limping, and crying hysterically, I ran back home, straight to my mother's arms.

"Who did I kill, Mameh? Who did I kill?"

Holding me tightly, she reassured me in a choked voice, "You didn't kill anyone, my precious child. Please, next time you are told not to go out, please stay home."

My mother held my bleeding face in her hands and studied my eyes, trying to discern how dark was the shadow that had formed in them. Until that moment, my mother had successfully shielded me from the occasional anti-Semitic outbursts of our neighbors. But now my eyes had seen their first act of cruelty, of my own friends turning against me.

Vera was my friend. We played in each other's yards. We shared dolls and fed the ducks. We walked in the same direction to school every morning. Why was this morning so different?

My mother's hands were firm yet gentle as they cleaned the blood off my bruised, swelling face. As a midwife and healer, her hands were used only to heal, to comfort, to bring life into the world for Jew and gentile alike.

"Lea'le," she repeated, as she hugged me close to her, "we live in difficult and terrible times. But you must know that everything Hashem does is always for the best." My mother's voice was soft and gentle, with no harsh edge of hatred towards the children who had beaten me. It was at this tender age that I internalized my mother's love for humanity. It was then that I learned not to hate. People who succumbed to subhuman brutality were to be pitied, but never imitated. I was taught to aspire to a lofty and exalted character with an eternal purpose.

Until this point in my early childhood, I had been spared the brutal side of my community's life. I lived in an almost idyllic world. My young mind, eager and quick to learn, was always questioning, absorbing, and searching for details.

As the youngest child, I was constantly cherished, nurtured, and educated by my loving and devoted parents and siblings: three full brothers, Nathan, Chaim, and Bentzion; and three sisters, identical twins Rivka and Liebe, and Devorah, the youngest before me; and my two half brothers, Avraham and Cesar, from my father's first marriage.

I did not know when I stepped out of my house that day that I had stepped into a world where the latent anti-Semitism was coming to the fore. Now, with my first beating, I had acquired my place in the ancient story of my people. At that moment, when I greeted my friends, I stood at a meeting point of my personal life and our history.

Besides being the adored youngest child in my family, I was a Jew. I was a representative of the Jewish people. For that fact alone, I was beaten till I bled. My clothing was torn, my braids were ripped apart, and my leg was pounded so badly that I could only limp home. Thus began my education in the dark side of world history. At the age of four and a half, that venomous reality was beaten into my bones: "You are a Jew? I will kill you for that, and for that alone."

After Easter passed, although I was hurt and confused by having been beaten, it was as though nothing had happened. Vera and I went back to being "friends," and subsequently, I heeded my mother's warnings.

For the next five years, my life continued along smoothly and peacefully, until that horrific night that brought my childhood to an abrupt and brutal end. Until that time, unbeknownst to my innocent heart, this beating was but a foreshadowing of the evil that was to come upon my family and upon our nation. Yet my mother's response taught me an eternal lesson. We must leave revenge for the Master of the World. We have always been, and must remain, a noble people.

These thoughts, memories, and emotions now pursued me as relentlessly as Gisela's telephone calls. One day, upon my return from a trip to Memphis to visit my eldest son Seth, his wife, Lisa, and their children, Jonah, Talia, Elaina, and Ariana, I found my answering machine filled to capacity with one message after another from Gisela. Finally, still fearful, I agreed to meet with her, just so that she would stop hounding me. But after meeting Gisela and speaking to her, I became convinced that she was right. I agreed to face the agonizing prospect of bearing witness to the horrors of Transnistria.

In 1941, as we trudged along on the Death March, starving and broken on the freezing roads, my mother, of blessed memory, would say to me over and over: *"Du muzt lebn, du muzt gedenken, du muzt dertzeiln der velt vos die Rumanier hobn tzu undz geton* — You must live, you must remember, you must tell the world what the Romanians did to us."

How did she know she should tell this to me? Did she know that I would be the only one of her children to survive? Did G-d grant her broken heart a hint of prophecy so that she could invest me with a larger purpose, and charge me with a historical mission? "Live! Remember! Tell the world!"

Now, along with Gisela's incessant pleading, I heard the lament of my mother's command. I realized that no matter what the sacrifice, I had to publicize my story.

But how is one to say, how is one to communicate, that which by its very nature defies language? How is one to tell without betraying the dead, without betraying oneself? And yet, I realized that to keep my memory in a vault was to grant victory to the deniers of the Romanian Holocaust. The executioner often kills twice: The first time is when he kills. The second time is when he tries to eradicate the evidence of his crime.

Our identity papers were destroyed but the Nazis and the Romanian gendarmes could never succeed in destroying my Jewish identity. Our killers tried to expel us from history or, worse still, to deprive us of our history altogether. They tried to prevent our lives and deaths from becoming part of human memory. I finally came to realize that by refusing to remember and then refusing to testify, I was becoming the enemy's accomplice. Whosoever contributes to oblivion finishes the killer's work. It thus became a vital necessity for me to bear witness lest I inadvertently find myself in the enemy's camp.

Gisela's pleading, love, and encouragement started me on another journey. I was compelled to return in my memory to that forgotten graveyard called Transnistria. I had to travel again and again through the agonizing loss of my family and childhood. I was forced to face the demons of my personal past, and in doing so, to affirm the miracles that saved me, and the prophetic mission of my mother's words. I was not merely one child who had survived. I had to become the collective voice for the hundreds of thousands of Jewish children who were brutally murdered and who perished on the roads, in the ghettos, and in the labor camps of Transnistria. Their souls are crying out to us. My story is their story. For the remembrance of our past, for the truthful identity of our future, we must listen.

CHAPTER 2

LIFE AT HOME

From the age of about five, I would occasionally have the privilege of accompanying my dear mother on her midnight journeys. I was the youngest of her children, often sickly, and very attached to her. It was hard for me to fall asleep without her soothing presence. On Shabbos, when my mother would take her nap, I would hold my golden braids behind my neck and gently put my ear against her chest. The rhythmic beating of her heart reassured me that her sleep was but a brief interlude in her active, loving life. Then I would go outside to play.

Mother's work as a healer fascinated and enthralled my ever-curious mind. In late spring, summer, and early autumn, she would take her special jar and we would walk hand in hand, past the attached houses of the town, down to the green wooded edge of the Hertzushka River, after which the town Herta (Hertza) was named.

My hometown of Herta, located between Dorohoi and Chernovitz, had a vibrant Jewish community with four synagogues, two cemeteries, and a hospital. It was established by Jews in the early 18th century. The lord of the province, Ghica, was given the land on which Herta was built as a wedding gift by Prince Mihai Racovita. Ghica had invited Jews from Poland to come to Herta and establish a town upon his land. Having seen the expansion of the province of Moldova that resulted from the Jewish presence there, Ghica had hoped that the Jews would build and develop his land and cause it to prosper[1].

As we walked to the river, my mother would point to the surrounding forest and warn me, "Never go there alone, Lea'le; it's dangerous." She knew it was a dwelling place for bandits, thieves, and highway robbers. People of Herta would say that when the town was first founded, the forest was so dangerous that residents leaving the city on a journey would first make a will, say *viduy*, and give their wives a bill of divorce, in case they never returned.

Once we reached the river, my mother would show me how to differentiate between various types of leeches. Only the ones to be used for healing were plopped into our jar. She made sure to tell me to scoop up some mud and river water so that the leeches would feel at home in the jar. When we got back home, the jar would be properly covered and placed on the shelf of the backyard shed, sharing a place with her herbal medicines.

In addition to being a midwife and a healer, Mother knew which foods were harmful and which foods were known to heal. She expertly made preserves and all sorts of unusual jams, such as rose petal jelly. Miniature pickled watermelon was a winter delicacy and the Shabbos table was incomplete without her Kiddush wine and *vishniak l'chayim* brandy made from sour cherries.

Mother, the youngest of many children, received all this knowledge from her mother, my Bubbe Leah, who lived to be 102 years old. Bubbe Leah was known for her righteousness and healing skills. How I wish I could remember details of the

---

1. *Encyclopedia of Jewish Communities, Romania, Vol. I*, Daf Chen Press, 1969, Jerusalem, Yad Vashem.

many amazing stories that were told about her. Although I never got to meet Bubbe Leah in person, the fact that I was her namesake made a very deep impression on me. I couldn't have been more than three years old when I stood up on a chair in front of a house full of guests and announced, "I remember Bubbe Leah — I'm named after her!" My latent desire to be a doctor must have been due to the family tradition of healing that began with Bubbe Leah.

When we would come to the home of one of her patients, Mameh would take out her *bankes* cups. These special round jars were used to draw fever and heat out of the body. First, she would wipe the inside of the jar with alcohol. Then she would quickly ignite it with a flame. Her hands moved with lightning speed as she placed the heated cup on the patient's skin.

I would watch in fascination as the cup turned blue, and I wondered if the skin would get burned. Miraculously, the skin only puckered into a bright pink ball suctioned under the heated glass. Many a midnight crisis responded to the *bankes* cup, blood-letting, and herbal treatments.

The most wondrous moments of my early childhood were when I went with Mameh to attend a birth. I would stand outside the birthing room waiting and listening for the baby's first cry. I was then invited in to look at and hold the baby. With a heart full of joy, I would cradle the newborn baby in my young arms. Even at my tender age, I knew I was witnessing the awesome and majestic Hand of the One Who creates new life.

In Romania, with rare exception, Jews were legally barred from the upper-echelon professions. Although there was a wealthy Jewish segment of manufacturers and distributors, most of the Jewish residents were craftsmen or merchants. My blond and blue-eyed father Shmuel was a textile merchant. During the day, he was out providing for us. In the evening when I wanted to see him, I knew I would find him in the *beis midrash*, leaning over his volume of the Talmud. When he saw me he always welcomed me warmly. I would climb up onto his lap, put my arms around him, and listen to the chant of his learning. I felt that I had entered a very special place. I loved both of my parents dearly. My mother, however, became my role model. Subconsciously, I must have decided that when I grew up, I wanted to be like her. My mother was very beautiful, with a pale complexion and dark brown eyes. I loved to see her all dressed up and ready for Shabbos or a *simchah*. When my parents would go out at night to a wedding, they always brought home something sweet for us. My children and I carry on this tradition.

I was extremely fortunate to have been a very loved, cherished, and delightfully pampered child. My mother was constantly concerned about my health and constitution. Afraid that she would lose me, she often took me to *rebbes* and *tzaddikim* for *bruchos*, *segules*, and *kameyes*, small silver charms that she pinned on my clothing and pillows or that I wore around my neck. I do remember being a fussy eater, and I was very skinny. I contracted every contagious disease that went around: mumps, measles, and chickenpox, to name a few.

When I had a contagious disease, our house was marked with a sign, and I even remember once being put into the hospital in isolation. With eyes full of concern my parents and siblings would look at me from the opposite side of the door's window glass. I had no way of knowing then that all this would prove to be for the best. I had no idea that all those childhood diseases would only serve to strengthen my immune system for what was to come.

Despite my sickly nature, I managed to be a very active and inquisitive little girl. Sometimes I just got into mischief, and other times I got into real trouble. At four years old, I was nearly trampled to death by our neighbor's horse.

I had decided to wander off and investigate life in the horse's stable. Being small for my age, I was able to squeeze through our backyard fence, squirm under the neighbor's fence, and crawl through a hay-filled opening under the barn. Despite my young age, I knew enough not to open gates anywhere because they would squeak and my whereabouts would be revealed.

I do not recall exactly what happened next. Perhaps as I stood up in the haypile, my head hit the belly of the unsuspecting horse. Before I knew it, the horse kicked me flat onto the stable's dirt floor. He bit down into my right cheek, tearing it open. By the time my mother found me, dazed, bloodied, and whimpering in the hay, she didn't know if my life could be saved.

She ran with me to the hospital and, *baruch Hashem*, after days and days of intensive emergency treatment and communal prayer, I recovered. People in the community encouraged my mother to take the horse owner to court.

"Berachah," I would overhear them saying, "that horse nearly killed your little girl. Take the owner to a *beis din*. Sue for damages. She will be scarred on her face for her entire life. You deserve compensation."

My kindly mother would reply, "Justice belongs to Hashem. I will not be the one to ask Hashem to bring the attribute of justice upon anyone. *Baruch Hashem*, my child is fine. He answered my prayers."

Unfortunately, soon after that, the owner of the horse became terribly sick. My mother went to his house many times a week to give him treatments. When he was nearing his end, he asked to see me. Despite my fearful protests, Mother insisted that I come with her. Trembling at being so close to the barn, I entered the house. Clutching my mother's arm, I allowed her to steer me into the sick man's room.

"Please forgive me for what my horse did to you," he said, with his eyes full of tears. "Please forgive me and ask Hashem to heal me." My child's heart bore him no resentment. In timid silence I wished him a *refuah sheleimah* and backed out of the doorway.

Soon after that, he passed away. But the impression of the kindness my mother demonstrated towards him will never leave me. Not only didn't she ask for compensation, but she also bore him no ill will. She treated him until his death and made sure that I forgave him. Such kindness can surely be called exceptional.

This was simply an expression of my mother's essence. Her faith in G-d encompassed every aspect and area of her life. She felt compelled to take care of our neighbor, even though his horse had almost killed me. For her to do otherwise would have been contrary to her character, which had been formed and educated according to the laws of our Torah. The nobility of her soul never wavered, no matter what the circumstances. Indeed, her practice of fasting every Monday and Thursday also indicates her lofty spiritual level.

Besides her professional work, my mother was involved in every aspect of our community, from giving charity in a hidden and modest way to the ritual purification of the departed before burial. Jewish funerals were always very different from those of our gentile neighbors. Much as my mother tried to shield me from these aspects of life, the fact that we lived on a busy main street made them unavoidable.

As soon as I heard her say, "Lea'le, this is not for children; stay in," I would take my post at the living room window until she left the house. When the coast was clear, I would run out the back door and find a hidden place behind the shul, where I listened to the *hespedim* (eulogies) and observed the motionless, white-shrouded body on the bier.

When someone in our community died, the purification ritual was held in the home of the deceased. Wrapped in *tachrichim* (burial shrouds), the deceased was then placed in a pinewood coffin that was adorned by a simple Jewish star. The body was carried to the front of the shul that the family attended. Everything was simple, and very plain.

After the *hespedim*, the deceased was then escorted to the cemetery. The chevrah kaddisha (burial society) and community members said Tehillim and Kaddish at various points along the way. The deceased was laid to rest inside the bare earth, and four members of the chevrah kaddisha carried away the empty coffin. When I saw them coming towards the shul, it was my signal to run back home.

Afterwards, my mother would have us help her prepare food for the deceased's family. If she had participated in the *taharah* (ritual purification), she would come home with a piece of the white linen fabric in her hand, as a *segulah* for long life. She didn't have to say anything. We knew life was precious and one did not take it for granted.

In contrast, when one of our gentile neighbors died, there was a large, colorful gathering in their home. The varnished, ornate black coffin was decorated with numerous wreaths of flowers. It rested in a wagon behind an elaborate horse-drawn carriage. The horses were adorned with ribbons and flower crowns. As the deceased was being taken to the burial ground, it was accompanied by a solemn musical procession. Afterwards, the community made a feast to which all were invited. When one of her non-Jewish patients passed away, my mother would go to comfort the family and to see what they needed.

As the embodiment of kindness, my mother never got angry, or raised her voice. It was not necessary for her to lecture us because she taught us how to live by example. She built our home into a miniature sanctuary through her kindness and strength of character. Everything she did was filled with love.

I loved school and excelled in all areas of learning. Every morning my mother or occasionally one of my twin sisters braided my long hair with colored ribbons and sent me off to school. I would take this short, familiar walk four times a day, five days a week.

We learned Hebrew and Romanian in what was a double curriculum. We were responsible for the same curriculum as that which was taught in the regular Romanian schools, in addition to a full day of Torah learning and a lot of homework. Inspectors used to come several times a year to check that we were on a par with the secular schools. My teachers called on me quite frequently to give the right answers. I especially excelled in writing. I loved to write poetry, stories,and plays for my friends. In school, my work was always on display in the classroom and in the corridors. We often had visitors at our home and my parents would call me into the living room, stand me on a chair, and have me recite what I had learned in school.

On my way home from school to our house on Strada Cucului (Peacock Street), I would often take a special turn to a little wooded corner where the beautiful peacock lived. My friends and I would wait patiently by the wooden fence, hoping for him to come out and give us an elegant display of his magnificent multi-colored tail.

"Here he is!" we would exclaim, and stretch our necks for a front-row view. The peacock looked as though he quite enjoyed our attention. He strutted along majestically through the tall green grass, as though his colorful tail were a royal garment. At the end of the fence, he turned his head to see if we children were still watching.

My next stop was usually the smith's workshop. I was fascinated by the way he molded fiery hot iron into various shapes. Very often, riders and horse-drawn carriages would pull up in front of his shop. I was captivated by the way the horses cooperated with the smith. The animal would raise its foot and place it in the smith's palm, allowing it to be measured. The horse must have known somehow that it could run better with new horseshoes.

Then it was on to the cobbler's shop, which smelled of leather and metal nails. Besides fixing shoes, the cobbler had various casts, which were used for custom-made shoes. Although our town had shoe stores, it was considered a very special treat to have cobbler-made shoes.

I was in grade three when, in 1940, the Russians occupied Bessarabia, Bukovina, and parts of Moldova. Our town of Herta was invaded and we were forced into a new educational system. Dramatic changes took place for the children of the town. Whereas before Jews and non-Jews had belonged to separate communities learning in separate school systems, suddenly the religious schools were shut down and we were thrown together by the Soviet authorities. This prepared me for what was to come. Hashem blessed me with the gift of learning languages easily, and I excelled in my studies. This gift was a crucial element in saving my life, along with my long blond braids, blue eyes, and sallow complexion.

The Russians introduced us to the concept of "peer teaching." Whoever excelled in any given subject had to be responsible for a group of children who were experiencing difficulty in learning that subject. Since my language skills were such that my Russian poems were already displayed on a bulletin board in the auditorium, I was given two groups of children to teach: one for grammar and one for poetry. My marks depended on how well the groups did. Little did I know then that I was being trained for my teaching career after my survival.

In spite of all the changes that were taking place, such as having to learn together with non-Jews and be taught by them, my mind was open to all types of learning. Still, my parents and siblings checked very carefully that I didn't internalize any foreign ideas and thoughts, so as not to become estranged from my family or my people.

Although I loved learning all the subjects in school, my core identity was nurtured and formed by the love of my parents and siblings and by the holiness of Torah and mitzvos that permeated every aspect of our lives. The traditional observance in our chassidic home, where we spoke only Yiddish and Hebrew, was vibrant and thriving.

Preparations for Shabbos started very early in the week. We would go to the local market to buy fruit, vegetables, and dry goods. Depending on the season, my mother would make either preserves or pickles. She had a unique system of food storage: apples, potatoes, carrots, onions, and garlic were placed in cartons in our basement and covered with sand so they wouldn't freeze during the severe Romanian winters.

In the backyard we had a chicken coop and a fish pond. We also kept geese. Every day I looked forward to the time when my mother would tie on my white apron with the wide pockets full of grain for the chickens and the geese. "Now don't go too close to the mother hens when the chicks are just hatched. She will do anything to protect them and she could attack you," Mother would caution me.

Once they could hop around, it was especially fun to catch a practically newborn chick and sit down in the grass with the tiny yellow fur ball in my lap. "Cheep, cheep, cheep, cheep," I would answer its cries. I would let the chick peck out the leftover grain kernels from my apron pocket, amazed by its instinctive ability to find every last bit of the food.

Then the goose eggs had to be collected. This job involved a basket and a chase. I would run after the squawking geese as they flapped their broad wings, sending feathers flying into the air. Then I would reach into their nests and pick up the warm fresh eggs, placing them gently into my basket. I would walk back to the house taking care not to rock my basket and crack open the eggs.

I always felt sorry for the Shabbos chickens. They were caught and brought to the shochet to be slaughtered early Friday morning. The wooden crate that held the squawking birds returned home silent and blood-stained with their limp, headless bodies.

My mother would declare, *"Lekavod Shabbos Kodesh"* (in honor of our holy Shabbos), and painstakingly pull out the feathers, making sure the skin was smooth and clean. Then she would spread out the chickens on a large board over the sink in the kitchen, sprinkling them with handfuls of coarse salt to draw out the blood and render them kosher.

I always enjoyed the sight of the kitchen table when it was covered with fresh challah, sweet challah rolls, cakes, pies, and cinnamon rugelach. On Friday mornings we had special onion-garlic rolls to take to school. My mother used a lot of garlic in her cooking. Without the benefit of contemporary research, she somehow knew it was very healthy.

On Friday afternoon before Shabbos the atmosphere in my house would be filled with anticipation and excitement as we were prepared for a long-awaited and beloved guest to come home. We all had our chores: cleaning, bed-making, shoe-polishing, table-setting. My favorite task was polishing the silver candlesticks. My mother lit nine candles, one for every member of the family. I would rub the soft cloth against the silver until my reflection was as smooth and clear as in a mirror's glass. This was my coveted chore and I refused to share it. At the Shabbos table on Friday night, the whole family took pride in my handiwork. But the gleaming silver paled in comparison with my glowing heart.

When my turn came to be blessed by my father, I knew that I was bound up with something of tremendous importance. He would place his warm hands on my bowed head, and stand in prayer as fathers have stood for millennia: "May G-d make you like Sarah, Rivkah, Rachel, and Leah. May G-d bless you and safeguard you. May G-d illuminate His countenance for you and be gracious unto you. May G-d turn His countenance to you and bless you with peace."

I would stand there innocently beneath his hands, not knowing that behind my father was an invisible chain of our ancestors that reached all the way back to Sinai. In my family, I was his youngest link in that chain, and unbeknownst to me, I would be the only living remnant who would transmit those ancient blessings to my children. The sanctity and love planted within me from my childhood home were to sustain me through the blackest and most difficult times ahead. My parents created a foundation of Jewish identity that nothing could destroy — not violence, not hatred, not terror, nor witnessing the deaths of my beloved parents and siblings.

Even when I felt as though my very being was shattered, there was something that still flickered within me. When all the externals were taken from me, my dignity and my pride remained intact. I was a Jew. That bare, essential fact of my existence set me apart from any worldly circumstance. I was a Jew. My very root was eternal.

Aside for my isolated Easter beating, I do have one other "foreboding memory." I remember my mother and father standing outside our house in Herta. When I looked at their faces, I saw that they were weeping. I could hear shooting in the distance. At this time we were under the Russian occupation.

Full of fear and concern, I approached my parents. "Why are you crying?" I asked them.

They said, "Go play; it's nothing."

Perhaps this is the reason why my parents sold our first home on Peacock Street along with everything in it. Although I was very young then, I remember our entire family riding on a train to Bucharest. My oldest brother Nathan lived in Cernauti, where he was a chef. We stayed in Bucharest awhile, and we got to know my half brothers from my father's side, Cesar and Avraham. These two incidents seem to be very much related. My family tried to leave Romania, most likely for Palestine. For some reason, we didn't succeed and returned to Herta.

Besides these two isolated incidents, my early life was untouched by violence, fear, or hatred. My parents must have made the decision to keep their home life as normal as possible and to provide me, their youngest child, with a secure inner foundation. All my learning, home life, and community activities revolved around the Torah. Throughout the Jewish week, month, and year, the moments of my childhood days were infused and illuminated by acts of kindness, love for the mitzvos, and preparations for Shabbos or the next upcoming holiday. There was always something to look forward to.

The Herta of my childhood was a world that will never exist again. Although we existed in an atmosphere of anti-Semitism, I have very happy memories of the holidays throughout the year. Every night, during the week before Rosh Hashanah, the *shamash* of our shul would walk through the town, banging on the doors of each home: "*Yidden*," he'd call out in a loud voice, "*shteit oif Sliches!* — Jews, get up for Selichos!" (prayers of repentance).

We would hurry through the midnight streets to the synagogue. Upstairs, the women's section was enclosed with thick curtains. While I loved to listen to the davening, I also wanted to see what was going on. Often I would find the seamed opening in the rough fabric of the beige curtain and peek down, searching for the covered heads of my father and brothers. Reassured by their presence, I would settle back into my veiled stance, only to peek out again a few minutes later. I found it comforting to be surrounded not only by the curtain, but by the heartfelt prayers of the people of my community and my family.

For Rosh Hashanah, my mother always baked two kinds of special challos. One consisted of a large round challah in the center, with smaller challah rolls attached all around it. It looked like a mother surrounded by her children. The other was a sweet challah shaped like a ladder. We understood this to be a symbolic way of asking that all our prayers go straight to Hashem.

Other Rosh Hashanah traditions from my home live on in my memory. The taste of the sweet apple and honey, for example, still lingers in my mouth, replete with the longing for a world that once was, and that will never be again. "Count the shofar blasts," Mother would challenge me in shul to help me stay quiet. "See who among you can count the most."

When we went down to the river for the Tashlich service, the bread crumbs that we cast into the water represented our sins. Happily, I watched as they were eaten by the fish.

After Rosh Hashanah we would count the Aseres Yemei Teshuvah (Ten Days of Repentance): "It is a much easier time to do better," she would tell us. On erev Yom Kippur, we did Kaparos (ritual of atonement), my mother and each of us girls with a hen, my brothers and my father with roosters. We would go out to the chicken coop to catch them. I was taught how to grasp the bird firmly and hold it gently in my arms. I would stroke the white feathered head of the chicken and feel the warmth of its beating heart close to mine. "This chicken will go to its death to feed a poor family, and then Hashem will judge us favorably," I would hear my siblings chant. The kindred life spark I shared with my chicken made me want to hide it and protect it from being slaughtered. But before I knew it, my mother was waving it over my head and placing it in the wooden crate for the *shochet*.

After the chickens were taken to the *shochet* and then cleaned and *kashered*, we learned a new lesson: *tzedekah b'seiser*, how to give gifts to the poor anonymously. My mother arranged for the chickens to be delivered to needy families through a messenger. They were not to know who sent them the chickens, to spare them from embarrassment and from feeling beholden.

Yom Kippur was a very solemn day spent in fasting and prayer. At that time, as a child, I always wanted to be happy. It was not until I was much older that I understood why such bitter cries and sobbing can be heard in the shul.

Right after my father broke his Yom Kippur fast each year, he would summon all of us to go out to the backyard and begin turning our shed into a sukkah. I loved to help adorn the sukkah with decorations hand-made from leaves and dried flowers. The sukkah was an enchanted home for me. On Sukkos night, when my father recited Kiddush, I would look through the *sechach* (foliage) up at the stars. I knew there was a G-d and that He was taking care of me, no matter what.

As much as I loved the beauty of Sukkos, it was the joy and happiness of Simchas Torah that I looked forward to all year. Until I was about three or four, I was allowed into the men's section of shul. My father would lift me up onto his shoulders, where I could watch all the dancing and festivity from a prime vantage point. Sitting there, clapping my hands and singing, I would throw kisses at the Torah when it came close to us.

When I got older, I was allowed to have a special flag with an apple on top of the stick. A small hole had been carved out of the apple to hold a candle. We would light the candles and march around, making our own *hakafos*, singing "*Torah orah, Sisu v'simchu b'simchas Torah*." We would eat lots and lots of candy, as we waited for the time when all the boys huddled under the big tallis for the special *aliyah* to the Torah, and the Hamalach Hagoel verse.

Chanukah came in the middle of the cold winter. The windows were always covered with ice. I used to write and draw pictures in the damp frost on the windowpane, while I waited for my father and brothers to set up their menorahs. My entire family gathered for the lighting. The house would fill with song and my heart would glow with pride. Hearing the story of the Maccabees imbued us with longing for Eretz Yisrael and hope for our future. In my memory I taste my mother's latkes and feel the top of my toy dreidel spinning beneath my fingertips. As long as the candles burned we sat together, affirming the continuation of our history. Since I do not have any photographs of any members of my family, it is difficult to construct a clear visual picture of them. Sadly, my last recollections of my parents and siblings are of the drastic changes wrought by starvation, cold, and disease.

Tu B'Shevat brought light and extra sweetness into the long, freezing winter. The table was set as though it was Shabbos. On top of the gleaming white cloth were platters of colorful fruits and nuts. My mother bought as many species of fruits and nuts as possible, and she always graced the table with her homemade cherry brandy and burgundy red wine. The seven species connected with the Land of Israel were arranged on special plates. It was as though the pomegranates, dates, and figs spoke to us, inviting us to taste of the sweetness of the land. I remember sitting at the table with a longing in my heart to see the Land of Israel.

The carob and the *rimon* (pomegranate) had a special significance. The hard carob that was practically impossible to bite into taught us a lesson: We must stubbornly pursue our survival and not let anybody break our will to do so. As for the pomegranate, when we received a piece of the ruby-seeded fruit, my mother would say, "Count the seeds, and for every seed, do a mitzvah." What a delicious way to internalize the importance of the mitzvos that we do. She taught us by her example that we become what we do. Actions build character.

Purim was the most fun. We children could pretend to be anyone and anything we wanted. I loved to be Queen Esther, and I had a beautiful costume with a white crown. Among my friends, we would decide, "I'm the good Esther," or "I'm the wicked Vashti." But one opportunity to dress up was simply not enough. We also liked to dress as one of our four mothers, Sarah, Rivkah, Rachel, or Leah. We put on plays, our favorite being about Yosef HaTzaddik and his brothers. I loved the tradition of delivering *mishloach manos* (gifts for the poor) around the neighborhood. Our task was not over when the gifts were brought; in order to receive the *mishloach manos* that our neighbors had for us, we had to sing or dance. I looked forward to these performances with the utmost anticipation.

The day after Purim, we began our Pesach cleaning. What a hustle and bustle of activity! We were all assigned a specific task to get rid of the enemy — *chametz* (leaven)! We searched every pocket and every corner. When we found a crumb, we got rid of it as quickly as possible. The house was painted, and everything had an aura of newness. Each day, we brought more dishes, pots, and pans down from the attic. At night the seamstress would come and put the finishing touches on our new clothing, which we couldn't wait to wear.

Sometimes, in the midst of the preparations, the longing to finish and to be sitting at the Seder table was almost unbearable. For me, this was especially true on erev Pesach, when my mother had us grate the *maror*. I would stand at our wooden kitchen table with a hand grater, shedding bitter tears.

"Why do I have to do this, Mameh?" I demanded.

"Lea'le," she would respond patiently, "do you think it was easy in Egypt? They truly had every reason to cry. Their children's lives were threatened, they were bound to slave labor, the men's and women's work was reversed — it was painfully difficult for them. But Hashem paid heed to our tears and saved us with great miracles. Not only did Hashem split the sea for us,

He also fed us manna for forty years. What would you prefer, to grate the *maror* now, or to still be a slave in Egypt?"

Although this didn't make me happy to grate the *maror*, I obediently accepted her explanation. When my whole family was finally seated around the Seder table and my gleaming silver Kiddush cup with my name on it was in front of me, I really felt happy that I had been freed from my grueling work.

On the day of Lag BaOmer, the entire school dressed in blue and white and had a picnic. We marched together to the wooded area. As we marched, we carried flags and sang Israeli songs. Our teachers taught us not to be afraid, despite the covert hatred of our Romanian neighbors. Memories of these very early times evoke in me a feeling of pride. At that time, I was not afraid of anyone.

How different this Lag BaOmer picnic march was from the Death March that later destroyed my family, my friends, and everyone I loved. Although I was ashamed to wear the Yellow Star that marked us as an object of hatred to the Romanians, I still maintained a cornerstone of faith from my childhood. Our house was demolished, my precious family was destroyed, but the sanctuary of my inner home that my family had so lovingly created was somehow, miraculously, left intact. In retrospect, this was the force that kept me alive. Knowing deep down my true identity gave me the strength to persevere and never give up.

After Pesach came Shavuos, at which time our home was filled with the scent of freshly cut green pine branches and fragrant fresh flowers. I remember climbing trees to help cut down the branches.

The whole town would go to the shul at midnight to hear the Rabbi's speech. I loved to peek at the *bimah* (prayer platform), which was adorned with greenery and flowers. Most of the men would stay in shul all night and learn. In the morning I couldn't wait for all the traditional dairy delicacies that we enjoyed after the first Kiddush. My mother made her own cheese, butter, and sour milk, activities that I loved to help her do. And her sweet blintzes and sour cream were Shavuos favorites.

Throughout the cycle of the Jewish year, my life was rich with the meaning of the festivals. Although I lived in an insulated bubble until the age of nine, I was a happy and cherished child whose home life was full of kindness and educational diversity.

My days were filled with schoolwork and play. Evenings in my house were devoted to homework, housework, and community service. I brought my homework to the kitchen table. I loved to be in the center of daily life and was loathe to isolate myself in another room. As the youngest, I learned to concentrate in the midst of much noise and activity.

After my homework was done, I had to get ready for bed. If my mother was home, she spent time with me until I fell asleep. I would say the bedtime "Shema" prayer and we would sing different prayers. Comforted by her presence and stroked by her loving hands, I would fall into a peaceful, happy slumber.

But on this last fateful summer night of 1941, my childhood was brought to a sudden and brutal end. The banging on the windows and the urgent cries of the Romanian peasants surrounding our house rang with an intensity I had never heard before.

"*Doamna Berachah*! (Lady Berachah) *Doamna Berachah*!" Although the term of respect before my mother's name was there, the panic-filled shouting of the Romanian peasant's voice echoed with a different tone than usual. "*Doamna Berachah*! Wake up!" There was fear in that voice and an urgency I had never heard before. The dread filled-alarm jolted me from sleep. Something was horribly wrong.

"*Doamna Berachah*! *Doamna Berachah*! Wake your family and run for your lives! Tomorrow you will be killed!" They knew. And in fact, the slaughter of Jews in my hometown of Herta began the following day.

As a child, I was often awakened in the middle of the night by the cries and incessant knocking of the Romanian peasants. Either someone was sick, or they needed a midwife. "*Doamna*

Berachah! *Doamna Berachah*!" they would shout, and frantically bang on the windowpane.

My mother woke us and dressed us in as many garments as possible, telling us to hurry and not waste any time. Leaving our home, I ran after my family on an unlit road that was crowded with people. That night was the first time I heard an airplane. It was a German plane, zooming down and dropping bombs. Those who were killed instantly were very lucky. But there were those who were mortally wounded and begging for help. People were running over their bodies, running for their lives to find shelter.

My parents instructed us, "Stay close to the side of the road where there are trees and bushes. The minute you hear the sound of the plane, run into the bushes and fall down on the ground." We pushed on, walking, running, hiding, until we came to the next city and discovered that all the Jews there were already dead. We moved into a house where the inhabitants had been murdered, and we lived in quiet fear with the shutters closed tight.

After a few days, we prepared for Shabbos. How different this Shabbos was from all the others of my young life. We sat at the table and listened as my father whispered Kiddush. Inside this ghost-like home of murdered inhabitants, we were sanctifying Hashem's Name, while outside were the vicious sounds of wanton destruction. Suddenly, in the middle of our Shabbos meal, we heard violent banging on the shutters and the door. The soldiers were searching for Jews. "*Open up! Open up!*" they shouted. The Romanians didn't need to take lessons from the Germans in how to hate Jews. They already knew. My mother and father motioned for all of us to run and hide. We children ran into the garden and found hiding places. My parents stayed inside and prepared themselves to face whatever came.

The soldiers burst in through the front door. They looked at my mother and father and at all the empty places at the table. My mother was forty-two, my father was forty-seven. The soldiers knew that they had young children. The leader demanded, "Where are the others?" My parents remained silent. He threatened, "If they don't come back, we will shoot you." At the thought of his children becoming orphaned, my father went to call us back to the dining room.

We were lined up to be shot according to height. They tried to save bullets, so that one bullet could pass through many people. I, being the youngest and the shortest, was at one end, and my brothers were at the other end. My twin sisters, another sister, and my parents were in the middle.

The soldiers picked up their rifles and took aim. We said our good-byes to each other, we said Shema Yisrael, and we were prepared. My parents told us, "Soon we will be together in Paradise." I don't remember crying. I had already seen many families lying dead on the road and in the forest. Although I was only nine, I felt this to be my destiny. I internalized that very quickly.

Just at the moment they were ready to shoot, the head of the firing squad ordered, "Put down your guns!" The others looked at him — had he lost his mind? "Put down your guns!" he cried out in a booming voice.

To this day, I can hear the sound of that order reverberating inside my head. The soldiers lowered their guns and looked up for an explanation. "You see that lady?" he said, in a much softer tone, pointing to my mother. "She brought me into the world. She healed me, and members of my family, many times. I can't kill her and I can't kill her children. Let's go." Through the sight of his gun, he had recognized my mother.

So you see, my mother's kindness saved us. But in retrospect, the soldiers would have ended our suffering if they had killed us, because what was to come was so much worse. It was beyond our imagination. After that, we were ordered to go back to our town. I didn't recognize Herta. It was in shambles after the massacre. Our homes had been emptied of all our valuables and belongings. The peasants had come while we were gone and taken whatever they wanted. Except for money and small items he could carry, my father dug holes in the backyard to bury what remained of our valuables.

We were able to take shelter in our ransacked house for a short period of time. Again, in the middle of the night, the Romanian soldiers came with their dogs, shouting, "Out, Jews, out! To the market place." And the official "Death March" began. We were ordered to leave our home, taking the bare minimum of possessions. My father stuffed any portable valuables into his pockets. Mameh dressed us in as many clothes as we could find, and snatched up some bread and cheese in a sack. We left the house and became part of the crowd that was driven towards the village square.

After some distance, I broke away from my family and before anyone could stop me I ran back to our home. I knew that our Pesach dishes were still in the attic. I remembered my silver goblet with my name on it. I wanted to take it with me. Of all the possessions I could possibly have chosen to return for, why was I longing for that silver cup? Perhaps to reassure myself at all times of who I was, that I had some identity as a Jew and as a member of the human race. Perhaps I wanted to see the silver against the backdrop of the night, to reassure myself of hope for a better future.

Across the street from my house lived my non-Jewish "friend" Vera. Although she and her brothers had beaten me up one Easter, we had remained "good friends." When she saw me return, she ran into her house, grabbed a long chopping knife from the kitchen drawer, and chased me down the street, trying to stab me with the knife. Fortunately, I had always been a better runner. Driven by fear, I fled from my playmate-turned-murderer. I didn't manage to salvage my cup, but I later rationalized that having it might have caused me even greater pain. To hold the cup in my hand and remember what it had been like to celebrate the "Festival of Freedom" would have been too constant a reminder of my precious family and childhood home. I didn't know what was facing us. I didn't know that over the months of the Death March to Transnistria, my entire family would perish, and I would be the only one left alive.

Although most of my childhood memories have been shattered, my earliest Jewish identity, built on a foundation of joy and love, remained whole. This wellspring of love and holiness remained with me even during my darkest and most horrific times. It was the source of my determination, my dignity, and my pride. No matter what happened, I was always grateful to be a Jew.

Throughout those black years, I learned that hope and faith reside in the goblet of the heart, even when it overflows with pain. I couldn't carry my actual Kiddush cup on the Death March. I had to become everything it stood for and carry it forward in my life.

Running as fast as I could, I darted through the crowd, looking for my family.

CHAPTER 3

THE DEATH MARCH

Breathless and shaken from my narrow escape, I joined my family. In their frantic search for me they had managed to slow their pace. To stop completely was too great a risk. This was not the time to speak of my terror, to tell my mother of the harrowing experience with my neighbor and so-called "best friend," who had tried to kill me with a kitchen knife.

This was the beginning of the end of my normal childhood. The Holocaust destroyed our lives, but the deepest form of damage was the shattering of the self – the feeling of absolute nothingness. During this darkest period of my life, my so-called existence was reduced to dust – nothing.

After the war, it took many years before I regained the self-confidence that I had had as a child. I always felt as though I were being punished for something that I had done. I had no one to help me straighten out my thinking. I was not to blame, but children always think they are to blame. It took a long while to realize that I was a victim of religious, political, and social persecution. The free world did precious little to protest or free us from our torture and destruction.

Nevertheless, I became acutely aware that even a horrendously dreadful life was to be lived with hope of survival. The vicious incident with Vera initiated my struggle for physical existence on the Death March. As long as there was a living spirit within me, I had to move on. Clutching my mother's hand, I merged into the moving crowd of people.

It was a dreadful, rainy September night. The foreboding weather reflected the end of my innocence and the end of normal life. The dark, endless road that stretched before us led to hopelessness and despair. The wet night air chilled us to the bone. The remnants of our community, those who hadn't fled or been murdered, were herded together in the village square. All around me people carried whatever they had been able to snatch up that was precious to them as they were rousted out of their homes. My father and brothers had hidden small valuables under their clothing.

Our Rabbi stood at the head of his congregation, his arms wrapped around the sefer Torah that he held tightly against his heart. I looked up and saw hundreds of men with their prayer shawls draped over their heads. They knew they were wearing their burial shrouds. They looked like multi-dimensional angels against the looming darkness of the black sky.

"Where are we going, Mameh?" I asked. She pulled me closer to her and stroked my face, but answered me only with her tears.

I began to cry, my tears falling on my rain-soaked cheeks. My mother's inability to answer or comfort me left me colder than the rain. The void in my heart became one with the night. I would soon learn to reach through that void and grasp onto my faith, holding it tighter than my desperate grip on my mother's hand.

This childhood nightmare began just before I was to start grade four. The day before we were driven out, I had been to the school to see my grades, which were posted before the beginning of each school year. I was full of happiness, because my name was one of those at the top. How I loved school and anxiously waited for the first day, which would never come. A different kind of school started for me at age 9. Over the coming months, I began to learn about the true meaning of Jewish suffering – about hunger, fear, homelessness, and starvation. Death was all around us; even the living were walking corpses. Anguish and humiliation became my new reality. Each and every one of us knew that our life was like the flickering of a candle – the slightest breeze could snuff it out.

Thus torn away from the last peaceful sleep of my childhood, I began another midnight journey. But instead of a journey of healing or birth, it was a journey into terror and destruction. From that time on, fear, shock, and uncertainty pulsated through my being with every heartbeat. It was not enough for our tormentors to mutilate and destroy us physically. Their goal was to make us feel worthless, to rob us of our humanity, and to eradicate our uniquely Jewish image.

Even before the Death March began, the old people and the little ones who couldn't walk were shot right there in the marketplace. As we began to move out, the gendarmes had whips with rocks at the end for anyone who refused to cooperate. If they hit someone with the whip, the person would be mortally wounded. We walked in the middle of the masses of bereaved and ragged marchers to avoid that whip. At this time, life was worse than death. Yet we clung to life, hoping that somehow this torture would soon come to an end.

The merciless killing began immediately. We were forbidden to stop and to help those who were injured. If one of us would bend down to pick up an abandoned child, he would be shot. The roads were covered with bodies; the air was full of the cries of the wounded. How difficult this must have been for my mother, whose life was devoted to healing and kindness, to witness this brutality and to be driven on. Overcome by fear and a determination to live, we restrained our human impulse to help the dying, and walked forward into the darkness.

As Professor Radu Ioanid documents in *The Holocaust in Romania*, "...Two stages of the deportation of Jews from Bessarabia and Bukovina can be distinguished. The first phase occurred between the summer and early fall of 1941, when the Jews living in rural areas were herded into transit camps and urban Jews into ghettos. The second stage took place from September to November, when Bessarabian and Bukovinian Jews were systematically deported to Transnistria to complete implementation of Ion Antonescu's orders. These expulsions were accomplished by administrators ... the most ruthless and toughest of the entire police force."[1]

Ioanid brings an example of how the fascist press prepared the public for the deportations. A Romanian newspaper, *Porunca Vremii*, stated, "The die has been cast...The liquidation of the Jews in Romania has entered the final decisive phase...[He] will no longer have the opportunity to wander; he will be confined...within the traditional ghettos...To the joy of our emancipation must be added the pride of [pioneering] the solution to the Jewish problem in Europe. Judging by the satisfaction with which the German press is reporting the words and decisions of Marshal Antonescu, we understand ...that present-day Romania is prefiguring the decisions to be made by the Europe of tomorrow."[2]

This Death March lasted for months. Our ranks diminished by the hour; at least seventy to eighty people per day died from hunger and exhaustion alone. Those who could not continue were shot. The roads were covered with the victims' bodies, some not dead yet, with no one to answer their pleas for help. I learned not to cry, not to hesitate. To move was to live. Thus, dressed in barely enough winter clothing, I followed my family,

---

1. Ioanid, Radu, *The Holocaust in Rumania: The Destruction of Jews and Gypsies Under the Antonescu Regime, 1940-1944* p. 122.
2. Ibid., pp. 122-23.

walking along a dark, dirt road. We kept pace with the crowd of living corpses, and when necessary, we stepped over the bodies of the dead.

Right at the beginning of this march, a Nazi car speeding by screeched to a halt next to me. There were two Germans sitting inside. One had a machine gun pointed out of the window. I was the image of every Nazi's dream child. My long blond hair had never been cut. It hung like thick golden ropes down my back. My large sky-blue eyes shone from beneath my bangs. Despite the effects of my hunger and fatigue, the Nazis saw a pretty little girl and they wanted me for their blue-eyed, blond nation.

One of the Nazis got out of the car, pointed at me, and beckoning with his finger said, *"Cummin zi! Cummin zi!* (Come here! Come here!)"

He demanded to take me away, shouting, "She's not your child! You kidnapped her! She's coming with us!" Over and over again, these brutes insisted that I was not my parents' child. My mother, father, and all my siblings fell to their knees, begging and pleading with them to leave me alone. It was a miracle that they didn't kill us all and that they relented and drove away. But at that moment, the possibility of my survival was planted within my mind without my even being cognizant of it. If the Nazis believed that I wasn't Jewish, then certainly the Romanian guards and the Ukrainian peasants who had settled in our country during the Russian occupation would believe me as well. Maybe these peasants would even help me.

The extreme conditions of the harshest winter in memory only increased our suffering. The temperature dropped to forty degrees below zero.[3] The snow was up to the rooftops. As far as the local people were concerned, we Jews brought the cold and we also brought the snow. The Romanian gendarmes were brutal to us. The police confiscated our shoes, which could be

---

3. Hilberg, p. 495.

sold, and forced us to walk barefoot on the frozen ground from one place to another.

Now and then they stopped us, not out of pity, but so that the guards could rest. Most of us fell to the ground, exhausted. We were not given any food or water. Bread was more precious than gold. Whatever valuables we had were traded for sustenance. It is documented that "the German military attaché in Bucharest reported that one of his agents, who had mingled with countless uniformed Romanians on furlough from the front, had discovered that every one of these officers was loaded down with rings, furs, silk, and other valuables taken from Jewish deportees."[4]

The military dictator of Romania, Ion Antonescu, decreed that death was too good for the Jews. We must first be humiliated, tortured, starved, dehumanized, and brutalized. After that, we would be shot; that is, if death didn't claim us first. We had to sleep on the ice-covered ground or in pigsties and stables without any windows. The pigs were luckier than we were because they were fed. I learned to steal food from the pigs. When caught, I was beaten, but it didn't stop me from trying again.

The final mortality rate was eighty percent. Very few of us reached our destination — Transnistria. Jews who weren't hanged or beaten to death fell ill and died from the cold, starvation, and disease. Life became so unbearable that many victims simply gave up hope and died. It is impossible to describe the horror, pain, and grief, the utter hopelessness that I felt when I lost all the members of my family one by one.

I rapidly developed survival skills. Intuitively, I watched faces and listened unconsciously to the rhythm of language around me. I always felt an invisible Hand guiding me towards life. With a hint of prophecy, as we trudged along, my mother, an ashen-faced skeleton of her former self, constantly repeated the words which became my life's mission: *"Du muzt lebn, du muzt gedenken, du muzt dertzeiln der velt vos di Rumanier*

---

4. Hilberg, p. 494.

hobn tzu undz geton — You must live, you must remember, you must tell the world what our Romanian 'friends' and neighbors did to us."

My mother's words, spoken with the kind of pain that the imagination cannot fathom, became the inner driving force of my life. I used to flee from danger like a bird stretching its wings in flight, telling myself over and over: "*Du muzt lebn, du muzt gedenken, du muzt dertzeiln der velt vos di Rumanier hobn tzu undz geton.*" Numbed with fear and loss, she was able to summon from within herself the ability to empower me, her youngest child, with this universal task. Now I was no longer an individual trying to survive. I was carrying the banner of remembrance, a banner that I would not display for another fifty years.

Early on "The March" my mother very much wanted us to have a chicken for Shabbos and she had an idea how we could get one. All four of us girls had pierced ears from the time we were young, and with my mother's, we had five pairs of gold earrings among us. As we were marching, the Romanians stood on the sidelines watching us and trading things. My mother traded all our earrings for a chicken. She sent me with it to a *shochet* who was on the march. Even on the Death March, my mother wanted to try to create a feeling of Shabbos. This would be a reminder of our identity and purpose in the world. Perhaps this would infuse our hearts with hope and the strength to continue.

When I brought back the coveted chicken, she plucked the feathers and opened it. The liver didn't look quite right to her, so she sent me back to the *shochet* who looked at the liver and told me, "This chicken is *treif*." Although we were tortured and starving, my mother said, "*Kinderlach, mir torren dos nisht essen* — My children, we are forbidden to eat this." My mother was desperately concerned for the spiritual purity of her children. In these life-and-death circumstances, Jewish law would have allowed us to eat it. But my mother wouldn't feed it to us. We were raised to understand that real life was the life of the soul. Physical vital signs of life did not necessarily mean that a person was spiritually alive. True life existed beyond this world. It was given by G-d and nourished by His Torah. Sadly, my mother and my brothers and sisters never ate chicken again. But they perished in utter sanctity and purity.

We were driven on and on, and beaten mercilessly. With each bare footstep, we sank further and further into hopelessness and despair. Death seemed like a welcome end to our misery. Nevertheless, somehow I was always looking for a way to survive. The gendarmes walked on one side of the unpaved road while we trudged on the other side. The dirt roads were mired in mud, with ridges of frozen earth that had been formed from the wheels of the army wagons. My red, swollen feet were frostbitten, numb, and bruised.

I couldn't walk anymore. I studied the faces of the gendarmes. Although most of their faces were twisted with meanness, one of them didn't look as cruel. He was leading the horse pulling the wagon that bore their food and water. We Jews were not allowed near their food supplies. We weren't even allowed to cross the road to the other side where the gendarmes were marching.

I decided to risk running to the other side. This humane-looking gendarme was very tall. As little as I was, I took a chance and ran as fast as I could across the road to him. I stretched out my arm but all I could reach was the edge of his jacket. Taking many steps to keep up with his long stride, I grabbed hold of his jacket hem and pulled.

I waited, my life suspended in that moment. It was decreed by Divine Providence that I would not be shot for walking out of line. The gendarme looked down at me with a puzzled expression on his face. In that instant I saw a spark of compassion in his eyes.

"What do you want, little girl?" My faith was kindled by his response. Perhaps beneath that uniform there was some semblance of a heart. He saw me as a child, not as some inhumane creature to be taken out and murdered.

I said, "What is it to you if I die? I can't walk another step. If you make me walk you may as well kill me. But I want to live."

"So what do you want from me?" he asked.

"Please, just let me sit in your wagon. I won't touch your food or drink. I just can't walk anymore." I pleaded, "Don't let me die."

To my surprise, he stretched out his long arms, picked me up, put me in the wagon, and covered me with a blanket! My parents and siblings saw me sitting there but they didn't envy me, contrary to what most children would feel. Perhaps my brothers and sisters knew, somehow, that I would be the one to ultimately survive this ordeal. In any case, that is how I made it through the March. Every now and then my fifteen-year-old brother, Bentzion, would come to check on me, bringing me news from the family and scraps of things to eat.

We traveled to a place called Ataki, where the gendarmes wanted to make sure that we were carrying no gold, extra clothing, or possessions. They took everything away from us. My father and my brothers, Bentzion and Chaim, were carrying whatever valuables we had left. When the Romanians tried to rob my father, he resisted and was shot. That night my brothers also disappeared, never to be heard from again.

I was still traveling in the food wagon when my mother approached me, her face white as snow. She said to me in Yiddish, "*Du bist a yasom, mein kind* —You are an orphan, my child." With this news I wept, but there was no time to mourn. One mourns when one has hope to live. Besides, at the age of nine and a half, I did not know how to mourn. It would have drained all my strength and I would have perished in my grief. We all knew that we, too, would be killed sooner or later. It was only a question of time.

We hadn't eaten for days. We were not given provisions of any sort, and we had no jewelry left to trade. When I was thirsty, I used to bend down like a dog and drink the murky water that settled in the mud holes. As historian Ioanid describes, "Food was not provided...Many Jews sought edible plants growing near the roads, and often they were reduced to drinking rainwater from ditches and puddles."[5]

Very few of us who set out on The March survived. The SS Einzatzgruppen were the most vicious, cold-blooded, trained killers. They used to bring their wives and girlfriends to show them with pride how they murdered Jews. It was the German SS Einzatzgruppen execution teams, the Ukranian police, and the Romanian Gendarmerie who were such experts at killing off the Ukrainian Jews that they had no time for us. Orders were given for us to stop at a place called Yedenitz, where we were detained outside in the raw elements for several weeks. The gendarmes barely gave us enough space to sit or lie down. Our tormentors had to have complete control over us, at all times. At any given moment, spontaneous killing could occur.

Although, "Besides Germany itself, Romania was thus the only country which implemented all the steps of the destruction process...,"[6] there were no standardized killing procedures in Romania and Transnistria, what Hilberg calls "the Romanian East." The methodology of murder was left up to the bestial impulses of each individual general, prefect, governor, soldier, policeman, or civilian.

At times the Jews were victimized due to the political tensions between Germany and Romania. The impulsive, earlier deportations of Jews across the Dniester River resulted in the deaths of thousands of Jews because the Romanians didn't like to take orders from the Germans. During the month of August 1941, in response to orders given from local authorities, thousands of Bessarabian Jews were expelled from their homes and marched towards the German-occupied area across the Dniester. When the Germans, who were unprepared to "handle" such large numbers of Jews, saw them coming, orders were given to send them back. The Romanians ignored the orders and threatened to open fire if the Jews were sent back. "Again

---

5. Ioanid, pp. 122-123.
6. Hilberg, p. 485.

and again the German Einsatzkommando turned back Jews, and again and again more Jews came across. In the process of shoving back and forth, thousands of Jews died on the road-sides from exhaustion and bullet wounds."[7]

Romanians were unsurpassed in creative savagery. The Bogdanovka killing center had a bakery where one loaf of bread was sold for five gold rubles. When the gold ran out, the Colonel Isopescu had the Jews put in stables and killed. The stables were set on fire and the corpses were burned. The remain-ing Jews were marched to a cliff overhanging the Bug River. "There, they were stripped of all their belongings and their ring fingers were chopped off, if the rings could not easily be removed...after that...standing stark naked in a temperature of 40 degrees below zero, they were shot. The corpses fell over the precipice into the river."[8] While my family perished, the fields, countryside, and rivers of Romania became a mass graveyard for my nation.

As fate would have it, our stopping place in Yedenitz was right near a bakery. The delicious smell of the freshly baked bread made our hunger pangs worse than ever. Small as I was, I was always a fighter. There must be some way we can help ourselves, I thought.

While everyone else was lying down, I would sit up and watch the door of the bakery. My mother would say, "Lea'le, lie down."

I would answer, "No. I'm not tired." I refused to simply lie down and die. I was looking for a way to get some bread to keep us going.

I was never as close to G-d as I was on that Death March. I always felt Him guiding me, surrounding me with circum-stances for my survival. "Dear G-d," I whispered, "maybe there is someone my age who can help us." Suddenly, my prayer was answered! I saw a little girl coming out of the bakery with her

7. Hilberg, p. 492.
8. *Ibid.*, p. 496.

school bag under her arm. She appeared to be about my age. I called out to her in Romanian, "Where are you going?" I had to speak very quickly because she was running.

When this child heard me speak to her in Romanian, she stopped dead in her tracks. She had probably never spoken to a Jewish child before. We were supposed to be bugs to be exterminated – not real people. But she was somehow caught off-guard when I spoke to her in her own language. At that moment the wall between us fell.

With a shocked expression she turned around, came over to me, and said, "What do you want?"

"How old are you?" I asked eagerly.

"Nine and a half," she answered. Exactly my age. I blurted out the next question.

"Where are you going?"

"I'm going to school," she answered with downcast eyes.

"What grade are you in?"

"I'm in grade 4."

That was my grade, the grade I would have started. I looked at her books and longed for the luxury of being a little girl on her way to school. "Do you like school?" I asked her.

"No. I hate it because I'm stupid." You're stupid, I wanted to say, only because you don't know how fortunate you are. Here I was, my future and my hopes totally destroyed. I was deprived of everything, including the chance to learn, and this lucky child hates school.

Beckoning with my right hand, I said, "Come. Come close to the fence. Show me your books. Show me what's hard for you. Maybe I can help." I stretched my arms through the wooden fence and she placed her books in my hands. I took one look at what she was learning and thought to myself, I'm going to be her tutor! "Don't go to school today. Sit with me and I'll help you. Tomorrow you'll know your lessons very well," I assured her.

And so began my teaching career, at the age of nine and a half. Although we sat on opposite sides of the fence, we were temporarily united in purpose, as I helped her. During the time I tutored this lucky peasant child, I felt human again. I was giving, I was using my mind. I felt so good to be in a position to help this little girl learn her lessons – for her to see that she wasn't so stupid after all.

When her mother came out of the bakery and saw that her daughter had not left for school, she was furious. "You stupid child, you'll never learn anything. Why do you speak to a Jidan (a dirty Jew)?"

My newfound pupil answered, "Mother, she is not a Jidan. She's a child like me, only she's much smarter. Don't worry. Tomorrow I will go and I will understand my teacher much better."

The mother, a simple peasant woman, asked her daughter sarcastically, "And how will you have learned so much so quickly?"

"The blond girl on the other side taught me and I know my lessons for tomorrow," she said. Her mother was so pleased that she went into the bakery and brought out a loaf of bread and a cake. And as long as we stayed in Yedenitz, we had food to eat every day. My mother would take the bread and the cake and share it with as many children as she could. She used to say, "*Kinder darfn lebn*. Children must live. *Kinder darfn gedenken*. Children must remember."

For a few weeks we were in Yedenitz, outside the bakery. Then the orders arrived to march again. Through the freezing rain, the ankle-deep mud, and the cold, we were driven on. The March would kill us slowly and horribly. We would be tormented as much as possible. Bullets were too expensive; we weren't worth it.

As we walked, I was always on the alert, scanning the countryside and forest for signs of life. When the Russians occupied Romania in 1940-41, we had been forced to learn Russian in school. With my fair-skinned appearance and my command of the Russian language, it was easy for me now to pose as a Russian child. I would often sneak away from the March and find a Russian family who had settled in the woods during the occupation.

I would tell them, "I'm a Russian child. I've lost my family and I'm very hungry." The peasants would give me crusts of bread. Sometimes they would take me into their fields to let me dig up a few potatoes. A real treasure was to find a goose or chicken egg. Since it was impossible to divide up and share it, I would drink it quickly. On the way back, if I could, I would dig up a frozen beet or a frozen potato from a roadside field. Whatever I managed to bring back to my family, though, was never enough to quiet our hunger pangs, or even barely sustain us.

Each day, hundreds perished from hunger, cold, and disease. All the young men and women had been taken away. The men were sent to slave labor camps. When their jobs were finished they were shot. The women were abused and then shot. There were instant orphans all over the roads all around us. These poor little children were lost, with no one to care for them or to console them. It is said that Mashiach is going to come when the world is *kulo chayav* or *kulo zakai* —a totally evil world or a totally perfect world. Now my mother couldn't imagine a more evil world than the one we were thrown into, so she was convinced that we would be saved at any moment. Only Mashiach could save us from this horrible, inhuman predicament.

On one of these freezing nights in the stable, my sister Devora'le cried all night. She was sick, cold, hungry, and very broken. In the morning, she was silent. I have no idea what happened to her body because the command came for us to move on. The ground was too frozen to bury her.

The following morning we were to cross the Dniester River into Transnistria. There was one very primitive barge that was used to ferry the people across. We were ordered to step onto the deck of the barge, but there were too many of us. People who couldn't squeeze themselves onto the barge were thrown into the Dniester by the gendarmes. They drowned in the icy water in a matter of seconds. The sound of their unanswered cries for help and the sight of them drowning will be with me for the rest of my life.

We reached Moghilev Ghetto, on the other side of the Dniester. The ground was covered with snow. But worse than the snow was the scene that greeted us. It stands forever like a haunting still-life picture in my memory. Against a house there seemed to be a great number of people sitting. Many had babies in their arms, children clutching parents and grandparents. Many had their hands over their children as if trying to protect them. But they were all dead. I don't know how long they had been that way. The killers didn't have a chance to remove the dead. So we got the message loud and clear that we were not there to survive. Death awaited us.

We weren't allowed to stay longer than one night in Moghilev Ghetto. The trains couldn't run. The frozen ground couldn't be opened to bury the dead. Frozen corpses lined the streets in every direction. Dogs roamed the area freely.

Starving and frostbitten, we were driven on to a village called Shargorod. The Romanian starvation policy resulted in the deaths of thousands and thousands of Jews. They were dying at a rate too fast for the Romanians to be able to dispose of the bodies in a sanitary way. In Shargorod there was a rampant typhus epidemic. The gendarmes were afraid of being infected so they didn't allow us to stop; they drove us on to Kopaigorod, which was our final destination, in Transnistria.

We were forced into a stable that was known as the "house of death," with barely enough space to lie down. We tried to warm ourselves in the damp, foul-smelling hay. Again, the snow was as high as the rooftops. The cold was bitter. The populace spoke Ukrainian or Russian but, except for a few of us who had learned it in school, the Romanian Jews knew neither language. The fact that most of the Jews couldn't communicate with the local people added to the cruelty of the situation.

The Ukrainian peasants lived in utter poverty, with very primitive ways. These villagers had no love for the Jews who were thrown into their midst, forcing them to share the little that was available to them. Nonetheless, some of the peasants had more heart than the gendarmes, men with education who should have known better. We were in this stable without food and without water. I thought to myself, someone has to be a provider.

My family was decimated. All that remained was my mother, my identical twin sisters and myself. Rivka and Liebe couldn't go outside to search for food because they were already thirteen and very beautiful. Throughout the Death March they had covered their faces with mud after shaving the hair from their heads to hide their beauty from the soldiers. If the soldiers caught them, they would be abused and killed. So it was up to me. I told my mother in no uncertain terms, "*Ich loif zuchn epes tzu essen* — I will leave this stable and try to find us some food." Before my mother could answer me, I took a sack and left.

I was not afraid to die. I had seen so much death that I now thought, it would be the end of my suffering. What was there to fear? My little emaciated body slipped easily under the fence and I approached some Ukrainian peasants. In Russian I told them, "I'm a Russian peasant girl. My parents died in an air raid. I'm hungry and I'm cold. Could you please help me?"

"What can you do?" they asked.

"I'll do anything you want me to. I'll help you dig up the potatoes. I'll clean. I'll do whatever you want," I pleaded.

My non-Jewish appearance helped me survive. There was a spark of humanity within these simple folk. The peasants shared with me the little that they had. In exchange for my work, some of the villagers did give me a bit of bread. That was a big sacrifice for them. Some of the peasants gave me a potato. Others gave me a piece of cheese. With these treasures I would go back to the "house of death" where my mother and my two sisters were. Although my return was a festive and grateful moment, the meager food was never enough to sustain us for long. One day one of my twin sisters, Rivka, lay on the ground motionless. Her face had the mask of death.

I went over to my sister and I put my ear to her chest. Naively, I asked my mother, "*Mameh, zi schloft?* She's sleeping?"

"*Nein, mine kind, zi is toit,*" she said, matter-of-factly. "No, my child. She's dead."

The bodies of the dead were stripped of their clothing and piled one on top of another at the entrance to the stable. From time to time, men would come with a wheelbarrow and remove the corpses for burial elsewhere. No one thought of following to see where and how these people were brought to their eternal rest. We didn't ask about Kaddish.

My sister Rivka's body was dragged along the ground and put on top of a pile. A few days later, Rivka's twin sister, Liebe, died in exactly the same way. She, too, was dragged away and put on the pile of the dead. Every time I went in and out of the stable I saw their corpses, and I don't remember crying. I had become numb from the pain, hopelessness, and grief. The reality that my beloved sisters lay dead on a pile of bodies was a fact of life. I knew that sooner or later, that is where I would be as well. Looking back, I'm awestruck that marching under the noses of the Romanian gendarmes, the German *einsazguppen*, and the Ukranian police, my sisters merited not to be defiled by the savage soldiers.

I don't know how my mother kept on living with so much loss, dehumanization, and pain. But as long as I was alive, she lived for me and I lived for her. At forty-two, my mother had become a mere white skeleton. She looked so old, with so much despair in her eyes. Yet she reassured me constantly: "*Du, mein kind, vest lebn* — You, my child, will live."

One day I went out with two of my friends who were in the stable with us, Basha and Raizel. We tried to strengthen each other, to give each other hope. Maybe they too could procure some food. This time, my companions seemed to be luckier than I because their small sacks were soon full. We met at a secret place where they told me that they were going back to the stable at Kopaigorod. Upon parting, I requested, "Please tell my mother that I will stay another day because I haven't any food to bring back."

The Ukrainian children didn't go to school. At ten years of age, they were taken from their families to serve as menial army workers. These young boys saw people being killed all the time. Everybody was killing, so why should they miss out on the fun? When these Ukranian boys met one of us, they would test us to determine whether we were truly non-Jews, as we claimed. "*Ijidovka,*" they would jeer, assuming that we were *Ijidovka* (a dirty Jew), even though I looked more Ukrainian than they, "*skajee kokorooza* — Dirty Jew, say corn." Ignorant as these peasant children were, they knew that language forged a common bond. The secret was to roll the "r" correctly. That was how the spoken test revealed whether or not one was truly Ukrainian. A properly rolled "r" meant life. A child who couldn't roll the "r" was killed slowly, torn limb from limb.

I passed this test many times. But my two little friends must have failed. The following day as I made my way to my mother, I was confronted with a sight that shredded my already broken heart. There, cut up and discarded in the snow, were the bodies of Basha and Raizel. Had they just killed them it would have been merciful, but the boys had tortured them slowly until they were dead. You could see by what was thrown across the snow.

Unfortunately, even now we are living in a time, when Western society and culture has produced children who kill. Raising children without values and without morals results in cold-blooded violence. When you teach children to worship their own whims and desires, they become capable of murder, like the children of the Ukrainian peasants.

When I came back from the forest to the stable with my little sack of food scraps, I discovered my mother's body lying naked on the floor. Someone had already stolen her ragged garments. Any clothing of the dead was needed by the living to help them live another moment, another hour, another day. Some other people who were also foraging for food had seen what happened to my friends and had informed my mother. Upon learning about Basha and Raizel's murders, my mother must have thought that I, too, had been killed, as I had not yet returned. My mother had nothing left to live for. She was placed on the ever-growing heap of bodies by the entrance, on top of her beloved twin daughters.

Although I was starving, I traded my meager food supply for a slip. As little as I was, I felt that it was undignified for my mother's body to be exposed. My mother had maintained her humanity under the most inhumane circumstances, and the preservation of my mother's modesty took precedence over my hunger.

She had been such an elevated soul in her life. Even in the midst of the worst suffering, my mother, known to all as *Doamna* Berachah, always treated everyone with respect. The one who had lovingly cared for me and given me my nobility of self could not be allowed to lie there in such a degraded state. I walked up to my precious mother, covered her body with the slip, and kissed her and my sisters goodbye. From that moment and forever afterward, I became nobody's child.

CHAPTER 4

LYDIA IN THE LION'S DEN

With the death of my mother, my intuition warned me that I had to move on. *I have to leave this house of death. There is nothing to keep me here. Maybe I can escape to a place where I have a better chance of surviving, of honoring the memory of my beloved family and of telling the world what happened to our lives.* Forlorn and totally broken, I picked up my empty food sack and walked through that stable gate for the last time. My starving, wasted body, along with my crushed spirit, again slipped through the wooden fence. Heaving with sobs of grief and anguish I disappeared between the trees, becoming just another creature of the forest of Transnistria.

For weeks, I trudged along on the desolate road, living on what I could find, steal, or beg. Deprived of any rites of mourning, I wept constantly. Haunting me were the images of my beloved family members, along with the memories of the torture and the terror that they had endured. Many times, I was ready to give up. But my mother's words welled up from within me with her command for my destiny: "You must live. You must remember. You must tell the world what the Romanians did to us. You are my last hope. Never, ever, give in to despair."

I decided to try to make my way to Moghilev Ghetto where I hoped to find some members of my mother's large family. With the brutal slaughter of Basha and Raizel branded into my memory, I dragged myself onward, knowing that I had to constantly be on the lookout for cruel children and large, vicious dogs. First, I would sneak up to a house to see if there were children inside. Then I would listen very carefully for any growls or barking. If I saw any children, or heard any dogs, I would run away.

One time, I heard a growl, but I didn't run away fast enough and two ferocious German shepherds attacked me. One of the dogs bit down on my cheek in the exact same place that the neighbor's horse had bitten me when I was five years old. The dogs slashed open my face, my lip, and my right hand, which was left limp and hanging. The peasant lady of the house ran out shrieking and pulled me out from under the dogs. Not knowing if I was dead or alive, she dragged me into her hut, sat me down on a chair, and brought a basin of warm water to clean my injuries.

Holding my blood-soaked face in her hands, she helped me swallow some brandy against the pain. With firm, steady hands, this kind-hearted woman sewed up my face with a needle and thread. Then she took a piece of moldy bread and held it against my fresh wounds. This was the villagers' homemade penicillin. Thank G-d, my wounds didn't become infected, although I was left with a three-inch scar on my right cheek. The peasant woman hid me in her home until I recuperated somewhat. But every day that I stayed there was a risk to the lives of my rescuer and the members of her family. One morning she gave me some food and sadly told me it was time to move on.

I walked the roads of Transnistria all alone, not yet ten years old. At times I would stretch out my arms and pretend to be a bird, imagining that I could fly away from danger. Hashem was always guiding me, showing me which way to turn and giving me strength not to be afraid.

Cold and starving, I was a wanderer, running from one hamlet to the next. One day, I saw a little hut. I sneaked up to the window and saw a very petite young woman cradling her baby. Relieved that there were no older children or ferocious dogs around, I told myself that this seemed like a safe place. I knocked on the door. With the baby in her arms, the woman came to the door and opened it a crack. When she saw me, the woman, whose name was Maria, motioned for me to come in and started crossing herself furiously, weeping as though someone in her family had died. "Come in, my daughter," she whispered through her sobs.

Upon hearing those words, my heart ached for my own mother, whose body might still be with my sisters' bodies on the pile of corpses awaiting burial. Standing there with tears flowing down my cheeks, I must have been a pathetic sight. Maria pointed to a wooden chair for me to sit on, and she quickly brought me a bowl of hot soup. The warm liquid was delicious and satisfying. After I ate it, this heaven-sent protector told me to take off my rags and she handed me one of her dresses. All the rags I had worn were completely infested with lice. Maria removed the food from the oven, took my clothes, and threw them into the oven to delouse them. Then she took kerosene and explained to me that she was going to kill the lice on my head. She rubbed the kerosene onto my scalp and combed out the lice. I was overwhelmed by her kindness.

After that, Maria prepared a bed for me in the warmest, most coveted place in the house — the alcove right above the oven. I must have slept for hours, and when I awoke she gave me another bowl of soup. How wise this wonderful stranger was. If she had given me too much to eat at one time, I could have died.

As I hungrily ate the soup, Maria's husband, Vasil, walked in. Without asking any questions, he said, "*Zidovka* — Jew."

I knew better than to lie. I said, "Yes."

Looking directly at me, he asked, "Where are you from?"

"Kopaigorod," I replied.

He then said the strangest thing to me: "Lucky *Zidovka*!"

At that point, I broke down completely. Weeping uncontrollably, I cried, "Please, please, tell me why, why am I so lucky? I've lost everyone I love, I have no life, and I'm being hunted like an animal." Between sobs, I told him the whole story: My mother was a midwife and a healer. Even the townspeople loved and admired her. Then, in the middle of the night, they banged on our windows. I thought it was for a birth, but it was to warn us to escape the massacre and first phase of the deportations.

Vasil stared at me with his head tilted and his mouth partly open. I told him how my life was destroyed overnight, how I lost everyone that I loved. How I was robbed of the opportunity to learn and to grow. How I was thrown into this hell of death and misery.

"I have no family, no home, no school. Why then am I so lucky?"

Vasil banged on the table and I jumped. In a loud voice he commanded me: "*Zidovka*, stop crying and I'll tell you why you are lucky." This uncouth peasant had lost his patience with me. But I was a little child and he had a baby. I looked like one of his own people, not at all like a Jew. Somewhere, beneath his rough exterior, was some kind of a heart. I tried to muffle my weeping. Vasil fixed his gaze on my face and pointed at me, saying loudly, "You, *Zidovka*, you were picked to be saved! The day after your mother died and you left Kopaigorod, the gendarmes drove all the remaining Jews into the forest, beat them senseless and burned them alive. You were saved! That is why you are lucky!"

Shocked and stunned by this news, I tried to grasp the impossible: Had my mother lived one more day, I would have been among those burned in the forest. So the painful and ironic truth was that even in her death, my mother took care of me. My mother's death released me to life.

Something happened to me at this time that kept me going throughout the war, its aftermath, and until this day. When

Vasil shouted at me, "You were picked to be saved," I felt that for some reason, unknown to me then, an invisible Hand had plucked me out of Kopaigorod, where my mother and twin sisters had died. I then realized that I must survive in order to remember my loved ones. My mother's message to live, remember, and tell filled my pitiful existence with a goal. My entire purpose was to survive for the sake of completing my mother's command of remembrance. *"Zachor...lo tishkach"* (Remember, do not forget) (Deuteronomy 25:17-19). Driven by this imperative, my will to survive gave me strength, intuition, and guidance throughout those nightmarish days, as well as the courage to rebuild afterwards.

Vasil and Maria kept me for a few more days so that I could regain some strength. I had to sleep in a haystack because there were periodic inspections. The Nazis had lists of the inhabitants of each and every village. If the police found an extra person in the house, they asked no questions, they simply killed every-one. If I were discovered in their haystack, my keepers trusted that I would never betray their kindness to me.

After a few days, Maria told me with tears in her eyes that they couldn't risk hiding me any longer. She gave me whatever rags they could spare to protect me from the bitter cold. In the winter of '41-'42, thousands of children froze to death on the roads of Transnistria. I could have easily been one of the dead because I fainted with a high fever on one of the harsh winter roads of Transnistria. I had contracted a terrible case of malaria. Someone found me, took me in, kept me until I was well, and put me back on the road on a warm spring day.

Who were the angels that risked their lives to save me? Who healed me? I don't think I will ever know. Whoever these people were, they told me how to find my way to Moghilev Ghetto. They taught me how to ask for a ride from people who were driving their horse and wagon. When those people completed their journey, I would ask someone else for a ride and continue on my way.

I returned to the Moghilev Ghetto in the spring of 1941 and found my Aunt Esther, my mother's eldest sister. She had only one surviving child, my cousin, Arele, a little boy the same age as me. Aunt Esther suggested that I go to live in the orphanage. Again, to my amazement and confusion, I was called lucky. She told me, "You are luckier than Arele. Arele can't go to the orphanage because he has me. You can go because you have no parents." Some luck, I thought. But from Aunt Esther's perspective, I had a better opportunity than her son. At least at the orphanage meager provisions were supposed to be available.

The orphanage accepted me but it, too, was a death trap. As I.C. Butnaru writes, "But one of the most bitter aspects of the tragedy taking place in Transnistria was the state of the orphaned children! Living a vagabond existence, naked, hungry, sick, and uncared for, these children presented a living image accusing a criminal regime of unforgivable deeds."[1] Butnaru quotes a memorandum forwarded by Dr. Wilhelm Filderman, a wartime leader of Romanian Jewry, to Marshal Antonescu on January 2, 1942. He states: "In one orphanage alone, with 140 children, 26 have died within a single month. They are naked, sleeping on beds without any bedclothes, in unheated rooms without any windowpanes, so that they cannot get up out of bed to take care of their needs; they live in a pestilential atmosphere."[2]

These were exactly the "living conditions" that I found when I entered the orphanage in Moghilev Ghetto. It was a cold building, without doors or windows. The people in charge shaved off the long blonde hair that my mother and sisters had combed and braided so lovingly, hair that had never been cut, and it was taken from me. I looked like a little boy. I thought I must be silly to mourn this loss when I had already lost so much, but my hair was all I had left from my childhood.

"Breakfast" in the morning was a small amount of coffee, hot water mixed with coffee grounds, along with an ounce of

1. Butnaru, p. 144.
2. *Ibid.*,pp. 144-145.

Photo reproduced with permission from *Dorohoi*, published by Rumanian descendants of Dorohoi and surrounding area.

A formal picture at the orphanage. I am at the far left in the second row.

bread. I remember a case in which one young boy couldn't walk to get the bread because, like many of the children there, he had sores on his feet, probably from frostbite, and as they healed, the skin of his feet had grown together so that he could not walk. His little brother went to get the bread for both of them. One of the portions was slightly bigger than the other.

The older brother said, "Give me the bigger piece because I'm older." The little boy responded, "You're going to die. I'm going to live so I need the bigger slice. The smaller one is good enough for you."

Even the orphanage was not a haven. From there the Kapos often sent children to death camps. When the Kapos (Jews who collaborated with the Nazis) needed numbers and they couldn't fill the quota, they took the helpless children who were unprotected and easy to kidnap.

We slept four to a cot, two pointed in one direction and two the other way. There was no bedding, only wooden frames. The girl who faced me had tuberculosis. Surprisingly, I never contracted tuberculosis even though it is a highly contagious disease. After liberation, the disease claimed the girl's life. Children were disappearing constantly, but others took their place. Barely fed or clothed, we were a thoroughly wretched lot.

Thrown together in that inhuman, disease-ridden circumstance, we nevertheless were still children, and we tried to befriend and help one another. At night, lying side by side in our hunger and loneliness, we would reminisce about our parents, our siblings, and mostly about the food that we needed so desperately in order to survive. We remembered the food we had left over on our plates at home and how we now wished we had it to eat. We had no nurturing; no loving hands to feed or bathe us, no gentle words or human contact. We longed for our families and the normalcy of home and school life. We all cried ourselves to sleep every night.

The children talked about ways to make things better. One night, we sat up and talked about crossing over to the other side of the ghetto, the Christian side. Scraps of discarded food were more available there. "It's a little easier to get food there," my roommate Bella said. "Over there, when a piece of bread is thrown out, you don't have so many people fighting over it. Over there, if you follow a funeral procession, they have a feast afterwards right in the cemetery. Anyone can come and eat. They don't chase anybody away."

Through being the provider for my mother and sisters, I had already been exposed to the Christian sector. I knew it was possible to get along with the peasants and to offer to do work for them. With this in mind, four of us decided to sneak out of the orphanage and try our luck in the Christian sector.

The Almighty had prepared me for this survival in a number of ways. As a young child at home with my family, I had contracted every contagious disease. On the Death March, when other children got sick, I stayed well. Hashem also endowed me with the gift of learning languages with ease. I could communicate with the local populace. Speaking their language saved my life countless times. With my Aryan appearance, they didn't view me as a total outcast. I also was given the ability to observe people and to be able to sort out kind faces from the evil ones.

My greatest asset, however, was my faith. Even when I was pretending to be a Christian, I would chant my Hebrew prayers in a whisper, saying, "Please, Hashem, forgive me. I am doing this because I want to live." The many nights I spent all alone in haystacks or bombed-out houses, I wasn't really alone because Hashem was with me. He was there by my side, guarding me and watching over me. Moment by moment, He helped me to survive.

Once we reached the Christian side, outside the Moghilev Ghetto, each one of us found a hiding place in a bombed-out building. Like solitary birds, we collected rags and bits of hay to use for bedding on the freezing ground. At night, I would pull my shirt up over my face and exhale my warm breath onto my body to try to generate heat.

We were a loyal group. The few of us on the outside of the Jewish ghetto used to meet every morning to acknowledge our survival together. Each day that we survived was a new reason to rejoice, to give another prayer of thanks and a *Shehecheyanu,* thanking Hashem for keeping us alive. Thinking about our pain was a luxury that we couldn't afford. We needed to conserve our energy for survival, moment by moment, hour by hour, day by day.

We lived with hope. We told one another how wonderful our future would be when the world would hear what happened to us. People would try to heal us, protect us, and defend us at all times. We imagined how they would see to it that we always had shelter, food, love, and education. They would nurture us and give us back our lost childhood, we thought. It was a beautiful fantasy.

We made each other a *neder,* a promise, that if one of us was caught, we would never, ever tell the police where the others were hiding. We never did. While I was in hiding, living as a Christian, those little vagabonds were my secret friends, my connection to my true identity, to the person that I really was.

Once I had secured a place to sleep, I had to look for a way to find some food. Surviving on the other side was very hard, but my "living conditions" afforded more opportunities than the orphanage.

On a street close to the Dniester River, there was a big restaurant on one side of the street and a little café on the other side. This café was a singularly run establishment. *Pani* (Madame) Bukovska, the proprietor, made her living from the *SS Einzatzgruppen*. I learned later that Himmler made a special effort to recruit from among the educated class. Many *Einzatzgruppen* were professionals and other college graduates. They proved to be among the most ruthless of the *Einzatzgruppen* murderers.

In the Moghilev Ghetto, they were all over the place! Their every movement was meant to inspire terror in a person's heart. The boots of their uniforms were designed with hobnails nailed into the heels. The sound of those nails pierced the air like bullet shots with their every step.

Bukovska served both the *Einzatzgruppen* and the *Gendarmerie*.

I studied the face of this tall, blond Ukrainian lady and decided that she did not look cruel. Finally, I gathered the courage to approach her and ask if she needed help at her café. She looked at me curiously. I hadn't had enough food to grow in more than a year, so I probably appeared to be only five or six years old.

"What can such a little girl like you do?" she asked me. With this response, it was clear that she saw me as a child. I felt hope rising up in my heart. Maybe she would let me work for her in exchange for food.

I said to her, "I could wash your dishes." There was no sink or running water in this restaurant. There was only a water pump across the street.

"All right, then, try these." Bukovska handed me four plates and pointed to the other side of the street where the pump stood. Starting the pump was no easy task for me. I had to muster the little strength that I had to push down the iron handle. After three or four pushes the water finally came gushing out.

I washed the dishes and brought them back to the restaurant counter. I could have easily stolen the dishes and traded them on the black market for bread, but I couldn't bring myself to do it. I had to bring them back. Bukovska looked at the dishes and then she looked at me.

"What's your name?" she asked.

Now quickly I had to give myself a name. Since my name is Leah I said, "Lydia." It was close enough.

"I'm *Pani* Bukovska, Lydia. You washed only the front of the dish. You have to go back and wash the other side of the dish." And so I got my first lesson in washing dishes. By helping *Pani* Bukovska in the café, I learned many useful things. With time, I would hide pieces of bread left over by the *SS Einzatzgruppen*, and give what I could to my friends. Slowly I gained her confidence and she took a liking to me. One night she asked me the most amazing question: Would I like to go home with her to sleep in her house?

I said, "Of course. I would love to."

I had been living like a homeless vagabond, sleeping on the frozen ground. A real bed in a real home had only been something to dream about. Now, though, being in a warm bed must have brought back memories of the night I was driven from my own bed at home. In my sleep, I had a nightmare. I screamed out in Yiddish, and *Pani* Bukovska shook me awake.

She said, "Lydia, Lydia, what language are you speaking and why are you screaming?"

I had to tell her who I really was. "I'm a Jew," I said, with fear rising in my heart. "I was crying out in Yiddish. I had a nightmare about my family being killed." I was afraid that after Bukovska heard my confession, she would ask me to leave.

To my surprise and relief she said, "Lydia, my child, your secret is safe with me, but you must not tell another soul, because if the Nazis find out that I'm keeping you, we will both die." From that time on, I was always with her, doing my daily restaurant chores in exchange for food and a place to sleep.

The strangest part of our relationship was that this Ukrainian lady named *Pani* Bukovska didn't even like Jews. When she had friends over, they would sit at one of the restaurant tables, huddled around a bottle of vodka, and drink. When the Ukranians reached a certain level of drunkenness, their vile anti-Semitism would spill out with as much ease as the vodka pouring from the bottle. When I heard my benefactor cursing the dirty Jews and passionately declaring her patriotic, Ukrainian hatred for us, I would cower in a corner of the restaurant and shake with fear. But when she was sober, she truly loved me and defended me. Without her, I felt that I would not have survived.

One day a group of *SS Einsatzgruppen* came into the café to eat and drink, the sound of their hobnailed boots filling the air with a foreboding terror. After those Nazis were finished they said to each other in German, "Why should we pay? We'll break up the place." They charged around like wild animals, breaking dishes and smashing furniture, laughing wildly in their drunkenness. Lights were shattered and glass fragments littered the tabletops and the floor. This horror was the Germans' idea of fun. The more they destroyed *Pani* Bukovska's café, the more they laughed.

Afterwards, huddled in a corner, still holding onto each other hysterical with fear, I said to her, "Yiddish is close enough to German that I understood what they said. *Pani* Bukovska, they were planning it!"

Bukovska stopped crying and looked at me. "Lydia, how do you know?"

I said, "I heard them talking and I understood every word they said. These Nazis didn't want to pay. They wanted to have fun."

Then Bukovska started laughing instead of crying. She hugged me and kissed me. Her laughter was so loud and deep that I thought she was losing her mind. She said, "Lydia, you will be my child. You will never have to worry again. You will be protected." She repaired the little restaurant and we developed a secret code between the two of us. Whenever I learned that the SS men were planning trouble I did something clumsy, like drop a glass. That was the signal for her to run across the street and bring an equal number of Ukrainian soldiers. When the Nazis saw the Ukrainian soldiers, they would pay their bill and leave. We thus protected her business, and I was relatively safe.

Then suddenly, my tentative world was destroyed again. From time to time Madame Bukovska went into the ghetto to buy things. One day I was alone in the restaurant. There were turncoat Jewish men who collaborated with the Nazis. Known as the Kapos, they usually wore distinctive armbands. This time they didn't. The Kapos came over to me and tried to ask me if I knew where any Jewish children were hiding. But because they couldn't speak the Ukrainian language, they couldn't make themselves understood.

I was so naïve that I betrayed myself and asked them, "What other languages do you speak?"

They said, "Romanian." Once I started speaking to them in Romanian, I was doomed, because the only child who could speak Romanian in Transnistria was a Jewish child!

The Kapos kidnapped me, but I never broke my promise. I never revealed the hiding places of my friends. These men dragged me away from the café and took me to the train station. As the train was leaving, they pulled an elderly man off the last car and shoved me onto the train in his place. I then witnessed one of the most degrading sights. One of the Kapos went over to the Nazi guard and, with a smile, put out his hand. My life had been traded for a package of cigarettes. I was shocked, terrified, and enraged at this injustice. How could fellow Jews do that to a little girl who tried to help them? Not even in my worst nightmares did I imagine that I would be betrayed by my own people.

This cattle car of tortured human cargo was destined for the worst death camp in Transnistria — Pechora, near the Bug

River. Only three people are known to have escaped from this death house: One lives in Montreal. One lives in the Ukraine. The third one is me. When the Nazis wanted to inflict the most terrible punishments on their captured Russian soldiers, they sent them to Pechora.

In despair, I looked around at the other people packed together on this lifeless train. I saw a woman next to me who looked either dead or very near death. She had a piece of bread in her hand. I took the piece of bread and quickly ate it. Other people came and searched her for the bread, but it was already gone.

When this airless journey of summer 1942 was over, we were marched through the forest to Pechora. In Pechora, there was absolutely nothing to eat and nothing to drink. Like an animal, I chewed on grass and I got down on my hands and knees to drink from puddles. No one there looked human. The prisoners were walking skeletons encrusted with dirt. When someone died, some of the remaining victims tried to chew off pieces of his body.

People went mad with hunger. The stench inside was beyond imagination. I went into one of the barracks and I ran out as if I had seen a ghost. Everyone there was very close to death. From somewhere within me, I decided that this was no place for me. Here I wouldn't live, I wouldn't remember, and the dead don't tell. My mother's wish mustn't die here. *I must get out of here in order to survive and tell the world. I must keep the memory of the brutal destruction alive.*

Determined, I sat down under a little bush, near the entrance gate. Starving but resolute, I stayed there day and night. The guards were watching me and I was watching them. I don't know why they didn't shoot me for staying out of the bunks. On the third day the gate was open and there was only one guard on patrol. This guard was joking with the Ukrainian girls. I could see that he was totally engrossed.

I said to myself, "If I'm caught it will be good to die. But maybe, just maybe, I will live." I girded myself with the mission of my mother's words. Whispering to myself, *You must live. You must remember. You must tell the world about this place,* I raised myself up slowly with as little movement as possible and walked out as if I didn't belong in there, blending in with the crowd outside the gate. I often asked for directions and sometimes rode along in a wagon with the local peasants.

Wandering for months along the crowded roads, my nightmare began all over again as I had to constantly be on the watch for children and dogs. A few days later I reached a Jewish Ukrainian community. I asked the people there for help.

Seeing that I was walking around barefoot and almost naked, they asked me where I had come from.

I replied, "Pechora."

They called everybody together. "Listen to this child. She says she comes from Pechora." When I described to them what Pechora looked like, the men believed me.

The people in the community gave me some food and warm clothing. Help was being sent from the Jews of Transylvania who remained in their homes until 1944, and from the Jews of Bucharest. The remnant of the Jews in Transnistria were freed in 1944, whereas tragically, the Jews of Transylvania were shipped in cattle cars to Auschwitz. Most of the life-sustaining relief was channeled elsewhere, in particular for the families of those in charge. We saw precious little of it. The orphaned children got very little help.

I was determined to try to find my way back to Moghilev Ghetto, back to *Pani* Bukovska. I decided, *That's it. If fellow Jews can betray me and send me to my death for a package of cigarettes, then I can't be a Jew anymore.* But I wasn't very good at giving up my heritage. Back with *Pani* Bukovska, I found that the more I lived like a Christian, the more I became a Jew.

When I went to church and crossed myself, in my heart I was saying, "Please, Hashem, forgive me. I want to live." When I ate non-kosher food, I asked G-d to forgive me and I resolved in my heart that if G-d would let me survive, I would fully return to my roots and raise a completely Jewish family. I looked for my friends who had escaped with me from the orphanage, but found no one. No new children appeared. I don't know if any of those children survived that terrible winter of 1942.

Living as a Christian, I had a deep need to affirm my Jewish self. I was raised to know that being a Jew meant living as a Jew. I needed to somehow declare who I was even though I was only ten years old. When autumn came, I would decide, *This day is Yom Kippur, and I'm fasting.* On that day, from sundown, I would pretend not to be hungry and I would find reasons to avoid eating the food that *Pani* Bukovska wanted to give me. When spring came, I decided, *The time for Pesach has come. For the next eight days I am not eating any bread.* Although bread was a staple food for us, it was more important for me to stay connected to my people.

My heart would burn with the memories of our Seder nights at home. In my mind's eye I saw our Seder table with the hand-made matzahs, the wine, the horseradish, egg, celery, and the shankbone — all in their gleaming silver dishes.

I remembered my mother's words when I would grate horseradish root and ask why we had to eat something so bitter. "If we keep the Torah, no matter what happens, even if sometimes it is bitter, we are free," she would answer me. Now, I was living the bitterness.

In contrast to my life in the café, these memories could have shattered me, if not for my strong survival instinct. Instead, they became my source of strength and determination. Through these secret, self-declared acts, I remained connected to my people even though I lived like a "painted bird."[3] Although outwardly, I looked and acted like a Ukrainian peasant girl, in my heart and soul I was loyal to my family and to my people.

While I wasn't very good at pretending to be a Christian, something inexplicable happened to me. I completely lost any memory of how to speak Yiddish, Hebrew, and Romanian. At that time, those languages represented death; a Ukrainian

---

3. Kosinski, Jerzy. *The Painted Bird* is a book about a child.

peasant girl simply wasn't educated in so many languages. I needed to forget them for the sake of my survival disguise.

On the street corner, adjacent to *Pani* Bukovska's café, was a pharmacy. Our Sages tell us that, "A man is known by his wallet, his cup, and his anger."[4] This pharmacist epitomized the negative side of this axiom. He was coarse and unruly; a jealous man prone to violent outbursts. One day he tripped over the café entrance, drunk.

"Bukovska, that girl is a *Zidovka,*" he slurred, "and that's why you're getting rich. You are keeping Lydia, and she understands everything the Nazis say." Of course, he was right. From that moment on, every time I would hear the clang of the hobnails from the Nazis' boots, I felt more than my usual sense of dread.

In the winter of 1944, more than a year after the pleas for repatriation of the Jewish orphans had been submitted early in 1943, on one of *Pani* Bukovska's trips into the ghetto, she found out that children from the Moldova province were being brought back to Romania as part of a repatriation plan. After the Nazi defeat at Stalingrad and the increasing possibility of an allied victory, and the incessant intervention of Jewish community activist Dr. Wilhelm Filderman, the Romanian dictator Ion Antonescu agreed to plans to repatriate Transnistrian orphans with the understanding that various international organizations would be involved in their eventual emigration to Palestine.[5]

I remember that my kind guardian returned from the ghetto. one day in October 1944. *Pani* Bukovska came to me and sat me down. With tears in her eyes she said, "Lydia, we must part. You must go back to Romania so that we can both live. The druggist is on to us. And if he tells the authorities, we will both die."

Twice she took me to the repatriation commission to report that I was from the Dorohoi region, and therefore eligible to return there. Only children under the age of fourteen were able to apply. Although I met the age requirement, twice I was

---

4. *Eruvin,* 65b.

5. Ioanid, pp. 238-258.

rejected. The committee didn't believe me when I said I was Jewish. I had forgotten how to speak Romanian, Yiddish, and Hebrew. I only understood and was able to communicate in Russian, Ukrainian, and German. The languages of my childhood had spelled death for too long.

Encouraged by Madame Bukovska, we decided to try again. Once more we walked freely, as non-Jews did, into the ghetto, which was abuzz with the news of the repatriation of the Jewish orphans. Posters in Russian were plastered on the walls. After more than a year of struggle, the repatriation plan received final approval by the Romanian government. It had been initiated by Jewish leaders, Chief Rabbi Alexander Safran and Dr. Wilhelm Filderman, and backed by Romania's Queen Mother Elena, the International Red Cross, and the Swiss Ambassador to Bucharest. This enabled the 5,000 surviving orphans in Transnistria to return to Romania, provided that the majority of them would be sent to Palestine.

For the third time, we walked into the school building and down the long gray hall to the large auditorium where the judges sat. Life and death were in their hands. In desperation, mothers would go to the train station and cry, clinging to the train, begging, pleading with the authorities to take their only surviving child and to place him on the train with a ticket to life.

I stood in front of the panel, petrified because I couldn't remember a word of Hebrew, Yiddish, or Romanian. All three had become languages of self-betrayal. In order to assure my survival, and hopefully to somehow "live, remember, and tell," I had transformed myself into a total *shikse* (non-Jewish girl) in every way, beyond all suspicion as to who I really was. As a result, in my heart and soul I became a stronger Jew, fully committed to my Jewish survival and to my destiny.

The experience of having been kidnapped and taken to the Pechora concentration camp had left me mute to the languages closest to my heart. I was devastated and determined to live "on the other side." It was an ironic twist that after all the time I spent hiding my Jewish identity and living in the lion's den, serving the Nazis, suddenly my future now depended on convincing the panel that I was a Jew.

The committee quizzed me as to who I was, where I had lived, and who my family had been. This time, my former teacher, Yaakov Schechter, sat on the commission. He stood up and proclaimed in an anguished tone, "This child is my former student. She is the only surviving child from the entire Hebrew school in Herta who has come before us so far. I knew her parents and she is, without a doubt, a Jewish child." The committee accepted his testimony.

It was a tearful parting. *Pani* Bukovska came with me to the train station and stood before me with her hands on my shoulders. "Lydia, we must part so that we both can live. May G-d watch you always." Along with a group of orphaned children age fourteen and below, I stepped onto the train and found a seat by a window. We orphaned children were sent back to Romania on luxury trains with sleeper cars. We, who were without families, without homes, and of broken spirits, were traveling first class as Romania began to try to wipe the blood off of her political hands and face. That was the last transport out of Transnistria for the orphaned children.

G-d didn't want me to pose as a Ukrainian child forever. He wasn't going to abandon me in Transnistria where I would be lost forever. He had other plans for me. First, I had to survive. Then, slowly, I was led to my destiny, step by painful step.

Sitting on the train and watching the Ukrainian countryside move behind me, I was on my own again, riding into the void, without any grounded framework of existence. It was not easy for me to leave *Pani* Bukovska. She had been kind to me, and I had grown very attached to her. Moving towards danger and the unknown, once again, I belonged to no one. Looking out the window with sadness, fear, and uncertainty of what future I would have as nobody's child, my mother's words coursed through me with my pounding heart. *You, my child, must live, you must remember, you must tell the world what the Romanians did to us.*

CHAPTER 5

SURVIVAL AFTER SURVIVAL

n that winter of 1944, the "luxury" train that took me away from the Transnistrian hell transported me to an unknown future. I had nothing and no one to go back to. Can a person return to nothing?

Suddenly, I was a Jewish orphan who, according to the arbitrary standards of the "Romanian Führer," qualified to be on the train to life and hope. My change of status was directly related to a paradox in Romanian politics and policies. As Ioanid reveals about Antonescu towards the end of his book, "He was a harsh, even violent, anti-Semite. But a comparison to Adolf Hitler, whom he admired and who admired him, shows him in a different light. A direct or indirect dialogue between the German dictator and the leader of the Jewish community in Germany would have been inconceivable. In spite of his apparent inflexibility though, Antonescu tolerated, even encouraged, contact with minority leaders in his own country..."[1] It was this openness

_____
1. Ioanid, p. 282.

to dialogue that made possible the appeals for the repatriation plan. Inwardly, I was reeling from the sudden turn of events. My heart churned faster than the wheels of the train.

Under normal circumstances, when a young child loses a parent, the entire community becomes united on behalf of that bereaved child. Everyone tries to comfort him, to provide him with shelter, and to care for all his needs. For us, no such provisions could be made, as we were part of a community that was persecuted. In an exceptional case, people barely managed to bring comfort to their very own.

My traveling companions became instant siblings – sisters and brothers who shared the same trauma and pain of a lost childhood. To us, this was a journey into the unknown. We were amazed at the comfort. We had warmth, food, and a berth to sleep in. Above all, we shared a hope for a better future. We were certain that once our stories of torture and terror, of loss and destruction, were told, people would go out of their way to protect us, care for us, and help us to rebuild our lives.

We lived with these fantasies of a warm, loving home, a normal school life, a fulfilled identity with encouragement and assistance in dealing with our pain. Had we known then what the free world knew, that most people were conducting "business as usual," we would have been devastated.[2] Our will to continue living our lives stemmed partly out of ignorance of the world's indifference towards us. Driven by our dreams of "royal" compensation, we persevered.

My seat on the luxury train represented a shift in the political and historical interest of Romania. Whereas before Romanian dictator Ion Antonescu had been one of Hitler's closest and most important allies, with recognized "special status" in the German war machine, tension was beginning to develop because of German criticism about how Romania was handling its "Jewish problem."[3]

---

2. Lookstein, Haskel *Were We Our Brother's Keepers? The Public Response of American Jews to the Holocaust 1938-1944*, p. 223.

3. Ioanid, p. 241.

Although Germany's preference was for Romania to deport its Jews directly to the German death camps in Poland, "...even Romanian fascists did not want to be told what to do with 'their Jews.'"[4] The Romanian *gendarmerie* and local populace were only too happy to vent their hatred towards the Jews – but they would do it in their own way. The German need for Romanian resources, in particular, oil – had forced them to exercise restraint with the erratic Romanian policies.

However, in Raul Hilberg's *The Destruction of the European Jews* (1961), he documents that: " ...what was true of personal opportunism in Romania was true also of personal involvement in killings. Repeatedly the Romanians threw themselves into *Aktionen*. Witnesses and survivors testifying to the manner in which the Romanians conducted their killing operations, and in some cases...the Germans stepped in to halt the killings that seemed offensive even to so hardened an establishment as the German Army." This was not, however, because the *SS Einzatzgruppen* objected, in principle, to the brutality; it was because in their estimation Romanian killing methodology was disorganized, inadequate, and would "affect the prestige of the German army."[5]

In the Bucharest pogrom that began on the twentieth of January 1941, perpetrated by the Iron Guard, it was reported that "...the victims had not merely been killed, they had been butchered. In the morgue bodies were so cut up that they no longer resembled anything human, and in the municipal slaughterhouse bodies were observed hanging like carcasses of cattle."[6]

But the German defeat at Stalingrad in 1943 compelled the Romanian dictator to face what his fate might be after an Allied victory. In an attempt to slow down the torture and deportation

---

4. *Ibid.*, p. 238.

5. *Ibid.*, p. 239.

6. Hilberg, p. 489.

of Jews, and to begin to elude the ultimate responsibility for brutality and hatred, Marshal Ion Antonescu opposed and cancelled some of his original deportation plans with the Germans and began to negotiate with the allies, with the goal of severing Romania's subservient relationship with Germany.[7] The very same committee that was to be involved in deportations now began to focus on the repatriation plan. This governmental shift was mirrored by certain political parties that suddenly began to claim that Germany was forcing Romania to act against her "humanitarian traditions."[8]

In short, with the prospect of Germany losing the war, Romania became anxious about her level of responsibility for the mass murder of hundreds of thousands of innocent Jews. She had to try to cover her bloody tracks and, in doing so, reverse her public image. All these factors — the pride of a madman, Germany's defeat at Stalingrad, and fear of international accountability — were fuel for the luxurious repatriation train that sped Jewish orphans back to an unknown future in a blood-stained land.

To the background of the rhythmic drone of the train's wheels, we sang the following songs:

Ich fohr aheim, Ich fohr aheim
Ich vill nit zein in land in deim
Shoin oisfarkoift di zach'n biz tzum letzn shtik
A leibn iz tzait tzu mach'n, ich fohr aheim tzurik
Ich fohr aheim, Ich vill nit zain mer kain ger
Vi gevezn biz aher, Ich fohr aheim.
I am going home, don't want to be here anymore.
My possessions are sold to the last.
Hard to survive here, I am going home...what home?
Tzi bin ich fun a shtein geborn
Tzi hob ich kain mameh gehat
Tzi iz den di velt oif hefker geshaf'n

---

7. Wiesenthal.com web site, *Encyclopedia of the Holocaust.*
8. Ioanid, p. 248.

G-t zei alien, G-t.
Oy Mameh shtei oif fun dain kever
Un kum tzurik tzu mir
Un tomer kenstu nit kumen tzu mir
Mamenu, nem mich tzu dir.
Has a stone given birth to me?
Have I never a mother had?
Has the world been created without purpose?
G-d, see for Yourself.
Mother, dearest, rise from your grave,
Return to me in haste
If you can't come to me,
Mother, please take me to thee!

After the war it became clearer and clearer that humanity had suffered because of the free world's callous indifference and inhumanity. Uppermost in my mind and in my heart was forever looming the question: When and under what circumstances would I be able to fulfill my mother's command to "Live! Remember! Tell the world!" Who could I trust to listen?

Hashem taught me and guided me to recognize the proper role models to emulate. He helped me to move from situation to situation, enabling me each time to set goals, to fulfill them, and then to set more goals. Hashem gave me the gift of learning languages, and created the circumstances for me to be able to achieve scholastically and to choose my friends.

Hashem gave me life again and again. What I did with my life was up to me. I had to turn every opportunity for growth into success. Not because of the fact that I had suffered, but in spite of my suffering.

When the train arrived in Dorohoi, it was bitter cold. The members of the Jewish community came out to greet us with food and clothing.

I was twelve years old and nobody's child. I had expected help, but whoever took me in used me and abused me. I spent time in orphanages, which were not nurturing places either. When I had lived as a Christian, I had had a protector. I knew where I would eat and I knew where I would sleep. Now I was liberated and dropped into the twilight zone of an abandoned, vagrant life. It was no "liberation" for me. It was entry into a new hell.

I eventually made my way from Dorohoi to Bucharest. My mother had a brother in Bacau who had sent me some money. You couldn't buy a seat on the train, but the cost of a ticket secured me a place on the train steps in the bitter cold. Every now and then, I managed to squeeze inside the train to warm up. As I stood, freezing, on the steps, I gazed at the passing fields, which were covered with the bodies of young Russian, Romanian, and German soldiers. Evidence of war and bloodshed was part of the landscape. From without and within, suffering was depicted everywhere.

Upon my arrival in Bucharest, I made my way to the office of the Joint Distribution Committee. They sent me to the Caritas Hospital to find out about orphanages. My former teacher, Mr. Yaakov Schechter, was one of the administrators of the orphanage. He warned me that I should not enter the orphanage because the Russian soldiers were coming to claim the children who were from regions that had been under Russian rule. In 1940, the Russians had invaded the region including our town of Herta. Although they left in 1941, I was still at risk of being designated a Russian citizen. Five hundred children met this sad fate. But, thanks to my former teacher's warning, I was not among them.

At the end of the winter, Mr. Schechter located a high-fashion dressmaker, *Doamna* Croitoru, who had applied to the orphanage on the pretext of looking for an "apprentice." Since I did not dare go into the orphanage because of the Russian threat, I seemed like the ideal candidate. I had no "baggage," and didn't have to answer to anyone. But this turned out to simply be a way for her to find a free maid. She never taught me dressmaking; with practice, though, my Yiddish and Romanian languages came back. I never even learned how to hold a needle or sew a single stitch.

I was her servant. I cleaned her dishes, beat her oriental rugs, scrubbed her fancy parquet floors, and made sure the glass in her display window was crystal-clear. As I rubbed the glass and checked it for streaks, I remembered polishing the silver candlesticks for Shabbos in our home. Standing on the ladder, making sure my tears didn't fall onto the dry polishing rag, I wondered what would become of my life. On the train we had all been so hopeful.

At night, I slept on the floor of the workroom. I would gather together the discarded scraps of fabric to create some semblance of a pillow. Stretched out on the floor, with only a threadbare blanket for a cover, I was surrounded by the fancy dresses *Doamna* Croitoru designed for her wealthy clientele, some of whom were dignitaries. I wore rags while she was sewing taffeta, velvet, and silk.

The rest of my waking hours, when I wasn't cleaning, I was sent to stand in lines and wait for the daily rations. Her children would go off to school, and she would send me to wait for our rationed supplies of bread, meat, and kerosene. I never went all the way to the end of the line, I would sneak up to the front of the line. Thus I always came home with supplies, while those at the very end often left empty-handed. I would have to go back and forth a few times a day. When I would see her children leave for school, the injustice would burn within me. I, too, wanted to learn. I wanted to rebuild my life and develop my mind. My family would be forever lost to me, but I did not plan to always remain a victim of the tragedy of my lost childhood and my bereavement, while being deprived of proper growth and education.

Wandering through the streets, as I went on errands for *Doamna* Croitoru, my eyes were constantly confronted by reminders of our pitiful state. Hundreds of homeless, dispossessed people walked about as though they were searching for something. Expelled from their homes, deprived of property and any cash resources, the returnees looked for relatives, for food, for assistance from social welfare organizations. When I saw their vacant, blank expressions, I knew that they, too, were among the haunted. They had no possessions to carry; instead they bore the eternal weight of the suffering that they had somehow managed to live through. Now, making their way through a second hell of non-existence, they searched the streets for signs of hope.

In his description of this wandering population, Butnaru records, "...their presence was looked upon with reserve, and even enmity by the Romanian population. They wanted – as was natural and legitimate – to go back to their houses, and that they couldn't do! They wanted to resume their small businesses, but they did not have the right to engage in them. Many handicraft shops did not function because they did not have the raw material or any place where they could carry on such activity. The homes of the Jews were occupied by new owners, who considered themselves to be the rightful heirs and legal beneficiaries of Romanization and did not want to renounce their benefits at any price.

"Personal possessions, furniture, clothing, and everything that once had made up their households had long since been stolen or bought up at the so-called auctions organized to turn the property of the Jews into cash. The new owners, those who had come from various regions of the country during the war years and had become established in those respective localities, considered the demands of the Jews to be absurd.... Having been dispossessed of their property, and lacking any possibility of resuming their occupations or exercising their professions, the majority of the Jews found themselves completely dependent on social welfare from the very first days of their 'liberation.' The problem of sheltering, feeding, and clothing them, and especially providing them with medical help, became acute...The truly disastrous effects of the stress of the camps and ghettoes in which they had lived began to be felt."[9]

---

9. Butnaru, p. 164.

Until the Communist Party established a strong foothold, only a minority of the Jewish returnees were able to resume their previous employment or reopen their shops. However, most of the population was homeless, jobless, and desperate. Despite the dangers involved, people had no other choice but to become involved in trading on the black market. Even simple commodities like matches could bring in some kind of an income.

One morning, as I returned from my daily food excursion, I saw Russian soldiers marching a group of Nazi prisoners across the street at gunpoint. In their ragged, torn uniforms they looked shrunken, starving, and scared. Hashem granted me the merit of seeing my enemies vanquished.

As I passed them by, I remembered my life in the café of Madame Bukovska. The Nazis would enter haughtily, preceded by the armored clank of their hobnail boots. I would have to serve them food and drink. They would sit down in the café, drinking until they were drunk. Their raucous, harsh voices would become louder and louder. When, finally, they left without violence or damage, both Madame Bukovska and I would breathe a sigh of relief.

Now, on the opposite side of the street, they passed in front of my eyes as broken, starving prisoners. I bore no hatred in my heart. I knew all too well what it was like to be starved and driven. I quickly took a portion from the food that I carried and threw it across to the Nazis.

As I stood there, watching my enemies groveling over the food I had thrown them, my mother's voice echoed within me, from the time the horse had nearly killed me, "Revenge is Hashem's work, not mine. My child is alive. Hashem answered my prayers."

As I watched the Russians march the Nazi prisoners across the street, I was grateful to be alive. The dignity of my childhood upbringing would allow me neither to rejoice nor to hate. The legacy of my mother's kindness and strength of character had not been scarred by being a victim of their persecution.

I carried my mother's example and teachings within me. They had formed the inner structure of my identity and guided my behavior, my choices, and my response to circumstances. The image of my parents was constantly before me. I never envied the gentiles, even when I was on the Death March. Now, as I saw the Nazis reduced to starving animals, all I felt was pity.

Around this time, I began getting severe pains on the lower right side of my abdomen. I didn't tell the dressmaker. I don't know if anyone ever saw me doubled over in pain, crying. I had become so accustomed to suffering that I simply accepted this as a new plague in my life. I ignored these attacks and continued my daily tasks of cleaning and standing in lines. One day in the spring, when I was in the front yard beating one of the dressmaker's fancy carpets, a young man appeared at the steps of the garden.

"Are you Leah?" he asked.

"Yes," I responded.

"I'm your half brother, Avraham!" he exclaimed. "We found out through the Red Cross listing that you were still alive. My wife, Betty, has been looking for you, but every time she came here you were always away, standing in line for something. Last time she came it was freezing cold and raining. When she found out you were in line again, Betty got so angry that she lost her temper and started screaming at the woman you are staying with: 'It is scandalous how you are abusing this child. Don't you know what she has gone through? How can you treat her like a slave? She came here to rebuild her life, to learn a respectable trade, not to stand in lines!' The woman became furious and called the police, so Betty wasn't allowed to come back again."

I was shocked and overjoyed to see Avraham again. He was my half brother from my father's first marriage. When my father became a young widower with two sons, he married my mother. I remembered meeting Avraham when I was a small child. At that time, before the war, we sold all of our possessions and took the train to Bucharest, trying to secure passage to the Land of Israel. Unfortunately, our attempt failed and we returned to Herta. Because they had been living in Bucharest, they were not deported. Avraham's sudden appearance saved my life. I was only too happy to leave my "apprenticeship" and go to live with him and his wife, Betty.

Avraham and Betty lived in a tiny courtyard basement apartment. Even with the best of intentions, their living quarters could not accommodate a third person. Nevertheless, they kindly took me into their meager residence and it temporarily became my home. I would have surely perished at the home of the wealthy dressmaker, either from pneumonia or from the infected appendix that I didn't know I had.

Concerned for my future and my education, Avraham and Betty convinced me to try the orphanage again, reasoning that the regulations might have changed and explaining that the opportunities were greater there. The orphanage was housed in a wing of the Caritas Hospital of the Jewish Community of Bucharest. It was described in the Memoirs of Rabbi Alexander Safran, Chief Rabbi of Romania during that time, as "...one of the most outstanding hospitals in the country and the glory of the Jewish community of Bucharest. The children from Transnistria had been brought to the hospital yard and from there were assigned to orphanages and foster families. In the same building, a rehabilitation program for those children was instituted in order to reintegrate them into a constructive way of life."[10] It was to this program that I applied.

This time, when I applied, I was told that a friend of mine, who had been living in the orphanage, had died. She was not under the rules of the Russian occupation and had not been in danger of being taken back to Russia. They had no right to claim her because she had been from a part of Romania that hadn't been occupied by the Russians. It was therefore arranged for me to take on her identity. That explains why I entered the orphanage in the Caritas Hospital as Surika Furman.

---

10. Safran, Rabbi Alexander, *Resisting the Storm, Rumania, 1940-1947, Memoirs,* p. 181.

This rehabilitation program was housed in a brand new wing of the Caritas Hospital. We had clean bedding, nourishing food, and people from different Zionist organizations who came to seek followers. I learned that there is a country called "Eretz Yisrael" that wants us to come home.

My parents, of blessed memory, had been religious Zionists. They had longed to go to the Land of Israel, and at one point before the outbreak of the war had tried, unsuccessfully, to leave Romania. On Shabbos, my father only spoke Hebrew. If he didn't know the word for something, he would point and say, "*nu, nu.*" On Tu B'Shevat, the New Year of the Trees, my mother would buy special fruit from the seven species of the Land of Israel. Sweet dates and pomegranates would grace the table alongside grapes, figs, and honey wheat cakes.

Most of the girls in this program were older than I was, but I fit in easily because of the emotional maturity I had been forced to acquire. Besides, from Transnistria, I had "business experience" which served us well when we would go out shopping for food. Since my friends became members of the Zionist organization *Habonim* (the builders), so did I. This was my first experience in a social organization since the time that we were driven out of Herta three years before. It was there that we learned how to laugh, to sing, to dance Israeli dances. The songs opened my heart and gave me renewed hope and a vision for the future. We were being processed and prepared to leave as soon as possible for Eretz Yisrael.

At that time Palestine was a British mandate, and since they enforced strict immigration quotas, a good portion of this rescue work was illegal. The boats that the Zionist organizations had procured for the secret sea voyages were structurally incapable of carrying the large number of people who crowded aboard. Nevertheless, with supernatural determination, hope, and vision, our longing for our "Promised Land" propelled us on, despite the many obstacles and hazards.

After a few months in the program at the Caritas Hospital, at last we were ready to leave for Eretz Yisrael. We had just one more day until we would undertake the midnight journey to the seaport. The night before our departure, I went to the infirmary complaining of an upset stomach and nausea. The young, inexperienced doctor didn't examine me or ask me any questions, and I didn't say anything to her about my frequent attacks of excruciating pain. She simply gave me something to settle my stomach.

I had barely raised the potion to my lips when suddenly my appendix burst. I went into a coma with a very high fever. Since the rehabilitation program was located in a wing of the hospital, I was rushed to the other side, straight into the operating room. This was one of the ways that Hashem ensured that I would be taken care of immediately.

Upon examination, however, the Chief Surgeon said it was futile. The infection had spread so rapidly that he was ready to give up. Dr. Fux, a resident orthopedic surgeon said, "You have given up. Let me try and save her." And he did. After the surgery, for two months I remained in a coma, fighting for my life. During this time, my mother appeared daily in my dreams in my comatose state and she nurtured me. The director of the orphanage later told me that in my comatose state, I had conversed with my mother as she fed me. This was the last time I saw my mother until my son Baruch's engagement. She then appeared to me with a smile on her face, although I couldn't make out her other facial features.

For six months afterwards, I was connected to tubes to drain the infection. Until I could speak again, Dr. Fux never knew my name. He always referred to me as Peritonito, a term referring to the burst appendix!

My friends threatened the staff that if I died they would dynamite the hospital. The next day they left for Eretz Yisrael but never reached the Promised Land. When I recovered and inquired about the fate of my friends, I learned that while I had been lying in a coma, close to death, consumed with fever and a systemic infection, my friends had boarded a small vessel from the port of Constansa. This ship, the *Mefkurie*, met the same fate as the *SS Struma*, in February of 1942.

The *Struma* was a boat with very little food and no sanitary facilities. Built to carry no more than one hundred people, it was laden with 778 Jewish refugees escaping to Eretz Yisrael. Wooden platforms had been built on the deck, to accommodate more people. Down below, in the hold of the ship, passengers had to lie shoulder to shoulder in the airless space. After three days, the engines stopped working.

The *Struma* was detained in the Istanbul harbor for seventy days, during which time, "The British refused to grant permission for the *olim* (immigrants) to enter Palestine, and the Turks would not let them repair the engine, disembark, or remain in Turkey."[11] During this time, the refugees were sustained with food from the local Jewish community. Living conditions were unbearable, and many people became sick.

On the night of February 23, 1942, Turkish police forcibly took control of the ship and "towed it out into the Black Sea." It drifted in the deeper waters until dawn, whereupon a single torpedo hit from a submarine was enough to tragically sink the failing vessel. There was only one surviving passenger, David Stoliar, who, upon his permitted entry into Eretz Yisrael, was advised by the British to say that the ship was sunk by a "mine."

Although I did not know any of the details about my friends, I learned that their ship had sunk and knew that they had all died. Much later, I read an account of a report in *The New York Times* (August 17, 1944) that said, "The *Mefkurie* with 350 passengers on board did not just sink. Her crowded deck was machine-gunned; the ship was torpedoed; and the survivors were again machine-gunned as they swam in the water. Three hundred and forty-five out of the 350 escapees from the Nazi hell were killed." It was reported in *The New York Times*

---

11. The Struma Project, www.struma.org, p. 1.
12. Perl, William R., *The Forefront War*

that "among these 345 who perished were sixty orphans from Transnistria."[12]

With all my soul, I had longed to be on that ship with those orphans who lost their lives at sea. Lying in my hospital bed, I realized that my burst appendix had actually saved my life!

When I was fully recovered, the chief nurse, Sara, took me under her wing. Sara had no children of her own, so she was exceptionally nurturing towards me. Having been fed nourishing foods, I gained back not only my strength but much of the weight I had lost as well. I didn't look as young as I was. My face was aged and weather-beaten by physical hardship and emotional trauma. Now, in 1945, at age thirteen, Sara declared me to be sixteen. She also decided that nursing was just the right career for me and prepared me for nursing school. I passed all the entrance exams, and was immediately accepted. I received a white coat and a nurse's cap. With great pride and a sense of a new beginning, I started classes.

I was beginning to regain my life when a man claiming to be my cousin, Yoeli, who had survived in Russia, showed up at the orphanage asking for Leah Buimaz. He was told that no one by such a name lived there. When Yoeli presented a picture of me, he was told that my name was Surika. Needless to say, Yoeli informed them that I was indeed Leah.

This cousin invited me to come live with his family in Dorohoi, and somehow convinced me that I would have a "home" with them. My longing to be part of a family was greater than my intuitive fear that if I went, I might become a maid again. Yoeli had a growing family: his wife Ruchi was expecting and they had a little boy of one and a half, Dov. They lived in a tiny apartment with a mud floor.

My worst fears were realized. I became a full-time maid and cook. Although Yoeli had good intentions, he simply didn't understand the importance of receiving an education. His outlook on life was not to set one's sights beyond the fulfillment of basic needs. My requests to return to nursing school fell on deaf ears. I had no one to turn to.

Once again Hashem came to my help. In the summer of 1945, I fell ill with the typhus that I had not contracted in Transnistria. I was extremely sick and afraid to tell them lest they would think I was faking and looking for a way to return to the hospital. Once, after taking my temperature, I was simply too weak to shake down the fever reading from the thermometer.

When Yoeli saw that it registered 104 degrees he asked, "Who used the thermometer?"

I admitted to doing so. They took me to the hospital where, thankfully, the doctors kept me for a long time. But when I was released the nightmare began again. I timidly begged to go to school. In response I got an angry outburst.

Finally, Ruchi gave birth to a girl and named her Bracha. These children were my life. I did all the laundry, including the diapers, by hand. All the cleaning and cooking was soon delegated to me as well. I never stopped working. At night, I would gratefully collapse into sleep, but not for long. I was the only one who attended to the babies at night. I gave them love, comfort, and a bottle.

Once, after a particularly severe argument about my desire for an education, I decided to run away to the orphanage. They accepted me back and happily allowed me to continue my studies. I was in heaven.

But my cousin had lost a nursemaid. Yoeli came and announced that I had a home and that I didn't need to live in an orphanage. When the directress explained how well I was doing in nursing school, Yoeli said it was too much responsibility for me.

I went back to live with him and his family. But, though he didn't know it, Yoeli was acting as an agent of Hashem. I wasn't meant to become a nurse and stay in Romania. The Communists were soon to take over and destroy whatever remnant was left of the Jewish population. Had Yoeli allowed me to leave his home, I could have been lost forever. Again an open miracle had occurred, which propelled me further on the path of my destiny.

My I.D. cards –
Polish and Romanian

One day, Yoeli and Ruchi announced that we were going to Bucharest. They took me with them. I was delirious with happiness. Perhaps I could go back to the orphanage or to nursing school. When we arrived in Bucharest, we found out that the Romanian government wanted to rid Romania of the Polish immigrants who had fled there when the Nazis conquered their country at the beginning of the war. They were even offering a certain sum of money per person to return to Poland. Yoeli and Ruchi managed to procure Polish and Romanian I.D. cards.

Then, one of Ruchi's friends came up with an idea. She took me down to the bureau and swore that I was born in her city of Gurbachov. The ruse worked. My Polish I.D. card turned out to be my ticket to freedom. Our plan was to take the train to Budapest, Hungary, sneak off at the first stop, and then "cross borders," into Austria. Getting me out of Romania at this point was the most wonderful kindness that Yoeli and Ruchi did for me. For this I am eternally grateful. I shudder to think what might have become of my life had I stayed in Romania.

Even during the war years, due to the devoted leadership of Chief Rabbi Alexander Safran and Jewish community leader Dr. Wilhelm Filderman, structures of Jewish life were maintained. As Rabbi Safran records in his section on "spiritual resistance," "The Jews were besieged, secluded in a situation in which we ourselves did not know whether we would survive to see the next day, and nonetheless our Jewish instinct, our Jewish desire to live, determined us to act with greater and more deliberate intensity in religious and spiritual domains, to educate our children and to shape our youth as if we were sure we would survive. All this proves our unflinching Jewish belief in the everlastingness of the Jewish people."[13]

This determined spirit of resistance led Rabbi Safran, Dr. Filderman, and other Jewish leaders to establish their own system of Hebrew day schools, which included the Onescu College and the Bercovici Polytechnic School. Conferences, cultural activities, Shabbos programs, and artistic presentations were part of the ongoing educational programs for all ages. They even managed to produce a Hebrew textbook for their pupils.

"We organized important cultural and musical programs at the Choral Temple; regular Torah lectures in the synagogues, and special Talmud lectures for the yeshivah students who had sought refuge in Bucharest. All these programs constituted acts

13. *Safran*, p. 72.
14. *Ibid* p.191.

of extraordinary bravery, moral resistance, and inspired courage and provided spiritual nourishment for those who were facing the scourge of all evils. These activities were moral sustenance for the entire Jewish population and constituted an impetus in resisting the brewing storm."[14]

After the war, with the Communist takeover, this entire Jewish communal infrastructure was destroyed. Hitler wanted total annihilation of our lives, but the Communists wanted to destroy our souls. They launched a campaign to ruin the names and reputations of Rabbi Safran and Dr. Filderman. As Rabbi Safran recalls, "...they employed moral, physical and political terror, hurling accusations that reminded us of the most crass blood libels conjured up by anti-Semites and Jewish apostates. The tactics reminded us of the Romanian and German police..."[15]

As Butnaru documents, both Rabbi Safran and Dr. Filderman were forced to "resign" their positions, and left Romania at the beginning of the winter of 1947. "The expulsion of Dr. Safran from the country...represented a turning point in the life of the Jewish community in Romania."[16]

The communal infrastructure was the external component of the inner foundation of Jewish life – the family – which Butnaru describes as the "very nucleus of society." "In Jewish society in Romania, the family had played an extraordinarily important role throughout its whole existence. Individuals in a profoundly hostile environment, living – or, more precisely, trying to slip unscathed – through cyclic periods of violent anti-Semitic demonstrations, found in the midst of the family moral and material support, shelter, kindness, and consolation. In his family, a Jew had a feeling of certitude and assurance, which mobilized his inner strength and gave meaning to his existence whenever it was threatened or when he was brutally struck.

---

15. Ibid, p. 73.
16. Butnaru, p. 174.
17. *Ibid.*, p. 176.

"In the crimes committed in the Holocaust in Romania it was not only individuals that were killed or destroyed. In that nightmare which darkened humanity, the Jewish family – with all of its moral system – was destroyed!"[17]

The first nine years of my life were formed and nurtured in a real Jewish family. My quest for survival and my ability to love and nurture Yoeli and Ruchi's children stemmed from those early years of my own childhood within the protective walls of my family. My spiritual identity, my ability to conduct myself in a moral fashion despite disguises, my driving desire to remain a Jew and raise my own Jewish family, were all part of a chain of ancestry much larger than any one particular individual. Had I stayed in Romania, this chain would almost surely have been broken. Escaping Romania gave me the freedom to choose to live as a child of my people.

Baruch Hashem, the escape plan worked. In November 1947, Yoeli, Ruchi, Dov, Bracha, and I left Romania as Polish citizens. The train made a lengthy stop in Hungary. At midnight, when the doors opened, we quickly descended and slipped down a muddy embankment. Out of the darkness came a voice calling *"Amcha"* (Your people). These young angels were volunteers from *Berichah*, the clandestine Jewish rescue organization from Eretz Yisrael.

They led us to a truck and helped us climb aboard. Once inside, we hid alongside wooden shipping crates with blankets draped over them. We were driven to a secluded house in Budapest, where we remained until it was safe for us to cross the Austro-Hungarian border into Austria. The rescue workers provided us with food and mattresses, which came primarily from American relief organizations. We were now part of the clandestine *aliyah* network of displaced persons on their way to the Promised Land.

As soon as the proper Hungarian authorities were contacted and bribed, we were able to leave for the border. In the dark of night I walked for many hours with two-year-old Bracha on my back. Yoeli carried Dov, who was three. After we crossed the border into Austria in November 1947, we were driven by open truck to Vienna. It was bitter cold, but we felt freedom in our heart and soul. It was a blessed feeling.

In Vienna, our accommodations were similar to those in Budapest. From Vienna, we were driven by truck to Salzburg and given shelter in a displaced persons' camp called "Bialik." Here we would stay and wait for news that would allow us to continue our journey to Eretz Yisrael. At this time, Dov fell very ill with diphtheria. He fought off the fever, and *baruch Hashem*, he survived through the night. I loved those children and would have given my life for them.

In Camp Bialik, we lived in primitive accommodations and each family received minimal provisions. Yoeli found out that orphaned children under the age of sixteen were to receive additional rations of everything. Off I was sent to the office of the UNRRA (the United Nations Relief and Rehabilitation Administration). The UNRRA and the Joint Distribution Project were desperately trying to find orphaned children under the age of eighteen to be sent to the United States, Britain, Canada, Australia, and South Africa.

Canada was one of the first countries to open her doors to Jewish orphans, although initially she was reluctant to do so. In response to tremendous pressure from both within and outside the political structure, she finally was persuaded to accept Jewish refugee children. "Like other Western nations, Canada was fearful about permitting young survivors of the Holocaust to enter the country. The authorities feared that these children would have been so damaged by their experiences that they would never be assimilated into normal life. And the Canadian public as well was quick to voice its misgivings about the troubles they would bring into the country."[18]

It is interesting to note that these initially unwelcome children later made great achievements and generous contributions

---

18. Martz, Fraidie, *Open Your Hearts, The Story of the Jewish War Orphans in Canada*, pp. 37-38.

to Canadian economic and cultural growth. In so doing, Canada became a haven for immigrants from all over the world.

Spearheaded by the Canadian Jewish Congress, the entire Jewish community of Canada, which then consisted of 40,000 families, pledged responsibility for the total care of the Jewish war orphans from Europe who would be brought by ship to Canada. With this mandatory governmental stipulation fulfilled, the government of Canada granted permission for 1,000 orphans to be brought into the country. Thus the War Orphans Project of 1947-1949 was born.

When I went to the UNRRA to receive an extra share of rations, the administration became aware that I was an eligible candidate for the program.

My destiny seemed to be preordained for Canada. A very kind and dedicated social worker named Gretta Fisher was assigned to my case. Born in Czechoslovakia, Gretta Fisher was a refugee who, prior to World War II, managed to escape to England, where the only job allowed to her as a foreign resident was as a domestic. She found work in the home of a medical couple who were impressed with how she cared for their children. Their colleague, Anna Freud, was searching for dedicated staff for the Hampstead wartime nurseries she directed with Dorothy Burlingham.

This job afforded Gretta the very training she would need in order to work for the UNRRA. Under Freud's tutelage, she learned how to run an institution as well as how to address the particular physical and emotional damages the children had suffered. In 1944, when the international appeal went out to professionals to join the UN relief teams, Gretta applied and was immediately accepted. She was assigned to Team 182, and stationed at the 16th-century Kloster Indersdorf monastery, which was converted into the UNRRA's International Children's Center.

In an interview with Fraidie Martz, author of *Open Your Hearts: The Story of the Jewish War Orphans in Canada,* Gretta recalled the world's hardened refusal to help the children. "For

---

19. *Ibid.,* p. 106.

the two long years of 1945 to 1947, we pleaded, we waited, we tried to convince the world of the Jewish children's membership in the human race. But the world remained closed to these children and nobody wanted them...By the time Canada's offer came we had almost reached the point of complete despair."[19]

When I first saw Gretta Fisher, she wore an army uniform resembling that of an American soldier, except that it had the letters UNRRA in large white print on her cap and on bright red shoulder patches on her sleeves. Although she was only in her twenties, she seemed to me to be an older, caring, and wise person. Gretta instinctively seemed to understand us and I sensed that I could trust her.

She asked me very serious and profound questions concerning who I was, what happened to me in my childhood, where I lived at the time, as well as what my plans were for the immediate future.

As to my future, I proudly announced that Eretz Yisrael is the only country I wished to live in. Gretta reminded me of my tragic past.

"There is going to be a war in Palestine," she told me. "You have seen enough war, enough tragedy. You need the peace, tranquility, and stability of a loving home. You need to continue your education and study a profession that will put you on the road to independence. Leah," she whispered, "you can always go to Palestine later, when there is peace. We have many families in Canada who are opening their homes to youngsters like you. There you will be supported by Jewish foster parents and you will be able to go to school. While you are waiting for us to arrange the sea voyage, you can stay at the Shtrobel School Orphanage."

Convinced that Gretta was right, I returned to my "benefactors" and told them the exciting news. But at the prospect of losing their nursemaid, Yoeli and Ruchi did their best to dissuade me. I knew better than to argue with them, and did not return for my next appointment with Gretta. I reasoned that it was just a matter of time until Yoeli would send me back for more supplies.

As our meager provisions once again ran out, I was sent to the UNRRA base to request the entitlement for orphans. I approached Gretta and told her that I couldn't possibly leave the children I loved so dearly. Having lived through refugee life, Gretta's instincts guided her to take the correct course of action for me. She was a heavenly angel. A strong-minded, fearless individual, Gretta was totally devoted to bettering the lives of the orphaned children. The very next day, Gretta arrived at the Bialik Displaced Persons Camp with a team of uniformed and armed companions from UNRRA. They had all come to inspect the "haven" which I refused to leave. Gretta knew that this was my only chance to regain my education and build a new life with a better future.

Through Gretta's concerned eyes, I was able to gain the clarity and strength that I knew I needed before I would be able to break away from my situation. As she spoke and then argued with Yoeli for my freedom, I knew in that moment that I was standing at the crossroads of my life.

"Mister," Gretta began gently, "Leah is a very bright and talented child. It would be a pity for her to miss out on this opportunity to further her education and better her prospects for the future. In Canada, she will have a loving home in a peaceful country. She'll be supported and will be able to go to school."

Yoeli stood outside in the front yard near the fence. His hands were raised and his right palm moved up and down rapidly. He answered Gretta in a harsh, loud voice: "You have no place here, interfering with Leah's life. She has a home, she has a family, I treat her like a little sister. We didn't ask for your advice. She doesn't need so much education."

As Gretta saw that it was pointless to argue with Yoeli, she quickly gestured to her armed, uniformed, UNRRA companions to take me, as is, to the waiting car. They stood on either side of me and lifted me up. I went willingly, although I felt my heart break. I felt awful leaving the children whom I loved so dearly. I had come to the difficult and stark realization that it was better to be alone and free in a strange country, than trapped by the "love" of these relatives. Their love would bind me to a miserable slave-like existence. In Canada I would be lonely, but I would be driven by my desire for education, to use my mind and make something of my talents. In November 1947, as the car drove away from the camp towards Austria, I felt that I had been placed under the care of a wise, protecting guardian. Gretta's decision was a "second liberation" into a new life.

When I arrived at the Shtrobel Orphanage, which was a world that I longed to be part of, I felt as if I were dreaming. The three-story building that housed the orphanage was a palatial structure that had belonged to a very wealthy family. The girls occupied the third floor, the boys the second, and the kitchen, dining room, and social hall were located on the main floor.

The classrooms were situated on the ground-floor level of a different building. It was there that we were taught English, Hebrew, math, singing, and Israeli dancing. I shared a room with Clara, who was from Iasi. Clara was a fireball; I was quiet. Although she was two years older than I, we complemented each other, and we became very close friends. I truly began to blossom at this orphanage. Yoeli did not know my whereabouts. As much as I loved and missed Dov and Bracha, I knew that this was the way it had to be.

With Gretta Fisher's help, I was finally on a path toward continuing my education and preparing for entry to Canada as a legal immigrant. Shtrobel was heaven. I loved school and did very well, easily forming friendships with many children. My English and Hebrew reading levels improved every few days. Once my teachers recognized my ability to learn, I was promoted rapidly to advanced classes.

From my arrival at the Shtrobel Orphanage in November 1947 to February 1948, I had a clean room, my own bed, and teachers who wanted to heal and teach their students. They would come to check on us at night because we never wanted to go to sleep! Despite our loss and pain, the time I spent at

Shtrobel was a happy time. Our days were filled with learning and hope for a better future. We had five meals a day, and I weighed one hundred and forty-seven pounds. Life at Shtrobel was my first measure of relative normalcy.

Amit, our Zionist teacher, sought to restore our fragmented spirits. He imbued us with a longing to see our people united in our rebuilt homeland, to see the prophecies begin to be fulfilled with the blossoming of the holy soil. The Hebrew songs he taught us were composed of melodies that implanted hope in our hearts along with a collective sense of unity. We, the children, carried the seeds of redemption for our people and for our Land. Listening to his inspiring stories, I began to feel guilty for choosing Canada. The yearning for Eretz Yisrael that he instilled in me during my Shtrobel days has always remained in my heart.

In the dormitory building, we had a piano. Some of the older teens knew how to play. Someone else had an accordion. We learned to sing, to dance, and to seemingly forget our pain. It was so good to be a child, to be alive and, above all, to be nurtured and cared for. Our teachers truly cared what would happen to us. Our future was of great concern to them. For that and much more, I am eternally grateful to them and to Hashem.

Most of us were destined to go to different cities in Canada. Clara and I had daily conversations about how rosy our lives would be. "Leah," she would whisper to me before falling asleep, "soon we will have a home. We won't have to escape from anywhere, ever again. We will have families to love and take care of us. They are already waiting for us right now." I would fall asleep with a heart full of hope. I couldn't wait to be on that ship.

After being in Shtrobel for four months, the day came when we had to leave this paradise. We were taken to the German Port of Bremenhafen to await the former military ship, the *SS Sturgis,* for our long journey to Canada. On the night prior to our departure, my worst fears were realized. Yoeli showed up to "save" me and to take me back to Germany where the family lived, waiting to go to Eretz Yisrael. He had gotten into Bremenhafen by using illegal papers and was so desperate to have me back that he had brought a set for me as well.

Secure in my decision, I was able to tell Yoeli firmly, "I will never return with you. I am grateful for the kindness and shelter that you gave to me, and I love your children very much. But I am leaving for Canada tomorrow to start a new life for myself, to try to have the kind of future that you would not permit me to dream of." Although he was angry, Yoeli knew he was defeated this time.

Convinced that there was no way I would willingly go with him, Yoeli left to rejoin his family. In retrospect, choosing Canada was the wisest decision I ever made.

All 150 children from Shtrobel boarded the *SS Sturgis* in January 1948. It was a dreadful journey. The ship was continuously tossed about in the turbulent waters of the Atlantic Ocean. The ship's struggle to survive the fury of the sea reflected my battle to survive in a violent world. We all became very seasick, vomiting and retching over and over again. The waves were so high and frightening that we were afraid that at any moment we would be swallowed up by the sea. Our sleeping quarters were in a large hold with three hammocks, one on top of the other. Many times in the midst of our misery we told each other that had we known how terrible this journey would be, we never would have agreed to make it.

While much of my memory of that voyage is of being dreadfully seasick, I also recall my worry regarding my friend Rosie's wristwatch. Rosie, one of the children on the boat, had two watches. I had none. She asked me to wear one of the watches in case of "inspection," such as occured in the labor camps. Despite the fact that I reminded Rosie that we were free agents now, she was genuinely afraid to be the owner of two watches. I did take the watch and was pleased to be able to tell time.

One day, we were all lined up on deck for a practice rescue drill with life jackets on. The storm was so fierce that the ship seemed to be climbing up and down mountains of sea. Never before had I felt so insignificant. I was a tiny dot in the raging ocean. At any given moment I expected to be washed overboard. I went over to Rosie saying, "Please take your watch back; I don't want to feel responsible in case it gets wet in the sea." I didn't worry for my life, as it was of no consequence. What was uppermost in my mind was not to get Rosie's watch wet!

When the sea was calm, we would gather together and sing Israeli songs, dancing the *hora* in a wide circle. That is, much to our horror and dismay, how we discovered that on board the ship with us, there were other new immigrants on their way to Canada from Eastern Europe who were anti-Semites. "You dirty Jews! You're on the wrong ship! You belong in Palestine!" they shouted at us through the music.

I had just lived through the truth of the words of Elie Wiesel's introduction to Butnaru's book, *The Silent Holocaust, Romania and Its Jews:*

"Hate is contagious: it is a cancerous cell that devours one cell after the other, one group after the other, and ends up by invading the whole organism. Those who hate Jews will later hate others, those who hate Jews will eventually hate everybody, and will unavoidably end up hating themselves.

"There is no evil more dangerous to a society than hate. It distorts the image man has of himself and of his place in history; it makes the person morally ill, just as others are mentally ill. Values are undermined by hate. Ideas lose their loftiness and ideals their humanity. The other is seen by the hater as an intruder, not as an ally, a friend or a brother. The other arouses suspicion, envy, jealousy, bitterness, instead of sympathy and compassion. Hate negates solidarity. It turns truth into falsehood, beauty into ugliness...Hate is the enemy of whatever lifts up the human condition and is the ally of whatever drags it down

---

20. Butnaru, Introduction by Elie Wiesel

to the basest and vilest instincts of man. But the hater is also his own enemy: Hate destroys the hater as well as the hated. Anti-Semitism imperils the Jews but also poses a threat to those who condone it." [20]

This hatred incited the brutal murder of European Jewry in the Holocaust. The victims included at least 93 percent of all Jewish children (not counting babies who died in their mothers' wombs), 80 percent of rabbis, and 90 percent of yeshiva students.

Here we were, 150 young fragments of the various Jewish communities of Europe. Our families, which had been the past, present, and future of the Jewish people, had been brutally murdered. Overnight, our homes had been destroyed. We were left to wander and to wonder what would become of us, and what any future had in store for us in this turbulent world. Finally, after grueling events and processes, we were given a temporary home. Our sickly, worn-out bodies were nourished, our souls were fed, and our hearts were filled with hope of a new country, a new life, and a better tomorrow.

We were the living remnants who had all been the objects of hatred. And we weren't going to stand there and be the target of attack. Our hope and our spirits were too high to be crushed. Naïvely, we had thought that with the lifting of the ship's gangplank, we had left such prejudice and persecution behind us. Instead, the ship's crew had to break up the fights that ensued between our boys and the anti-Semitic immigrants who were on the ship.

From the Death March out of Herta, to the deck of the SS *Sturgis*, once more I was on a journey into the unknown. Only this time, despite the anti-Semitism, I was full of hope that I was on my way to a new and better life. I carried the pain of my past, and I carried the memory of my loved ones. Bound up in my heart, along with the pain and sadness, was all the bursting potential of a young Jewish girl who also longed for her chance to forge a new life.

CHAPTER 6

ON CANADIAN SOIL

Through the cold, foggy mist of the evening twilight, the *SS Sturgis* approached the Canadian shoreline. After weeks on the Atlantic Ocean, I stood on the deck, gazing at the gray, choppy water of the winter sea. What now? I hoped nobody would be sent back. I wondered what new procedures we would have to endure and what challenges we would have to face. My thoughts returned to the immigration process I had already undergone....

While at Shtrobel, I remember being taken to the Salzburg D.P. (Displaced Persons) Camp to obtain my certificate of identity. In contrast to the love and warmth I felt in Shtrobel, the screening process had left me feeling more like an interrogated convict than a welcome new immigrant. We were subjected to countless tests and examinations: I had to declare that I didn't have a criminal record. I was given psychological tests to make sure that I was sane. I had to undergo x-rays to prove that my lungs were clear. I endured a dental check-up and passed the physical exam for general good health, which itself was a miracle. My fingerprints were taken, and I was photographed from different angles, recording details of my prominent features, like the scar on my face from the horse and dog bites. I had to submit the name of a Canadian family in good standing who was prepared to foster me, and the Canadian Jewish Congress had to guarantee that I would never become a burden to the government.

In retrospect, I know that Canada was the best place for me. However, after enduring all those inspections, I didn't feel as if they were eager to have me. Since my last name, Buimaz, began with the letter "B," I was always among the first to be called into the examination room. All the other young refugees would pace the floor of the waiting room, anxious for me to come out and brief them on what the committee wanted to know. We were still a group of scared, suspicious, and insecure kids who were afraid of not meeting the high Canadian standards. Rejection meant we had no home, no hope, no future.

These dehumanizing procedures placed every possible stumbling block in my path. They did not represent the welcoming hand of kindness one might have expected to find from a seemingly civilized world. It is not that we were treated cruelly — it was instead a prominent display of indifference that we sensed. There are no words to describe the things we had witnessed and the pain we had suffered. The resettlement authorities never acknowledged our trauma or our pain. The fact that we had emerged from a world destroyed by war meant nothing to the officials who conducted these examinations. Besides being found healthy, we had to prove our innocence. We went through these procedures with silent indignation and waited impatiently to leave Europe's blood-stained land.

On November 24, 1947, I finally received my D.P. certificate, to be stamped by the Canadian Immigration Department upon my arrival in Canada. I received my coveted Certificate of Identity. At the top it said, "This certificate is issued to refugees not enjoying in law or in fact the protection of any government, with the

My identity papers

approval of the American Sector of the Allied Commission for Austria, through the International Refugee Organization. Its purpose is to serve as a temporary certificate pending the adoption of an international travel document. In no way does it affect the nationality of the bearer."

In other words, I was now an official "Displaced Person." Our past did not provide us with a passport entitling us to the compassion and nurturing we so desperately needed. Instead, we were reduced to being an object, as if we were not human at all. Branded with a horrible past, we were viewed with mistrust, as if our past were suspect and our future unreliable.

Now, at the end of the dreadful voyage, I stood on that ship, identity papers in hand, a lonesome living remnant of what had once been my parents' loving family. I was a child in search of a future, but I was also a link in the continuity of my people. My mother's words lay dormant within me. The darkness of the sea seemed to reflect the emptiness in my heart. I was no longer escaping, and I wasn't running away. I felt like a solitary ship, traveling to the harbor of a new life.

Clara, my roommate from Shtrobel, stood next to me, clutching the railing. "Canada is such a big land. We must part now from our friends. It's good we are both going to the same province. We'll still be able to stay in touch and see each other."

As the lights of the Halifax, Nova Scotia port beamed their docking signals into the night fog, I came face to face with the reality of more impending farewells. My friends and roommate, who had become like sisters and brothers, were all being sent to different cities and provinces across Canada. Jewish families from the entire spectrum of the Canadian Jewish community had come forward to open their homes and hearts to all of us. As wonderful as this was, we were all sorry to leave each other. Our shared tragedies had given us a silent fellowship. Although we rarely spoke to one another about our losses, being together as a group had itself been a source of comfort to us.

❧❦❧

Our ocean voyage to Halifax and the train journey to Calgary represented the culmination of fourteen years of dedicated efforts by individuals, groups, and organizations on behalf of the victims of Nazi persecution. A majority of the 40,000 Jews of Canada had both immediate and extended family living in Europe.

From the time of Hitler's rise to power in the early 1930s, members of the Canadian Jewish community began receiving desperate letters from relatives in Europe describing the terror and brutality that they were witnessing, and eventually would succumb to without help. The individuals who received these pleading letters had no way to save their loved ones.

Canada had a history of anti-Semitic restrictions placed in response to requests for immigration. Fredrick Blair, the head of Canada's immigration department at that time, was a known anti-Semite. Although he accepted applications, he always found reasons to reject the applicants. While the stated concerns were possible economic, social, and psychological instability of the war orphans and adult immigrants, a glance at Canada's willingness to receive 6,000 British children during the first two years of the war tells a completely different story. Charlotte Whitton, social worker, feminist, and outspoken anti-Semite, traveled across the country, warning welfare councils and authorities of the problems of admitting "non-British," i.e., Jewish, children into Canada.

Despite this official policy opposition, the outraged and impassioned response of Jews in every sector of the Canadian Jewish community ultimately resulted in the reestablishment and strengthening of the Canadian Jewish Congress, the organization which bore the ultimate responsibility for offering refuge to the Jewish war orphans.

The Canadian Jewish Congress originally came into existence in 1919. As social worker Fraidie Martz explains in her book, *Open Your Hearts: The Story of the Jewish War Orphans in Canada,* its purpose was "to co-ordinate, on a national basis, efforts to cope effectively and judiciously with internal and external problems. It was the only organization which could call upon all the Jewish community to unite. In its acceptance by almost all Canadian Jews and Jewish organizations, it has no counterpart in the country."[1] Described as a "dazzling complex of synagogues, health services, *landsmannschaffen*" (mutual benefit societies often organized by people from the same region in Europe), the Canadian Jewish Congress was largely dormant until the reality of Nazism struck home.[2] The desire to help their threatened relatives, coupled with an increase of anti-Semitic events in Canada, shook and mobilized the national Jewish community. By 1938, the Canadian Jewish Congress was revived and firmly reestablished. However, it was not until the war was over that the major obstacles were cleared so that a small group of carefully selected and scrutinized war orphans could be allowed into Canada.

During the intervening years between the reestablishment of the Canadian Jewish Congress and the granting of permission for

1. Martz, p. 50.
2. *Ibid.,* p. 50.

the war orphans to immigrate, the Canadian Jewish community was faced with many seemingly insurmountable obstacles. How many hundreds of phone calls, private meetings, urgent letters, parliamentary appeals, educational programs on the radio, sleepless nights, and relentless efforts from anguished hearts culminated in the voyages and family placements of the orphans! Day after day, month after month, and year after year, requests to save the orphaned Jewish children had been denied. Barriers in the child welfare laws and structural restrictions in the federal government had to be overcome. In addition, all arrangements and costs for the War Orphans Project, "ocean passage, housing, food, clothing, medication, and social services — were to be assumed by the Jewish community."[3]

After years of attempts and appeals, in March of 1946, an interdepartmental government committee met with members of departments from external affairs, labor, health, and welfare. Participants of this forum acknowledged that besides the incessant internal pressure from the national Jewish community, "Pressures were mounting from the international community, and from Canadian officials working in External Affairs in Europe. A core of young, progressive, and well-educated personnel, often more open-minded on the refugee issue than those in the Immigration Branch, found themselves in the distasteful position of defending a government policy of which they were critical. Moreover, Georges Vanier, the Canadian ambassador to France, who was deeply affected by the plight of the refugees in that country and whose embassy in Paris was besieged by appeals requesting permission to join relatives in Canada, appealed repeatedly to his superiors in Ottawa, the capital of Canada. It was obvious, at least to External Affairs, that in order to avoid suffering an 'international black eye,' immigration authorities and the cabinet would have to change their position."[4]

---

3. *Ibid.*, p. 50.
4. *Ibid.*, p. 36.

In a moving letter to the Minister of Health and Welfare, Charity Grant — a member of a Canadian team of the United Nations Relief and Rehabilitation Administration (UNRRA) in Europe — wrote, "I wish Canada would offer to take a group of Jewish children. So far no country has offered any permanent haven to any of them. Canada says it must play the part of a major power. Well, let her show herself. Let her be the first to offer refuge to some of these children. We have here thousands of orphans all of whom have no place to go. I can't tell you what it would mean to thousands of people to think that at long last one country had offered to take even a small group of children. I would absolutely burst with pride if Canada were to offer a home to some of Hitler's victims. It would be a magnificent gesture."

However, it was not until April of 1947 that the government of Canada issued a renewal of a Privy Council Order, which allowed five hundred child Holocaust survivors to enter the country. This, of course, was only on the condition that the Canadian Jewish Congress took full responsibility for their support. Eventually, this number was to be expanded to 1,123.[5]

As much as I approached my new life with excitement, fear, and trepidation, the families, volunteers, and social workers who waited for us on the pier knew that they, too, were making an uncharted journey into the unknown. As Martz so accurately recorded in her book, "How...would it be possible to begin to find the right home for a youngster about whom one knew only that he or she had lost everything — parents and grandparents, shelter and safety, food and nurturing — and is left with only a story or, if lucky, one fading photograph of a family to bring to his new home? What constituted good parenting for these unknown orphans of differing ages and backgrounds? How and where were these surrogate parents to be found? And what could realistically be expected from parents already carrying their own family obligations?"[6]

---

5. *Ibid.*, p. 37.
6. *Ibid.*, p. 119.

Martz relates the experience of Dr. Joseph Kage, who was the national executive director of the Jewish Immigrant Aid Society, as he welcomed the very first group of orphans at the Pier 21: " ...As I proceeded to the ship to meet the children, my anxiety mounted. Many thoughts flooded through my mind — the sacrifice of Isaac; Tishah B'Av; the Spanish Inquisition; the massacres of *Tach V'tat* (1648-1649); the pogroms in Czarist Russia; and a vision of a mountain of two million shoes, shoes that belonged to the millions of Jewish children slaughtered by the Nazis.

"Here I was to face a group of children who had lost everything and everybody, who had been hunted physically, were emotionally deprived, incarcerated and tortured — children of the Holocaust. What should be my first greeting? What should I tell them? The Halifax reception committee was ready to welcome them with comforts, but this would not solve the basic problem of 'breaking the ice.' I tried to recollect the various social work interviewing techniques and approaches, but they all seemed empty, cold, and inappropriate."

⚜

"As I disembarked from the ship, something welled up in me and all of a sudden I knew the less said the better. The only valid greeting was the age-old basic precept in Jewish tradition. As I reached the group of youngsters who were waiting for me, I introduced myself, shook each one's hand, and simply said, '*Shalom aleichem, baruch haba*' (Peace unto you, bless your arrival). I knew that they understood me and I knew that they knew what I meant."[7]

Finally, on February 11, 1948, (1 Adar 5708), the *SS Sturgis* docked at Pier 21 in the Halifax port. As I walked down the gangplank and stood on solid ground, I still felt the sensations of the moving ship. The Canadian Jewish Congress had prepared a reception for us and we received our stamped Canadian Certificates of Identity with Landed Immigrant Status. Although they had tried to keep the fanfare to a minimum, many

---

7. *Ibid.*, p. 24.

people from the community arrived to welcome us. Volunteers had prepared food and warm clothing for us. Children who were to stay in Halifax were introduced immediately to their foster families. The orphans who were going to the larger cities, like Toronto and Montreal, were to first stay in temporary reception centers. We parted painfully, wishing each other a better tomorrow. Those of us who were bound for other cities were driven by volunteers to the Halifax train station.

In the bitter cold night, we boarded the passenger train to take us all across Canada. The inside of the train was divided into large, luxurious, curtained compartments with berths and washroom facilities. We were served kosher meals in the dining coach. We received a great deal of attention from the social workers, who had joined us at the port to accompany us on the long journey. Although they provided us with numerous opportunities to talk, none of us wanted to share our painful past, as we hoped, naïvely, that our pain had been left on the other side of the ocean.

At the stop in Montreal, a group of children disembarked. Clara and I had to say more painful farewells. The vastness of Canada seemed cold and impersonal. Every time more children left the train to join their new families, or to be taken to a temporary immigrant reception center, we felt as if part of us were left behind with them.

Finally, after a stop in Winnipeg, we were bound for our destination. The train continued towards Calgary, where Clara and I were to meet our foster parents and begin a new life. On the 15th of February, 1948, after four days and nights on the train, my wandering ended for now as the locomotive slowed and we pulled into Calgary.

Clara and I looked out the window. All we saw were ladies dressed in boots and long crinoline skirts. To us, they looked old. Clara whispered to me, "Maybe they are bringing us here because there are no young people in Calgary!"

Clara was picked up from the train station by the Switzers, and I was greeted by Chaya and Pinchas Hubberman, as well as the social worker, Roina Perelman, who was assigned to our case. Although there were only two of us arriving, the train platform was crowded with curious onlookers. Many members of the Calgary community came to see and greet the two girls from "hell."

I was brought "home" by the Hubbermans, who had three sons. They had requested a girl because they wanted a daughter. Sam gave up his room for me and moved in with Lou, while Morris graciously moved downstairs to the basement. We were able to speak to each other fluently in Yiddish, a language commonly known to the majority of the immigrant families. The Hubbermans spoke Yiddish only to each other and to their children. Although they were completely secular in their values and outlook, they felt that speaking Yiddish within the family would preserve Jewish continuity.

The Hubbermans lived in a magnificent three-story house. When I first entered their home, I couldn't believe that such ostentatious living existed anywhere on this earth. Because that day, the fifteenth of February, was my sixteenth birthday, my new foster family made me a sweet-sixteen party so that I could meet their relatives and friends. I was determined to put on a happy, grateful face, since this was the beginning of my new life.

Soon after my arrival, the inevitable dreaded questions began. "How many people were in your family? Did you have sisters and brothers? What happened to them?" Bracing myself, I tried to begin to describe the indescribable, to tell them how I had been awakened from the last peaceful sleep of my childhood and brutally forced to walk in sub-zero weather to the death camps of Transnistria. I tried to explain how I had watched my beloved family perish, one by one.

I suppose I felt that I had a certain obligation to answer their questions since, after all, they were kind enough to take me into their home. I wanted to tell them the truth, because I yearned for the real intimacy that comes with close family ties. Having been deprived of that for so many years, I was eager to establish a genuine bond with my benefactors. They didn't know how to look at me. Instead they looked away, at the walls and the floor, amid an uncomfortable silence. I was totally unprepared for and shocked by their response:

"*Maidele, du host a groise fantazie.* Little girl, you have a vivid imagination."

"What?" I wanted to scream at them, "You think I'm making this up! Even Vasil, the Ukranian peasant, who shouted at me about how lucky I was in the midst of my tears, knew I wasn't lying." Instead, silently, I looked down at the plush burgundy wall-to-wall carpet in their living room.

Stung by the implication that what I had said wasn't true, I decided then and there that I would never again speak about my past. In retrospect, this was one of the most significant decisions of my life, enabling me to raise my family, outside the shadow of my childhood horrors. At that moment, a part of my essence went into hiding. I was a survivor. When I lived in the forests of Transnistria and posed as a non-Jew, serving the Nazis in the café of *Pani* Bukovska, I was silent. Now I adopted another kind of silence, and wore a mask that met the expectations of my new-found family. Because it was their wish for me to become a happy child, free of my nightmarish experiences, I endeavored to begin to live the "happily-ever-after" life of which fairy tales are made.

After that incident, whenever I was asked about my parents or siblings, I would say, "They died."

"How?"

"There was a war."

I would never say anything beyond that, as there are no words invented to describe the pain that had been inflicted upon the survivors. And I remained silent for more than fifty years.

My predominant concern was to continue my education as soon as possible. My former schooling had stopped just before grade four. Most of the young immigrants who came to Canada had to find work right away. I was overjoyed that the Hubbermans were willing to send me to school. Yet, at the same time, I was afraid of failing. I had so many new tasks ahead of me. Besides having to learn English, I had to make new friends, adjust to Canadian culture, and function as a member of a family.

At the Canadian public school which I attended, Haultin Junior High, I was fortunate to have a most caring and loving teacher. Miss Grant, and her students welcomed me into their tenth-grade classroom and were eager to help me, both academically and socially. On the first day of school, Miss Grant asked me if I would like to also have an English name. "Leah is the name my mother gave me," I answered her. "I lost my mother; I do not want to lose my name."

Every morning, after Mr. Hubberman would drive me up to the school building, there would be girls from my class waiting for me. "Leah, come with us," they would call out, and walk me hand in hand to the classroom. In the evening they would invite me to get together with them. In retrospect, my classmates must have been briefed by the social worker about not speaking to me about my past. I was very grateful that they never asked me any questions.

Together with my classmates, I learned to derive benefit from my studies, and to have fun. When springtime came, the boys and girls included me in any activity that I could physically participate in. Learning how to play baseball was great fun for me. At first my fellow classmate would hold the bat with me, to help me steady it, aim, and practice my swing. I lost my first pair of sandals to baseball practice. Although I learned a difficult lesson by seeing my new sandals torn, I thoroughly enjoyed learning the game. Gym, math, geography, and home economics were also subjects that I loved and in which I excelled.

Clara and I stayed in touch with each other and occasionally slept over at each other's homes. We often went, either with her family or with the Hubbermans, to the resort lodge in the Rocky Mountains Banff, which was very near Calgary. The majestic beauty of the snow-covered mountains in the middle of the summer was breathtaking. It is one of my fondest memories of this time.

Walking the trails of the mountains, I had the opportunity to do a lot of thinking. Here I was, in a "free" country. I was free to fail, or to rise above failure and succeed. In reality, life in Canada was far from our dreams of people going out of their way to love and care for us. As Dr. Joseph Klinghofer, former director of the Toronto Reception Center for the orphans, expressed in Martz's book, "There was a tremendous gap between the hopes of these young people and the realities of Canadian life. For one thing, their will to survive was made possible by the hope that once peace came, the world would make up for their sufferings and all their dreams would come true. They expected to be received with open arms and to be compensated for their losses. Also, they had been fed the idea that they were coming to a golden land, and that they would be adopted by rich families who would give them the opportunity to study in high school and go on to…university. The reality was different. Very few were adopted, and in many cases the adoptions didn't work out well. For most of them life in Canada meant being assigned to a home where they were given room and board, and sent for training or work in manual occupations."[8]

I understood almost immediately that the sooner I could learn how to make a living, the better. But I wasn't encouraged to set my sights too high. When asked about my scholastic ambition, I announced that I wanted to become a nurse. Somehow I knew that being a doctor was an impossible dream. My foster mother told me that I was too short to become a nurse. I didn't know what I was going to do, but I knew I had to do well in school so that I could move on to the next challenge.

The Hubbermans worked very hard to provide their children with a materially comfortable life. Even though they had a magnificent home, they had no household help. Mrs. Hubberman would wake up very early in the morning and do everything herself. On Fridays, she was up by 4 a.m. Occasionally I would pretend to be sick, just so that I could stay home and help her.

---

8. *Ibid.*, pp. 109-110.

I would dust, polish, fold laundry, and clean the Venetian blinds. She never, ever asked for my help. I just couldn't stand by watching how hard she worked without offering to work along with her.

Often we would be in the kitchen together, peeling vegetables or rolling out pastry dough, and Mrs. Hubberman would speak of the sacrifices they made to achieve and maintain what they had accomplished. She measured all accomplishments according to material success. Money was the goal. Wealth was the highest attainment.

Although we had a common language, and there was good will on both sides, we never became truly close. The Hubbermans did the best they could to make me feel welcome. They called me their *"tei'ere tochter,"* beloved daughter. But even though I knew it would mean so much to them, and I was genuinely grateful to them for taking me into their home, I just couldn't bring myself to call them Mom and Dad. The memory of my dead parents was too raw to seemingly betray them in such a manner. My friend Clara, though, did call her foster parents Mom and Dad.

Life with the Hubberman family meant I was very comfortable and surrounded by beautiful things. As for my religious affiliation, I was Jewish by virtue of my identification with the Yiddish language, but there was very little to nurture the part of me that had been formed by the solid values and vibrant Jewish life that had been part of my childhood. Yet I was extremely fortunate that my foster parents were willing to send me to both public school and private Hebrew-Yiddish afternoon school. For this, I am eternally grateful.

The Hebrew-Yiddish afternoon school that I attended was privately supported by the Jewish community. I went to afternoon school at the Jewish Peretz Shul. I had two main teachers there, *Lehrer* (teacher) Melotik and *Lehrer* Heilik, both survivors from Poland. *Lehrer* Heilik, the principal, realized that I learned very quickly. He also noticed that, at every opportunity, I would play with the children of the younger classes. I loved to be around the children and to play with their toys as well. It was my way of trying to heal my spirit.

Lehrer Heilik saw in me the qualities of a potential educator. He decided to take me under his wing and tutor me intensively. One afternoon, in the middle of a grammar lesson, he looked up at me and said, "Leah, how would you like to become a Hebrew-Yiddish teacher?"

The question took me by surprise. I knew that I would have to choose a profession one day, but I didn't think it had to be so soon. Although I had received an excellent report from Miss Grant, and I was doing well in the after-school Jewish program, I was far from being able to apply to an advanced seminary. I stared at the deep lines in my teacher's forehead and asked softly, "How?"

He looked at me with his kind brown eyes — eyes that I knew had witnessed horror. With a clear, determined voice he answered, "I will help to prepare you. At the end of the year, you will apply, and we will see what happens."

With the approval and encouragement of my foster family, I harnessed myself to the goal of preparing to apply to the Hebrew-Yiddish Teachers Seminary in Montreal.

For my remaining time in Calgary, I studied around the clock. Between my secular studies in Miss Grant's class, my private Hebrew-Yiddish lessons with *Lehrer* Heilik, and the heavy workload of homework and research, I was learning constantly.

The day finally came, at the end of the school year, when *Lehrer* Heilik and I filled out the application for the Hebrew-Yiddish Teachers Seminary in Montreal. A countrywide advertisement had been published in all the major Yiddish papers. There was an increasing need for young Hebrew-Yiddish teachers. Under the directorship of Yona Braverman, the seminary undertook to train not only teachers, but future leaders of the Canadian Jewish Community. In retrospect, the project was a resounding success.

With much trepidation and excitement, I waited for the reply. When my teacher, *Lehrer* Heilik, approached me one afternoon with a beaming face and an open letter in his hand, I knew I had been accepted. I was overjoyed, and yet apprehensive at the same time. I developed a happy bounce in my walk.

I understood, young as I was, that my acceptance to the ranks of the seminary was a heaven-sent challenge. I had to make a success of every opportunity. I dared not fail, yet I was often overwhelmed by the fear that I would not succeed, and thus lose my only chance at a new and productive life.

Six months after my arrival in Calgary, in August 1948, I left for Montreal. Although I was again facing the unknown, my destiny was calling me. The same heavenly hand that had pulled me from danger to safety now plucked me from affluence and set me on the road towards the fulfillment of my mother's words.

The platform at the Calgary train station was crowded with people. My foster family, classmates, friends, and neighbors had come to see me off. Laden with chocolates and cookies, the outpouring of good wishes and warmth helped soothe my apprehensive heart. Roina Perelman, my social worker who had arranged with the Canadian Jewish Congress to cover the cost of my travel, schooling, and weekly stipend, gave me $35 for food for my three-day journey. However, I did not spend a penny for extra food of any kind on that trip. Too many times, I had lost everything, and so I kept the money for emergencies. As it turned out, it was a good thing. People who rented out rooms in Montreal wanted two weeks' rent in advance. I had just enough money to cover the taxi to the seminary and the rent for the first two weeks. Looking back, I feel certain some emergency arrangements could have been made if I had arrived with no money to pay the rent, but at the time, I felt quite proud of myself for my foresight.

Gazing at the beauty and vastness of the Canadian landscape on the trip helped me to forget my meager diet. When I looked at the mountains against the clear blue Canadian summer sky, I felt an immense yearning to learn and to grow. My intellect and my soul raced within me as the train sped across the country. How very different this train journey was from all my other journeys. For the first time, I saw a glimmer of hope for an independent and productive future.

A social worker who was traveling to Montreal on the same train evidently observed me eating chocolate and cookies throughout the day. She kindly invited me to join her in the dining car, and I gratefully accepted her invitation. Nothing could dampen my excitement for the opportunity I had been granted, but it helped to eat a solid meal.

I arrived at the Montreal train station on a Thursday afternoon. Clutching my suitcase, I stood and looked around. Most of the people in the crowd sitting on the brown leather covered benches were reading newspapers. For a moment, I panicked. I had no way to contact the seminary. If no one came for me, what would I do — where would I go? As these frightening thoughts were beginning to envelop me, a tall young man walked towards me holding a photograph in his hand.

Zavi Ettinger, one of the older seminary students, looked back and forth from the black-and-white photograph to my face. He was surprised to see a blue-eyed girl with two blond braids. "*Du bist a Yiddishe maidel?* Are you a Jewish girl?" He asked me in a doubtful voice.

"Yes," I replied, "I'm Jewish. That's why I'm alive here today, because of my blond hair and blue eyes."

Zavi picked up my suitcase and guided me to the taxi stand. Opening the door of the cab, he beckoned for me to get in. "Come, Mr. Braverman is waiting at the seminary for you."

I sat in the taxi filled with excitement and fear. A new world stood before me. *I must succeed, I must succeed. But I might fail. "You, my child, must live!"* The Montreal sun cast its late summer light on the passing streets. A resurgence of determination filled me as my mother's words echoed in my heart. *"You must live, you must remember, you must tell the world."* Her words were like a beacon. They kept me on the right path as I set about the task of constructing a new life.

The taxi turned onto Duluth Street, and pulled up directly in front of a clean, well-kept brick building. I watched timidly as Zavi carried my suitcase up the steps, and then I slowly followed him through the entrance and down the hallway to the director's office. Mr. Braverman, the founding director of the seminary, took my suitcase from Ettinger's hand. Although he smiled warmly at me, I knew how to read faces. I could sense a question in his eyes.

Mr. Braverman surveyed my appearance intently. I had wrapped my braids around my head in a coronet. *"Leah iz dain nomen?* Leah is your name?"* he asked gently.

"Yes," I replied.

"Du bist a Yiddishe maidel? Are you a Jewish girl?"*

"Yes," I answered him, again.

Unconvinced, he asked again, *"Leah, vaiz mir chotch ein tzeichn az du bist a Yiddishe maidel.* Leah, give me at least one sign that you are a Jewish soul."

For a moment, I was at a complete loss. I had nothing to show him. Could I show him my lost home? Could I show him the radiant Shabbos candles that I would never see again? Could I show him my anguish because I would never again feel my father's hands on my head as he blessed me? Could I show him my gleaming silver Passover wine goblet that was looted and stolen with the rest of our possessions? Could I show him my mother's cries and pleading when the Nazis tried to kidnap me because I was their image of the Aryan dream child?

With no tangible evidence of my Jewish identity, I innocently answered, *"Ich bin a Yiddishe maidel. Ich hob nit vos zu vaizn.* I'm a Jewish girl; I have no proof to show you." To this day, his deep, delicious laughter still rings in my ears. Now smiling broadly, he brought me into his office and told me to sit down.

The first order of business was to find me a place to live. Mr. Braverman sat at his wooden desk and opened *The Canadian Jewish Adler*, the Jewish newspaper, to the page that said, in Yiddish transliteration, "Rooms for rent." He explained that I'd have a stipend of twenty dollars per week, and found me a room within walking distance from the seminary so that I could save the eight cents daily carfare. My rent was fifteen dollars a week. The remaining five dollars a week would have to cover all my needs: school books and supplies, clothing, shoes, medical and dental expenses, and cultural activities.

After having lived with the Hubbermans in luxury, the plain rented room was a bit disappointing. Yet Montreal was where my life was truly to begin. Though my funds were limited, I had a remarkable opportunity to grow and aspire. Spiritually and culturally, it was at the seminary in Montreal where I was molded into the person I became.

Later, Mr. Braverman arranged for an older student to introduce me to one of my teachers, *Lehrer* Shtern. I was brought to his house on Jeanne Mance Street. He and his wife lived in an upper double parlor with one bedroom, a tiny kitchen, and a tiny room off the kitchen, which was shared by his two children, Esther and Shmerl.

From the very beginning, *Lehrer* Shtern and his wife, Sarah, took me under their wing and made me a member of their family. I spent every Shabbos and all the Jewish holidays with them. Even though they had very little materially, every Shabbos — as well during the week — the survivor teachers would gather in their home.

When classes began in the fall, it was *Lehrer* Shtern who took me to the seminary for the first time, and guided me in my studies. I was overjoyed to meet all the students and teachers in the seminary. Most of them became my friends for life. Our teachers at the seminary were brilliant, and totally dedicated to the continuity of the Jewish community. However, I felt very inadequate, overwhelmed by the numerous, demanding courses given at the seminary. I worked day and night, and still I did poorly the first term. Hard as I tried, I just could not achieve passing grades. Fortunately, my teachers were very supportive. Some even took me to their home after school to tutor me.

Following a faculty meeting held on my behalf, *Lehrer* Shtern asked me what I thought should be done. I suggested learning an extra year or two, to allow me to catch up to the high academic standards of the school.

The faculty liked the idea and inquired as to sources for my support. I informed them that the Canadian Jewish Congress was responsible for my support until I was twenty-one years old. There should not be any problem with extending my stay at the school. All parties agreed that another year or perhaps two at the seminary would allow me to compensate for my lost studies. However, it was ultimately unnecessary. By the second half of the first year, my persistent efforts bore fruit. I began passing my exams. Slowly, I worked my way up to the top of the class, and I graduated together with my classmates.

It was in Montreal, at the seminary, among my teachers, my close friends, and in that rich cultural environment, that the significance of my mother's message began to penetrate. The intellectual doors that my teachers opened for me allowed me entry into an entirely new world, and filled my life with meaning. There was no turning back. I seized the opportunity for academic growth and independence, and I decided to turn my pain into triumph. I became a student for life.

My teachers were devoted. Along with the knowledge they imparted to us, they imbued us with a love for learning itself. The seminary and my teachers occupied my mind and soul twenty-four hours a day. I devoured every book that came my way. My books became my constant companions and dearest friends. The wisdom nurtured me and began to heal my spirit. Slowly, I began to live in the world that I studied, the world of Judaism. Little by little, I fell in love with everything Jewish.

I began to develop a deep respect and reverence for all Jewish values. I realized there, within the simple walls of the seminary, that mere survival wasn't enough. My physical survival was the first step. But I was a living link in a chain of Jewish survival. To be a secure link, a thorough Jewish education was critical. To "live, remember, and tell," I had to know why I was living, what I had to remember, and how I was enjoined to tell it.

Live as a proud Jew. Be cognizant of your identity. Marry a Jew. Create a home filled with love for all things Jewish. Model the kind of person you wish your children to become.

Remember: Jewish memory must be filled with love of who we are, love for our rich heritage and tradition, love for each other and mankind. Don't look for what divides us. Find memories that bind us as a beacon of light to mankind. An *am segulah,* a treasured nation. *Mamlechles kohanim v'goy kadosh* — a kingdom of priests and a holy nation.

Tell — V'higadeta L'vincha: Delineate clearly to your children the history and treasured roots of our people. *Al hadevash v'al ha'oketz* — Let them learn about the "sting" we suffered and continue to suffer. But do not forget to emphasize the honey. How sweet it is to have such a rich spiritual heritage, and for each of us to be a link in the golden chain of Jewish continuity.

As a child of the Holocaust, I realized that I have both aspects of my people's history within me. Although I was torn away from the sweetness of my parents' home, I still retained it. The "sting," the terror and persecution that I suffered, did not accomplish its task. It did not extinguish my desire to learn my people's history and to live as a Jew. Once I discovered that I still had the potential for spiritual growth, once my teachers put me on the road to scholastic achievement, I knew that nothing could stop me.

Everyone worked hard at the seminary, as its program of learning was a very demanding one. We studied from nine in the morning until six at night, Sunday through Friday. Each teacher gave homework as though he were the only one doing so. I never gave up. I worked as hard as possible. I also struggled because the rooms I lived in were not conducive to study. While everyone slept, in the silence of the long nights, I worked till dawn.

The librarian was very good to me. She allowed me to do homework in the archive rooms of the Jewish Public Library. Once I spent the night there because the staff forgot all about me and locked me inside! I was happy to be in a quiet environment, where I could do my work. While the world slept, my brain churned in the Hebrew, Yiddish, and required secular curriculum. Although I was extremely poor, I felt very fortunate to be part of this richly cultured and intellectually nurturing environment.

By the second half of the first school year, my grades began to improve. It became clear to all my teachers that I would graduate on time. Knowing that I had overcome failure and was on the road to success gave me the daily strength and determination to persevere. Although at this time, at the age of seventeen, I yearned to be young and enjoy all the things I had missed in my abbreviated childhood, I harnessed myself to the goal of becoming a successful teacher.

Later, in retrospect, I learned that my relentless drive to succeed had been forged in the fur-

Upon receiving my teacher's diploma, in 1950.

nace of my tragedy. It was characteristic of child survivors to not give up. In a descriptive analysis of my selected comrades, Fraidie Martz writes, "What makes their story remarkable is that the inner mechanism of energy these youth acquired trying to overcome disaster, later served them in their pursuit of accomplishment...The inner mechanism of their minds was to want more, to work harder to get it, and to always move forward. They took with them from the netherworld where everything good had been denied them the knowledge that you had to work for your own miracles." [9]

Graduation from the seminary was a major high point in my life. My teachers were extremely proud of me, as were my schoolmates. I felt that from that day on, I was independent, "*a mentch mit mentchen glaich,*" an equal member of humanity. When my name was called to go up to receive my diploma, tears of joy filled my eyes. In my mind and in my heart, my parents and siblings were standing next to me. I could hear them whispering, "Lea'le, you are our living memorial. You must continue the golden chain in our family and for our people." I stood, clutching my diploma in my hands, knowing that this was my first significant step in the fulfillment of my mother's command: "Live. Remember. Tell the world."

---

9. *Ibid.*, p. 111.

CHAPTER 7

A BORN TEACHER

y seminary education and early teaching experiences were the beginning of a very deep healing process in my life. My mentors nurtured me with high expectations. My teachers opened their homes and drew me into their families. The intensive study of the Hebrew and Yiddish languages, as well as the celebration of the holidays with joy and festive singing, reconnected me with a part of my childhood home. Despite my quiet anguish, my family began to live within me again, as the love for all things Jewish could safely be expressed.

The school staff became like an extension of my new family. I was proud to be part of the school, with its Jewish values and cultural circles. A new me was being molded. I was very fortunate to have role models whom I hoped to emulate. I had three uniquely different mentors: *Lehrer* Shtern, *Lehrer* Zipper, and *Lehrer* Wiseman.

Lehrer Yechiel Menachem Shtern was of slight build, with an intense and serious expression. He was my first teacher and became my mentor and lifelong friend. Although *Lehrer* Shtern and his wife lived simply, their home was open on Shabbos and all week long. After school, we would often go to *Lehrer* Shtern's home to review our studies and to talk about our lives, our dreams, and our aspirations. We had discussions about *Tanach, Nevi'im,* Jewish philosophy, mysticism, and Jewish literature.

Although he had a serious demeanor, *Lehrer* Shtern's style of teaching had simple yet dramatic effects. For example, when we studied in *Bereishis* how Hashem created the heaven and earth, *Lehrer* Shtern went to the electric switch, flipped it on and, quoting from *Bereshis,* said, "*Yehi ohr!* Let there be light! *Vayehi ohr!* And there was light!"

Lehrer Shtern was fortunate enough to have immigrated to Canada from Poland before World War II. His home gave me a resting place, and a chance to heal. The people who gathered in his home shared losses similar to mine, but as teachers of the next generation, they were intent on building and restoring what could be restored. Although we shared the trauma of the *churban* (destruction), we were also the future. Their spiritual and emotional nurturing succeeded in making a tremendous contribution to the renewal of my Jewish identity.

As a young aspiring teacher, I tried very hard to internalize *Lehrer* Shtern's lessons on teaching, and to put them into practice in my classes. Through the years, *Lehrer* Shtern's rules and philosophy of teaching helped me with my hundreds of students, as well as in raising my own sons: Seth Ian, Boruch Dovid, and Joseph Shalom. These rules included:

• Be well prepared. Never enter a classroom unprepared for all eventualities. Structure your lesson plan so that you can review and reinforce what the students learned, and then go forward.

• Be well groomed at all times. First impressions count. Your students need to look up to you.

- Your students learn who you are, as well as what you teach. A teacher is a very important role model.
- Create a welcoming, warm environment in your classroom. Get there early to set the tone. Always be there to greet your students.
- *Shem Tov* — a good name is your most valuable asset.
- Never make promises that you cannot keep.
- Discipline, but it is not necessary to mention it. Don't impose rules of class management without first consulting the students. If they help make the rules, they will be more inclined to keep them.

For two years our teachers taught us psychology and methodology. They taught us theories of teaching, philosophy, and all the subjects within *Yiddishkeit* to build us up so that we, in turn, would impart what we learned to the next generation. Although the first year class of my seminary had only five students, it still had a vision — to groom its students to educate future generations so they would go on to be learned, informed, and dedicated members of the Jewish community. We wanted to help our students to be links in the chain of Jewish continuity. We did all this in Hebrew and Yiddish. In the same way our teachers modeled behavior that we wished to emulate, we, in turn, had to become role models for our own students.

I wanted my students to have a happy Jewish childhood, to learn and to love all the things that I had missed out on. Teaching them gave me back some of my childhood. My goal was for my students to be literate, well informed, thinking, questioning, knowing, and proud of their heritage. I believed it was important for them to identify with Jewish causes, to love and to care for each other, and to support Jews and Jewish values.

After graduation, new teachers didn't need to apply for a job. The principals of various schools would come to observe us teaching, interview us, and then let the seminary know who their preferred candidates were. As much as I hoped to work under the superb pedagogic tutelage of *Lehrer* Zipper, principal of the Yiddishe Peretz Shul, I feared the possibility of working under the awesome and commanding scholar *Lehrer* Wiseman, who directed the Yiddishe Folks Shul. Although I greatly admired *Lehrer* Wiseman, who had been one of my teachers at the seminary, I was afraid of him. He was known to be a tough and demanding principal. I did not want to place myself under his leadership because I did not want my fear of him to affect my daily relationship with my students.

Much to my joy, both schools wanted me. Even though the Yiddishe Peretz Shul existed on a "shoestring," and I was all but penniless, I chose to work under the kind yet brilliant mantle of *Lehrer* Zipper. I wanted to be molded and influenced by someone whose personality was closer to that of my parents. *Lehrer* Zipper embodied the values of my childhood home. All my mother's strength had come through the kind and gentle way she treated everyone — Jew and gentile alike. She had a quiet sense of power, and a profound ability to influence us to do good things. I recognized this strength through kindness in *Lehrer* Zipper, and I wanted to be influenced by him.

In the seminary, *Lehrer* Zipper had taught us Yiddish literature. He was *Lehrer* Shtern's brother, but when they escaped from Europe, the names on their papers were different. *Lehrer* Zipper was a mild-mannered middle-aged gentleman with a slight build. Always soft-spoken, with a warm smile he taught us that a gentle, kind teacher can also be firm, organized, and disciplined. Order was the vessel for imparting knowledge: order in our minds, in our classrooms, and in our communications with our students.

I was molded to become the kind of teacher I aspired to be because of the loving way *Lehrer* Zipper guided me. Being young and inexperienced, I naturally made many mistakes. But when *Lehrer* Zipper observed me in class he never mentioned errors to me. He would bring me books and articles to read that instructed me in ways to improve. Beyond the reading material, we would meet to discuss what I had learned, my students' progress, and how to enrich my teaching style, both for my own development and for the benefit of my students. With such a gifted class, and an innovative mentor who pushed me to grow, I steadily gained the confidence I needed to be an effective teacher.

In September of 1950, the Tuesday after Labor Day, I stood outside the doorway of my first classroom, frozen with fear and excitement. I was on the threshold of a new life, and I just couldn't bring myself to open the door.

A young colleague, Yankl Gladshtein, whom I had observed when I was a student teacher, came towards me saying, "*Leah, far vos bistu nit in dayn clas? Di kinder vartn oif dir!* Leah, why aren't you in the class yet? The children are waiting for you!"

"*Ich hob moireh.* I'm too scared," I answered in a whisper.

With an understanding look and determined nod of his head, Yankl gave me the best medicine for my fear. He opened the door, pushed me into my second-grade class, shut the door behind me, and held the door handle so I couldn't run out!

Petrified, I faced my class and immediately started laughing. But beneath the surface of my laughter lurked the images of my young friends who had been slaughtered in the snow of Transnistria. Then, for a split second, I saw myself reciting Russian poetry for the groups of children I had taught at age nine, under the Russian occupation. My mind flashed to the Ukrainian peasant girl I had taught with outstretched arms, holding her textbook through the fence on the Death March.

The children looked me over with curious eyes and then followed my lead and laughed along. Could they detect the remnants of my hidden past? Could they see my parents and siblings standing behind me? To compensate for my nervous reaction, I began singing the songs they had learned the previous year. Suddenly, after a moment of absolute silence, their voices joined mine. When we had finished the songs, they stared at me. I looked down at my lesson plan on my desk and touched the papers with trembling fingers.

"*Far vos kukt ihr oyf mir azoy?* Why are you staring at me like that?" I asked in a whisper.

My first class in the Peretz School

One little boy who sat in the front looked up and said, "*Du zingst azoy shein.* You sing so nicely." Then the entire class burst into applause! That was it. The ice was broken, and I breathed a sigh of relief.

I started to teach the material that I had prepared. Looking back to that first day, the faces of those children will always be in my memory. Their inquisitive expressions reflected the normalcy I had been deprived of as a child. These children had parents. They had a childhood. They were afforded the normal progression of development and education. They were eight years old. I was eighteen.

In 1950 the second-grade class divided according to ability. It was a one-time experiment, closely watched and monitored by my principal and mentor, as well as by my colleagues in the school. I used to prepare my lesson plan for the week and, much to my amazement, the students went through it in only a few days. I had to have a great deal of extra material prepared to keep up with their desire to learn.

The Yiddishe Peretz Shul was located in a modern building on Duluth Street, the heart of the Jewish immigrant community. A majority of the members of the school's staff had been teachers in Poland. These survivors found employment and cultural comradeship in their workplace. The school was new, clean, and beautifully designed for children's safety and convenience. The classrooms were bright, airy, and spacious. *Lehrer* Zipper's office had a window facing the schoolyard. He was always there whenever we needed him. He knew each student by his first name, and he was familiar with the details of each child's family situation. He believed that a child didn't exist in a vacuum; he was part of a home, a family, and a community. *Lehrer* Zipper knew that success in school was more likely fostered by a warm home atmosphere.

When I graduated from the seminary, I decided that it was too difficult to continue living the impersonal life of a boarder. I really had no idea where I was going to live; I only knew that I had no desire to continue living in rented rooms. I wanted to be part of a family. Divine Providence was such that Hashem continued to surround me with His kindness, love, and support.

Two years earlier, when I had first arrived in Montreal from Calgary, I was given the phone number of a young lady named Diane, a survivor from Romania who was living with the Bercusons, a family from Romania.

Sam and Dora Bercuson lived in a magnificent upper duplex at 669 Wiseman Avenue in Outremont, which was a very prestigious area. The Bercusons had employed Yvette, a full-time, live-in French-Canadian maid. Their children were married, and Diane had joined them because each wanted the companionship of the other. They were already like a family for Diane, and they were to become one for me as well.

Diane invited me to come for Shabbos. Every Friday night, the Bercusons' children and grandchildren would come for dinner. Being seated at their table, among their family, stirred memories of my own family in our home in pre-war Herta. As Mr. Bercuson made Kiddush, I could almost feel my father's warm hands on my head as I stood before him to receive his blessing.

Many times I could have burst into tears at their Shabbos table, as the memories that stirred within me brought fresh pain to my heart. Besides the agony of my loss, the warmth of their family served to accentuate my own lack. I was deeply grateful to be able to join this warm, loving circle of people. Silently, I cried my tears alone, beneath the muffled blanket of the night.

Mrs. Bercuson was a superb cook and baker. She always made sure to prepare enough of a surplus so that everyone went home with large *pekelach* (food packages). I was drawn to these wonderful people. Divine Providence orchestrated that when I graduated from the seminary, Diane got married and the Bercusons were again looking for someone to keep them company. Much to my joy, the Bercusons invited me to come and live with them.

Initially, the invitation was only for a room in their home, but did not include food.

I wasn't sure how I was going to work full time, prepare lessons, and find the time to cook my meals as well. Nevertheless, I liked the Bercusons so much, I just moved in. They took very little money from me. I am sure it was more to protect my pride that they allowed me to pay them anything at all.

Although Yvette helped Mrs. Bercuson in the kitchen and did all the cleaning, Mrs. Bercuson did all the cooking and baking herself. On my first erev Shabbos in their home, I offered to help her. She taught me her methods of food preparation, and I caught on very quickly.

The following Sunday, when they sat down to have dinner, I overheard Mrs. Bercuson say, "Leah helps me so much; she really knows how to work in the kitchen."

Mr. Bercuson paused before beginning to eat. "Devorah, you prepare so much food. Let the child eat with us." They summoned Yvette to set another place at the table and called me into the dining room. From that day on, I ate all my meals with them. Soon after that, the Bercusons became Aunty Dora and Uncle Sam.

My living situation then was close to ideal. All my needs were provided for. Yvette took care of everything: setting the table, cleaning up, doing the laundry, making the beds. This left me free to focus intensively on my professional development as a teacher. At that time, the school and its staff existed mostly on idealism. The school had almost no money and every so often I did not get paid. Aunty Dora was always there to extend a loan. She would say, "Leah, don't worry. When you get paid, you'll pay us."

In the meantime, Uncle Sam took me to school by car, as his office was not far away. I didn't have a warm coat. One evening, Uncle Sam came home with a large brown cardboard box under his arm. "Leah," he said, as he opened up the box and took out a beautiful blue wool coat, "try this on. It must have gotten lost among the stockpile of men's coats at the store. I spoke to the merchandiser. If it fits you — it's yours." It fit as if it had been made for me, and was so nice and warm besides.

"Uncle Sam, it's gorgeous, how can I ever thank you?"

"Leah, *trog dos gezunterheit*. Wear it well."

They were such loving and generous people. I am sure that Uncle Sam bought me the coat.

Another constant problem was my worn-out shoes. They had many holes and when it rained my feet got wet. One day, Aunty Dora noticed me hanging my wet stockings on the radiator. Without pausing, she took thirty dollars from her purse and handed it to me, saying, "Leah, go buy shoes. When you get paid you'll give me the money." At that time, a pair of shoes cost a week's pay.

In this phase of my young life, I felt that I was just beginning to fulfill the first part of my mother's words. *"Leah, du muzt lebn! Leah, you must live!"* Although torn from my home at age nine, I had been raised to understand that living was much more than physical existence. True life meant an intrinsic vitality of the spirit, and my spirit was just beginning to be restored within me.

My teaching was my life, my hope, and my future. And there's no better way to learn than to teach. As my knowledge grew, I deepened my bond with the Torah and with my people. Being part of the Bercuson family gave me a base from which to grow. The love, warmth, and kindness that I saw in their home enabled me to respond to the call in my heart, "Leah, you must live!" How often had I felt that core of nothingness to which our enemies tried to reduce us to. I was a remnant, yet as my awareness and knowledge increased, I began to see in my abilities the glimmer of continuity, productivity, and a healthy, loving life. Slowly, I continued to gain self-confidence within the classroom. Unfortunately, I still had very little confidence socially. Among my friends I was at ease but whenever I had to talk to the parents of my students, it was very traumatic for me. Nevertheless, I did it, as I had no choice.

The school policy was that new teachers were employed on a trial basis for two years. After I had been teaching a few months, a well-meaning friend of mine approached me one day and said, "Leah, what if you don't succeed as a teacher? You need to have some other kind of training just in case. Why don't you take a secretarial course?"

Being a survivor meant always having a Plan B. I thought over my friend's advice, and it seemed to be a reasonable suggestion. On top of everything else, I registered for a secretarial course in night school. After a few weeks of this impossible schedule, my principal noticed that on certain days, I was very tired. He walked up to me in the hallway and said, "Leah, is anything bothering you; is something wrong? You look very tired. It's not like you."

I looked up into his kind eyes, and earnestly said, "*Lehrer* Zipper, what if I don't succeed as a teacher? I'm on probation for two years. I'm attending secretarial school at night, in case my plan to teach doesn't work out." He put his hand on his forehead and laughed, saying, "Leah, come into my office. I have to speak with you right away." I followed him into his office and sat down opposite his desk. He took his seat and faced me with a serious expression on his face. He gestured gently in the air with his right palm and said, "Look, Leah, you are a born teacher. You don't need another job. You want to go to school at night? Go to university."

Most of my friends who went to seminary with me went on to the university. But they had attended high school. I hadn't. All I had had was an elementary school education up until grade three. I didn't take up his suggestion. I simply didn't believe in my capacities to that extent — not, that is, until much later in my life.

Reassured that my future career was secure, I happily dropped the typing and stenography night courses. As I began to succeed, I started gaining recognition from the principal, my co-workers, and the parents of my students. Now big decisions had to be taken. How would I educate students and continually motivate this brilliant class? I received wonderful guidance on a continual basis in creating new materials and integrating language skills. Both *Lehrer* Zipper and I were overwhelmed with the results these amazing students began showing. These especially bright and gifted students became fluent and literate in both Hebrew and Yiddish. They mastered both languages with ease. The principal used to come into the classroom and talk with me in Hebrew and I would tell him, "Please, *Lehrer* Zipper, be careful; they understand every word!"

Finally I successfully finished my first year of teaching, and then I began to dream again about moving to Israel.

Ever since I was a child, my parents, of blessed memory, had instilled within me a longing to live in the Land of Israel. When I allowed myself to be convinced to go to Canada with the Canadian Jewish Congress, I knew I was making the right choice. But now I had completed my education, or so I thought. I had language skills; I could teach. Perhaps I was ready to fulfill my dream. I knew some people in Zionist social groups who were enthusiastically making *aliyah*. I admired their courage and I wanted to do the same.

I was convinced that I wanted to go to live in Israel. Everyone tried very hard to talk me out of my decision, but I was set on going. Leaving before a five-year residency in Canada was established would automatically renounce my Canadian citizenship. I forfeited that, and went to Ottawa to obtain my traveling papers. I bought a one-way ticket, and packed my few belongings in boxes. I went to New York and stayed with friends for a few days. The ship was to depart from there.

Everything was set. On the day we were scheduled to set sail, I said my goodbyes and boarded the ship. But when the captain announced that it was time for all visitors aboard the ship to disembark, suddenly I decided to get off, too. In those last moments, something just held me back. It wasn't until I was actually standing on the ship that I realized that if I left, I would never have a chance to return!

Everything my friends had been saying had finally penetrated. I was being young and impulsive. I walked off the ship, not knowing what my fate would be. I had no job, hardly any money, and only the clothing on my back. Once again, my life was in the hands of Hashem. The ship sailed with my possessions, and I was again on my own.

I was faced with a very complicated situation. I couldn't remain in America and I had renounced my Canadian citizenship, because I only had landed immigrant status, which I had forfeited when I left. I had no country, little money, and even fewer possessions! I had nowhere to go. My friends thought that marriage to an American citizen would solve all my problems. But I didn't like any of the candidates! I tried to get working papers so that I would be able to teach, but that ended in a tangle of red tape. The tension of my tentative living situation was taking its toll. I finally decided that I was simply going to go to the Canadian Embassy and tell them the truth. What would be, would be.

I made an appointment with the Canadian consul and told him my story. "I am a survivor from Romania, brought to Canada by the Canadian Jewish Congress. I'm a teacher and I had made plans to travel to Israel but I changed my mind at the last minute. I want to return to Montreal."

The consul picked up the phone and called his head office in Ottawa. After a few minutes of checking my records, he concluded his inquiry with a big smile on his face and said, "Welcome back to Canada!"

Gratefully, I was able to return to Canada, back to Aunty Dora and Uncle Sam's house, but I no longer had my job. The position at the Peretz School had been filled. But my principal, *Lehrer* Zipper, found me an opening at the Adath Israel School, and that is how my Hebrew teaching career began.

Teaching became my passionate obsession. During learning time, I taught my students, and during recess and lunch, I spent time with my students and joined in their games. Thus I could act as the child I had never had a chance to be. The students' acceptance and devotion to me was a healing balm for my spirit.

Intellectually, I immersed myself in all the literature I could find that dealt with educational teaching techniques. I was continuously learning. I went to intensive summer teaching seminars to improve my skills.

In my two years as a student at the Hebrew-Yiddish Teachers seminary, I had only one negative experience. One morning, we were learning about the life of King David. My teacher then was a kind, religious man with whom I had a good rapport. When he taught about how King David sent the husband of Bathsheva to the war front and then married her after he was killed, I was confused and troubled. He was teaching the subject in a very matter-of-fact way, and I felt a sense of outrage at what I perceived to be the injustice of the situation. How could this be the dynasty of Mashiach? But beyond my outrage, I was devastated, because I loved King David and everything he stood for. After the class, I went to the teacher and I asked him, "How could King David do such a thing?"

I was surprised and taken aback by his response. He looked at me sternly and said, *"Talmidim yodim lo lishol sh'eilos ka'eleh.* Students know better than to ask such questions." Then he added, *"Kol mi she'omer sheDavid chatta, to'eh.* Whoever says that David sinned is mistaken."

I ran out of his classroom crying bitterly, both about David Hamelech and because of my own hurt feelings. I had never encountered such a harsh reaction to any question I had ever asked. I had been raised to ask questions about things that I didn't understand. In fact, as a young child I was praised for having an inquisitive and curious mind. For me, questions were part of living a Jewish life. I was never taught to simply accept things at face value. In this case it wasn't only the history of David Hamelech that disturbed me; my entire approach to learning was being challenged.

In the afternoon, I had a class with *Lehrer* Zipper, my literature teacher. He was an intellectual whose soul was permeated with a deep love for Jewish history, literature, poetry, and music. I brought my questions to him, and he smiled and gently answered me with an analogy:

"Leah, you like to wear white shirts, right? Let's say your blouse was stained with one little stain. Would you wear it?" I looked up at his kind face and said, "No, of course I wouldn't wear it. I would try very hard to take out the stain."

He explained, "This was David Hamelech. He was on such a high level that what he did was not befitting the nobility of his soul. It was totally out of character for him. Hashem allowed the circumstances to come about for our sake, so that we could learn how to do *teshuvah* from David Hamelech himself. That was his greatness."

Lehrer Zipper answered me in such a gentle, beautiful way. He gave me back my King David, David *Melech Yisrael*.

A teacher can destroy a child, as much as he can raise him up. Parents and teachers have to know how to understand their children. If the youngsters' spirits aren't shining through their faces, they must spare no effort to find out why. I never gave up on my students. If the parents had confidence in me, we worked together to determine the problems and help the child reach his or her full potential.

I tried very hard to gain my students' trust and to teach them that having good work habits, working hard, and loving learning will make life easier and happier for them. When a challenging student disrupted the lesson, I would ask him to write a composition about why his behavior was not constructive but unacceptable. This assignment would have to be signed by both parents. It wasn't meant as a punishment. It was an exercise in taking responsibility for his own behavior.

If I had thirty students and one didn't do so well, I worked especially hard on that one. Sometimes other teachers would say, "He's not my kid; why should I care? I only teach him. If he doesn't want to learn, it's his problem." That was not my philosophy. Teaching is not a one-way communication. The teacher is like a pitcher, pouring knowledge into new vessels. If the vessel isn't there to receive, what is the teacher accomplishing?

My teacher *Lehrer* Shtern had always taught us about the *Echad,* the One. We are one people with one G-d, and one Torah. Avraham Avinu was one person, yet he was endowed with the ability to transform the thinking of the entire world. We never know who is destined for greatness, but each child, in his own right, has to be endowed with a sense of his own unique Jewish self.

Whenever *Lehrer* Shtern taught us, it was focused around the principle of the *Echad.* He would draw a circle on the board, turn to face us, and say, "All of you are somewhere on a point in this circle. You will close the circle when you turn to the *Echad,* to the One." If any of the students were difficult or uncooperative he would say, "If you won't live as a Jew, you will surely die as one! Hitler taught us that."

At the center of my teaching was the eternal lesson of the *Echad.* I was not going to be the kind of teacher who let go of the One. I didn't want to break the circle.

Every year before the first day of teaching, I used to spend many sleepless nights. I would lie awake wondering: Will I succeed? Will I be able to motivate each and every child to learn and to grow? The new school year loomed ahead, frightening and overwhelming. Throughout all the years of my teaching career, I made a point of treating each student as an individual, always cognizant of their special needs. I had individualized materials prepared for both challenged and more gifted students, without them being aware of it. Once I saw that a given student was capable of doing more, my goal was to help him reach his potential in an assertive yet loving manner. By the end of each year, some of my most beautiful letters came from those students who had proved to be the biggest challenge.

Teaching at the Adath Israel School put me in touch with a more observant group of young people, some of whom were part of an organization called *Mizrachi*. Until this point, socially, I was so eager to recapture my lost youth that I attended a very wide variety of cultural events sponsored by every social group available. Perhaps because I had no family, I had an even greater need to participate. I think I was the only one from my peer group who belonged to two very different kinds of Zionist youth organizations, *Habonim* and *Mizrachi*. I enjoyed activities with both groups, just as I liked being among the young people who were members of each.

Through co-workers in my school, I was invited to become part of the executive committee of *Mizrachi*. Everyone from this group kept Shabbos and was very knowledgeable and interesting. I was drawn more to these people because their behavior was more refined. Eventually, my involvement with *Habonim* fell away, and my social and intellectual circle expanded.

One day, during one of my teaching breaks, Rabbi Bender of Adath Israel School approached me, and asked whether I could help in forming a young peoples' group under the auspices of the synagogue. These groups were very popular at that point in time, because it was a way of keeping young people connected to *Yiddishkeit* through the shul, which also functioned as a community center.

I helped to form a discussion group of young students wishing to meet other Jewish students. At each meeting, we took turns presenting a topic that was within our chosen specialty. I gave presentations about the cycle of the Jewish year. This discussion group became the nucleus of the young people's forum.

We had a number of marriages within this group, and it is where I met my future husband as well. On the 27th of June, 1954, at the Young Israel Synagogue in Montreal, Mark Kaufman and I were married. Although all we could afford was an afternoon wedding and a sweet table, our wedding was joyous.

Aunty Dora and Uncle Sam gave us two rooms in their duplex, and we lived with them for an entire year. When they decided to move to a smaller home, we inherited their furniture, curtains, and dishware. Our home on Van Horne Street faced the synagogue, where I was asked to establish an afternoon school. I worked in two schools and gave private lessons at home so that we could aspire to a better quality of life.

To have a family meant everything to me. Mark had parents and six siblings, but most lived in England. I felt that rebuilding myself and eventually having a family of my own was the greatest contribution I could make to the memory of my murdered family.

Before we were married, we both agreed that no matter what, our children would be raised in a totally Jewish home and receive a completely Jewish education. As a child survivor, I wanted to have children, and to give them all the happiness that I had missed.

The first home that we bought, in 1957, was a four-and-a-half room duplex, at 6660 McLyn Street. Mark and I painted the entire home, inside and outside, including the fence around the magnificent garden. Our home was ready for our family to grow.

Although I was supposed to give birth any day, students were still coming to our home for private lessons that autumn. In fact, on the 10th of November, 1957, I completed a private lesson and my student's father took us to the hospital. At the stroke of midnight, November 11th, our first son, Shmuel Yitzchak (Seth), was born. Although it was the Canadian Memorial Day for the fallen in World War I and World War II, Seth changed the day for me from one of sadness to one of joy.

After the birth of our beloved son, I continued with my private lessons, but decided to trade my teaching career for full-time motherhood. I never dreamed that I would be lured out of my "early retirement" to teach under my awesome and once-feared teacher — *Lehrer* Wiseman!

It was a cool spring morning in 1959. I was finishing my dinner preparations and was about to sit down to review the material for my private students. The phone rang. It was the secretary from the Jewish Peoples School, asking whether I could possibly come in the next day as a one-time substitute. After a moment's hesitation, I agreed. After all, even though I was still afraid to work under *Lehrer* Wiseman, it was only for one day, and I would welcome the chance to be back in the classroom again.

After the morning recess, as the students and I were returning to the classroom, I was a bit startled to find *Lehrer* Wiseman sitting on a chair in the back of the room.

"*Lehrer* Wiseman, can I help you? *Vi kumt es vos ihr bazucht dem klas?* What brings you to our classroom?" I managed to ask him.

"*Azoy* — like that," he replied with a smile, and gave no indication of leaving. I felt my panic rising, yet reminded myself that this was a single day and I was not really under his employ. *What can he possibly do to me? I'll teach what I've prepared and do my best — that's all.*

After the students were dismissed, *Lehrer* Wiseman stood up and said, "Leah, come into my office. There's something I would like to discuss with you." With a pounding heart, I followed him in. "Leah," he said in a softer tone, "the teacher is still sick. Could you possibly come in tomorrow?"

Relieved that this was all he wanted, I took a deep breath and said, "I will ask my babysitter as soon as I get home and let your secretary know right away."

The next day after recess, as I entered with the students, there he was again! "*Lehrer* Wiseman," I asked in a slightly puzzled tone, "*Vi kumt es vaiter?* Why again?"

"*Azoy* — like that."

Unnerved by his commanding presence and the brevity of his answer, I summoned my inner resources and began to teach. At the end of the lesson, once again, *Lehrer* Wiseman stood up and said, "Leah, please come into my office."

I followed him into his office and sat down, bracing myself. "Leah, I would like you to take the class."

"*Lehrer* Wiseman, I came for a day."

"That's what you think! The teacher will soon take maternity leave. Could you at least finish the year?"

I discussed the offer with my husband, arranged for childcare, and accepted to work under the tutelage of *Lehrer* Wiseman. I suppose Hashem thought that I was ready for the challenge, because He arranged it in this fashion. Besides, I kept telling myself, it is just to finish the term, and he invited me in; I didn't ask for this position.

Lehrer Wiseman ran his school the way a captain controls a ship. I don't think there was a single teacher who wasn't afraid of him. But he was a brilliant man, and an educator of the highest order. He never let a teacher know when he was planning to observe him. Either he would stand outside the window of the classroom and listen in, or he would sit down in the classroom during recess so that the teacher would find him there upon his return. He wanted real samples of his staff's daily work. He demanded excellence and punctuality. Once, I was five minutes late for recess duty. I was never late again.

But he was extremely kind to me, and asked me to continue teaching the following year. He saw that I was my own worst enemy. I was very hard on myself. In his school, teachers had to submit a goal report and an outline of lesson plans for each month. Then there were weekly checkups, semi-monthly reports, and end-of-month evaluations. I had to state what my goals and aspirations were, and what I had achieved. We had to do this every month. He would come and check every student and every teacher.

I wasn't quite as afraid of *Lehrer* Wiseman as I thought I would be, perhaps because I felt that either he could fire me or I could always quit. Then I would simply go back to "retirement."

On two occasions, I overstepped my boundaries. The first time was when *Lehrer* Shainblum and I decided to switch classes. *Lehrer* Shainblum was the art teacher in the seminary for first grade. He was an artist in every sense of the word. He could draw a picture and teach it in so many ways. But he admitted that he didn't know the songs as well as I did. I knew I couldn't teach art, as I had never had a chance to learn. But we both knew that I could teach singing. Ideally, every teacher teaches something in which he or she excels.

It came about spontaneously. One day during recess duty, we were discussing our creative limitations, when all of a sudden an animated look came over Shainblum's face. His eyes widened and he turned to me, saying, "Leah, let's switch classes. I'll give your class art and you teach my class the songs." We planned the switch for the very next day.

Unfortunately, *Lehrer* Wiseman chose that day to make one of his surprise visits. I glanced up in the middle of a song and nearly choked, but instead I beckoned him in with my right hand. Neither of us had asked permission to change classes. And suddenly *Lehrer* Wiseman had come in and seen me with *Lehrer* Shainblum's class!

"*Vos tustu du*? What are you doing here?"

"*Ich lern Yiddishe lider*. I'm teaching singing."

"*Un vu eez Shainblum*? And where is *Lehrer* Shainblum?"

"*Her iz in mein class*. He's in my class."

"*Vos tut ehr dort*? What is he doing there?"

"*Ehr lernt di kinder moin*. He's teaching the children art. That was not one of the things I love to do, so we decided to change."

"*Oy!*" said *Lehrer* Wiseman, as he clasped his hands together. "If only more teachers were able to do that." He was filled with awe that we had changed classes.

And *Lehrer* Shainblum and I were filled with relief at his response.

My next move was decidedly an act of *chutzpah*, but I was determined that my second graders were going to be prepared for Pesach. The Jewish People's School was technically not a "religious school," although it taught Hebrew, Yiddish, *Tanach,* and Jewish values and philosophy. *Lehrer* Wiseman himself was traditional in his values. If a teacher ever arrived in school without stockings, he would take money out of his own wallet, hand it to her, and say, "Here's two dollars. Go buy yourself a pair of stockings."

I remember one rare occasion when a teacher arrived with an inappropriate neckline. He told her, "Go home now and get a sweater. You'll catch a cold like this." We had no written dress code. It was assumed that as a teacher you embodied certain standards. *Lehrer* Wiseman, who was already eighty years old at that time, left no room for compromise. Excellence was excellence.

Unfortunately, *Lehrer* Wiseman suffered from chronic bouts of intense back pain. The following spring, as Pesach approached, he was at home, ailing. One afternoon I approached Bella Zuckerman, the school secretary, who was also a friend of mine, and said, "Bella, I need to order *Haggadahs.*"

She practically turned white before my eyes. "Leah, *Lehrer* Wiseman is sick. It's not on the curriculum for the second grade. Just teach them a few songs. I have no permission to order anything and I can't ask him now. Please, don't do it. You have such a good relationship with *Lehrer* Wiseman. Please, listen to me."

I was holding the edition of the *Haggadah* that I wanted her to order. I looked down at the front cover. In simple letters it read, *"Haggadah shel Pesach."* How could I possibly communicate to my friend how important this was? Was I going to tell the secretary, that in the hell of Transnistria, where a piece of bread meant life itself, I declared my own Pesach and refused bread for eight days? Could I, in a few moments, give to her what my parents, of blessed memory, had given to me? The image of my silver Pesach goblet with my name inscribed upon it rose before my eyes. No one knew the details about my past and my lost family. I was living in a self-imposed prison of silence.

"Leah," my friend repeated, "don't do it; it's too risky."

"Bella," my voice found its way out in a steady tone, "please order the *Haggadahs* for my class. What is the worst that can happen? Let *Lehrer* Wiseman fire me." I tried to sound as casual and nonchalant as possible. "Pesach is coming, and my students are going to know what the *Haggadah* is all about."

I proceeded with my lesson plans undisturbed. One day, as I was teaching the songs in Yiddish and Hebrew about the sorrow of our slavery, I noticed *Lehrer* Wiseman by the door of my classroom. Calmly, I walked to the door, opened it with a smile, and said, *"Kol dichfin, yeisei v'yeichol.* All who are needy, come and eat! *Lehrer* Wiseman, *zitz by mein tisch!* Come sit at my table."

Okay, now I am going to get fired. I must be prepared.

Lehrer Wiseman took his usual seat in the back of the room. I avoided his gaze and focused on the lesson. Five minutes later, I summoned the courage to glance in his direction. Much to my surprise and great joy, there was *Lehrer* Wiseman with a radiant smile on his face, singing the Pesach songs along with the children. Instead of the indignation I expected, he wore a softened expression of delight.

After I finished and dismissed the children, I followed him into his office. "*Lehrer* Wiseman," I began with trepidation, "I know I did this without your permission. You were home sick, and I wouldn't dream of disturbing you. I'm happy to see you have recovered. And I do apologize for having taken the liberty of ordering the *Haggadah*." I waited for his response.

"Leah," *Lehrer* Wiseman began, "I loved being in your class. You did a beautiful job. *Host doch shoin opgeton — vos ken ich dir ton?* You have already done it — so what can I do to you now?"

He paused and knit his long gray eyebrows together, pressing his fingers against each other.

Here it comes.

"There's one other thing, Leah. *Furan ein lerer vos hot far mir nit moire!* There is one teacher in this school who is not afraid of me."

"*Ver ken dos zayn?* Who could that possibly be, *Lehrer* Wiseman?"

"*Dos bistu, Leah.* Leah, it's you!"

With the birth of our second son, Baruch Dovid, I longed to return to my full-time mothering career, but the community never allowed me to retire for very long. During the course of fifty years, I taught in three schools, and in 1993, received the I.I. Segal Cultural Foundation Premiere award for excellence in Jewish Education, given in memory of my first principal and mentor, *Lehrer* Yaacov Zipper.

I remember one very moving moment with my first principal. We were gathered in the home of his brother, *Lehrer* Shtern, for Shabbos lunch. Filled with gratitude, I turned to *Lehrer* Zipper and said, "You opened a door for me. Without you, where would I be?"

"Leah, some of my most gratifying moments were spent watching you teach. You absorbed immediately and put as much of yourself as you could into practice. You did not let yourself rest. *Narish kind,*" he said tenderly, "foolish child, I taught so many. But I taught only one Leah."

My teaching anchored me as a Jew to my past, present, and future. It filled my entire being with the healing force of our historical wisdom. My outer life was devoted to raising my growing family and to my students. Yet my inner life was fraught with pain. Although I didn't realize it at the time, I was in the process of creating a different kind of hiding. The monster of my past was hidden deep within me. At any moment, painful, wrenching memories could surface, but I hid them beneath the smooth facade of a silent, normal life. I had struggled to achieve this public composure, and nothing, or so I thought, was ever going to make me break my silence.

CHAPTER 8

THE SILENT YEARS: PROTECTING MYSELF FROM MYSELF

With the births of our beloved sons, Seth, Baruch, and Yossie, I made up my mind to do my best to give my children a vibrant Jewish home, filled with educational resources and unconditional love. Although my past had left me so traumatized that I could not speak about all that had happened, I wanted desperately to raise my children in an environment of happiness and love. My parents and siblings had been beaten, starved, and murdered because they were Jews. As a result, I lost my family, my home, and my birthplace. Yet I was determined to give my children a solid Jewish education, without placing any of my burdens on them.

I wanted them to be inwardly free to form their Jewish identity without hatred or bitterness so that they could, in turn, build families of their own. I wanted my children to know that despite our bloody and oppressive history, they were sons of a noble people. I wanted them to become strong, powerful links in the chain of Jewish continuity, with no possibility of breaking that chain. I had no place in my present life for the demons of my past. I refused to scar their future with images from my terrorized childhood. My survivor identity remained hidden and silent, from myself, my family, my students, my friends, and my community. I was fiercely determined for it to remain that way forever.

Our sons today. L-R: Dr. Seth Kaufman, Rabbi Boruch Dovid Kaufman, Rabbi Yossi Kaufman.

Living in a different kind of hiding became second nature to me. I needed the buffer zone of my silence. I had to create a home, and a professional and community life that was based on a foundation of positive accomplishments. In my inner life, I was doomed to mourn for my lost family, my lost innocence, and the child I could have been. But to constantly bind myself to the tragedy of my past would have been an even greater catastrophe.

Why should I wrap the lives of my children in the shrouds of my inner torment? They were my investment in our Jewish future. My sons were my living memorial to my murdered family. Why should I make them the bearers of my psychic pain, when I could make them the bearers of our rich and glorious heritage?

From time to time throughout the "silent years" of my life, isolated incidents would occur that would threaten to shatter my thick, protective veneer of silence. The shadow of my past was inescapable.

One afternoon as I stood at the kitchen sink preparing supper, my four-year-old son, Baruch, ran into the house, sobbing. "Mommy, Mommy, do you know what the Nazis did to little children in the Holocaust?" He put his arms around me and buried his face in my apron. I felt panic rising up within me. I wanted to comfort my son, and I wanted to run away. Vulnerable and helpless, I had no voice with which to answer him.

Could I tell him that among those who were slaughtered, who perished from starvation, illness, and grief on the Death March to Transnistria...were members of his very own family? Could I tell him, "Yes, my precious child, I was one of those children in the Holocaust that you learned about today. I was one of the 'fragments of a million and a half murdered children' who were butchered, gassed, and burned. So many times Hashem sent angels to guard me and to save me from the gates of death. You, my son, along with your brothers, are the links of living continuity. Together, we must begin again and help to rebuild our nation, and to help make a better world." These words were locked away in the vault of my heart with my trauma, my pain, and my mother's words. I held my son as he cried and shook, and I stood there, frozen.

Suddenly, my older son, Seth, aged 6, who had been in another room doing homework, ran out, grabbed Baruch by the shoulders, and dragged him into their bedroom. "Baruch," he shouted in a voice far more adult than his six years, "never, ever talk to Mommy about the war, about children, or about Nazis!"

I stood there and held onto the kitchen counter, shocked and unable to take a deep breath. How does he know? He is only six years old. A memory flashed through my mind. Something had happened the previous year, when Seth and I were in a local bookstore. There on a display counter was an oversized book with a glaring red-lettered title: Transnistria. Seth had tugged at my hand, saying, "Mommy, isn't that where you were? Don't you want to buy the book?" I had pulled him quickly out of the store. Once outside, I bent down and looked deep into his eyes, which reflected confusion, and I said, "I don't want to know. I just don't want to remember."

Now, I stood at the sink with an icy chill spreading through my heart. Through the kitchen window I saw the rays of the mid-afternoon sunlight slanted towards the red geraniums blossoming in their white flower boxes. The memory of my first anti-Semitic beating lunged at me like a lion breaking out of its cage. I was four years old, standing in the kitchen of our home on Peacock Street in the town of Herta. The springtime sunlight cast its rays through our large kitchen window. My mother had warned me not to leave the house that day because my "best friend" Vera had a holiday. It was Easter. Not heeding her warning, I ran out to my friends, only to return torn, bloodied, and beaten, straight into my mother's arms. Sobbing hysterically, I cried, "Who did I kill, Mameh, who did I kill?"

Now, at the same tender age, my four-year-old son had had his eyes opened to the beastly element in man. I stood in my kitchen, at a crossroads between my past and his future. I could never uproot the horror of the past from my heart. Yet the ability to articulate my experience had been locked in the vault of my memory.

I had no language to begin to describe the suffering that I had seen. My silent years began the night of the Death March. As we trudged along in the freezing rain I had asked my mother, "Mameh, why are we being punished? Where are we going? When can we go home?" My mother wept in silence. She had no answer for me. From that moment on, I lived, fighting for my life, with a soundless cry in my heart.

"Silent" became my state of being. As long as members of my family showed signs of life, what was there to speak about? We were all in the process of passing from bare existence to the eternal silence of death. Dragging on through frozen mud, resigned to our fate, with no sign or possibility of hope, what could we wish to live for? To remain alive for another hour of starvation and hunger? At that time, death was my constant companion. MamehWith the demise of my beloved parents and siblings, I carried a voiceless mourning in my soul and waited to be released from my suffering.

Hashem had other plans for my life. Only He can accomplish the impossible. Just as our forefathers were formed in the fiery crucible of Egyptian slavery, I was being formed in the death furnace of Transnistria to become a link in the chain of our people. How many times, when I looked at the faces of my own sons, did the image of the martyred children rise like flames before my eyes? I saw again how they would scrounge for potato peels in the snow, to "silence" the pain of starvation. We had no strength to share our pain. We were silent when confronted with brutality, afraid to cry lest we be discovered. Silence was our blanket of protection. When living under an assumed Christian identity, we were forbidden to protest when we saw the atrocities towards fellow Jews. Silence then became the language of hope.

Mommy, Mommy, do you know what the Nazis did to little children in the Holocaust? Now, along with my memories of the screams of those who perished on the Death March, the cries of my son pierced my very being. How could I answer him without breaking down? How could I continue to provide my children with a silent, normal life if I allowed the atrocities of the Romanian *gendarmes*, the Ukrainian police, and the *SS Einsatzgruppen* of my hidden past to ransack and destroy our home? What would knowing the details about my past do to my tender, young children?

There had been one time, when I had first arrived in Canada at the age of sixteen, that I tried to describe what had happened to me, only to be told dismissively that I had a vivid imagination. I was filled with horror, yet I controlled myself and began to erect my fortress of silence. Some years later, as a young teacher, I overheard an older survivor colleague trying to interest his class in stories from his personal life. They laughed at him in disbelief. I vowed to myself never to speak to anyone. There had to be a better way to deal with my fate.

My childhood home had been stolen from me. For that, I was in eternal mourning. I had to protect my children from my past. I looked around and listened. There was no more sobbing or shouting from the boys' bedroom. I had private students coming that afternoon for their lessons. I forced myself to pick up the vegetable peeler, and continued my preparations for supper.

Yet in all other aspects of my life, I was anything but silent. I threw myself into domestic and professional activities. I successfully hid my past behind the collective identities of wife, mother, teacher, and community leader. I taught my class, gave private lessons at home, served on numerous committees at school, and for one year, was the highest-paid salesperson of World Book Encyclopedia in Canada. Our home was a center of learning. While I was teaching private students, my children were listening to stories from *Tanach* about the kings and prophets that I had recorded for them.

I began to suffer from horrendous headaches, and my doctor prescribed painkillers. I ignored my headaches and pushed on. I always had high goals for a better life for our family and for our children. I kept taking on new responsibilities without discarding any old ones. My days become longer, and my nights shorter. Who had time to think about yesterday, when I was busy meeting commitments of today and of tomorrow? As my activities increased, my headaches worsened.

As the years passed, somehow my family knew, "Don't talk to Mommy about Nazis." I participated in almost every cultural event in our community, except for Holocaust commemorations. I never appeared in public as a survivor.

My past seemed safely locked away. I avoided memorials and funerals. Not until Aunty Dora Bercuson passed away did I attend any funeral. The first Yom Hashoah ceremony I attended was when Seth was thirteen and participated in the program. My children knew that something terrible had happened, but they didn't know what. They didn't have extended family. They had no pictures of my early life. They merely knew that my parents and siblings had died in the war.

I would never say anything further; there were simply no words to describe the trauma that had been inflicted upon us. I remained silent, as I refused to reveal my personal legacy of pain. The term "child survivor" didn't mean anything to me, nor to my family, until the early nineties, when the child survivors began to gather and tell their stories to each other. But at this point in my life, I was unable to deal with survivor issues. I didn't want to associate with people who had been scarred the way I was. If I had not hidden my identity, I couldn't have accomplished anything. In retrospect, everything that I did with my life led me to the next step in the fulfillment of my mother's words, "Live! Remember! Tell the world!"

My sons, at different points in their studies, all did projects about the Holocaust. I found out about Yossie's high school assignment at a parent-teacher meeting. Hidden under my son Seth's mattress, I discovered books and papers for his project on Dr. Josef Mengele, the "Angel of Death" who conducted "scientific" experiments on children at Auschwitz. As my sons got older and learned more about our nation's history, my family formed a protective pact with each other. I would often sit down to read the daily newspaper, only to discover a large hole in the mid-section of the double page. "What happened to the paper this time?"

"Nothing, Mom; it tore." Eventually I caught on to the fact that something had been cut out, censored so that I wouldn't see it!

My fellow survivor friends and I knew that we shared losses in common, but we never spoke of anything except for the bare facts. I knew of other survivors who talked about their pain. I fled from these encounters as though from a fire. I was already too engulfed in the pain of my past. I had nightmares almost every night. I had almost daily headaches. I had experienced so much brutality, so much rejection, so much hatred. Did I have to bring my nightmares into my daily life as well?

Identifying myself as a survivor did not fit what I perceived to be my true identity. At that time, the stereotypical notion of a survivor was someone who had docilely obeyed his captors. Those who had perished in the war were depicted as meek sheep who had been led to the slaughterhouse. I abhorred the kind of pity that that image evoked. It had no place in my life. Although I was full of shame and guilt for a past that had been inflicted on me, I knew that had I been a passive victim on the Death March, I would have lain down and died. Instead, I had looked for ways to keep myself alive. At the risk of being shot, I asked the *gendarme* to let me sit in his wagon. I offered to tutor the Ukrainian peasant girl and then her mother brought us bread and cake. I offered to wash Madame Bukovska's plates at the water pump. Hashem gave me the strength and the inner resources to be a fighter. Now I was quietly using my strength to build my family, my home, and my profession. As always, the survival instinct was at work.

Only once during this period of my life did I receive positive validation for my silence. One Sunday morning, I sent my son Baruch to get some milk from the local grocery store. As usual, he took his bicycle. Within about twenty minutes, my neighbor's son came running into my kitchen screaming, "Baruch's been hit! Baruch's been hit! There's an ambulance!" As my husband, Mark, ran out to the street to catch the ambulance and go with Baruch to the hospital, several policemen suddenly appeared at my door begging for mercy. "The radio fell, Ma'am. I reached down and I didn't see your son. I'm a father — I have children too. He's not badly hurt, he was thrown onto the grass. Please don't press charges against me."

The policemen had been in an unmarked police car, following a wanted criminal. The driver, Officer Bundy, had reached down to pick up his two-way radio, which had fallen beneath his feet. For a split second, he took his eyes off the road and didn't see Baruch on his bicycle. The car hit the bicycle and, miraculously, Baruch flew off the bicycle and landed on the road. Although he had injuries, they assured me that he wasn't seriously hurt.

The policeman who was talking so excitedly was very tall. As I looked up at his worried face, I felt weak from shock and panic. For a moment, I was disoriented. Even though they had told me that Baruch would be all right, I felt as though my world had been shattered. Once again, I was a child on the Death March, studying the faces of the *gendarmes*, recoiling from their cruelty.

At that time, I could trust no one. The members of the Romanian police force who had once patrolled the sidewalks of my hometown to keep us safe, had, overnight, become our persecutors. My "best friend" who helped me feed our chickens and geese had tried to kill me with a knife. Our neighbors and townspeople, whom my mother had run to heal at all hours of the day and night, stood ready to loot and plunder our belongings as soon as we were driven out of our home.

"Please, Ma'am, I know I was wrong. I didn't see your son on his bicycle because I bent down to pick up the two-way radio. I made a mistake."

The pleading voice of the policeman jolted me back to the present. I saw that Officer Bundy was shaken and close to tears. His face was white.

"G-d willing, my son will recover," I finally answered. "We are not going to take you to court. We are not looking for revenge; we are just hoping that our son will be all right."

Baruch Hashem, our son recovered from his injuries but, for quite some time afterward, he was afraid to cross the street. The accident had cast a shadow over the normally bouncy nine-year-old boy, making him fearful and withdrawn. I was advised to take him for a psychiatric assessment.

The psychiatrist had a thick European accent. He reassured us that Baruch's reaction to the accident was only temporary and that, in time, he would return to his normal, active self. But

I had another question I had to ask the doctor. I asked my son to step outside.

"Dr. Lipman, are you a survivor?" I got straight to the point.

"Why do you ask?

"I can tell from your accent. I have to ask you a question. You see, I lost my family on the Death March in Romania and I never told my children about it. I didn't want to burden them with the brutality of my lost childhood. I never discussed this with anyone. Dr. Lipman, am I doing the right thing?"

He paused, took a breath, and looked up from his papers. "Mrs. Kaufman, you should be blessed for having the wisdom to do what you are doing. I was in a concentration camp. I have many survivor patients who are having problems with their children because of the wounds and scars of the war. Just yesterday, I received an anonymous phone call from a young woman, crying to me, 'Why can't my mother make a life for herself? I know she lost family in the war, but we were saved. We have to move on.' Mrs. Kaufman, by doing what you are doing, you are giving your family the gift of life!"

Dr. Lipman's words fortified my resolve to continue in the pursuit of silence. My past was sealed, and my professional identity was established. I probably would have lived out my life in hiding if not for the French Canadian separatists, the unexpected appearance of a fellow survivor from my town of Herta, Gisela Tamler, and eventually, the Canadian Holocaust deniers.

In the beginning of October 1970, when I turned on the seven o'clock morning news, I was shocked to hear that a group of French Canadian separatists from the Front de Liberation du Quebec (the French Liberation Front, FLQ), had kidnapped James Richard Cross, the British Trade Commissioner. A few days later, on the 10th of October, the Quebec Vice-Premier and Minister of Labor, Pierre Laporte, was kidnapped and subsequently murdered.

The FLQ, based mainly in Montreal, was a small separatist group "whose occasional declarations called for a Marxist/anarchist insurrection, the overthrow of the Quebec Government, the separation of Quebec from Canada, and the establishment of a workers' society."[1]

These terrorist events were part of over 200 radical actions including bombings and other murders that had occurred between the years of 1963 and 1970. In response to what came to be known as the "October Crisis," under the terms of the War Measures Act, Canadian Prime Minister Pierre Trudeau had declared a national emergency, and the army had taken over the province. Many people in the Jewish community panicked, and thousands left the province of Quebec. Historically, I knew that small nationalist groups spelled death for the Jews. In February of 1920, when the Nazi party published its twenty-five point program in Munich, it had only sixty members.[2] Twenty-five years earlier, in 1895, Romanian professor of political economy A.C. Cuza had founded the International Anti-Semitic Alliance. His dogma, with which he "infected the spirit of generations of Romanians," cultivated a nationalist passion for "a pure Romanian spirit, a culture to be exercised only by 'true born' Romanians."[3] Although I shared the apprehension of other people in my community, I wasn't leaving.

A few years earlier, when I first became aware of the FLQ activities, I had wanted to better understand this problem. I discussed it with my French Canadian milkman. "What are these terrorists seeking to achieve by such brutality?"

"To understand, you must learn French," he said.

I held the cold milk jars in my hands and replied, "Is that all?"

---

1. *Wikipedia*, the free encyclopedia, http://en.wikipedia.org/wiki/Front de Liberation du Quebec.

2. Gilbert, *The Holocaust, The Jewish Tragedy*, p. 23.

3. Butnaru, pp. 25-26.

My milkman seemed surprised at my somewhat bold response.

"Mr. Lapierre, I love languages. I teach Hebrew and Yiddish." I wasn't going to tell him that I knew how important language was in saving lives.

Years later, I learned that the Charter of the French Language, which was eventually passed in the government, had over 214 points, including the establishment of an Office of the French Language, whose function was to define and implement language policy. Even labels on toys were legally required to be printed in French, as well as English. In the preamble, the Charter explains that the French language "is the instrument by which that people has articulated its identity."

Even the French Canadian separatists had an intellectual recognition of the relationship between the preservation of language and the identity of a people. Almost as important as our religion, language was one of the three distinguishing characteristics that helped us preserve our national Jewish identity in the time of our enslavement in ancient Egypt. We kept our mode of dress, our Hebrew names, and our Hebrew language. It was the immersion in Hebrew and Yiddish in the seminary that had enabled me to reconnect with the prewar life of my childhood home. Language could insulate and protect, could act to preserve a people. And the lack of a mother tongue could cruelly isolate the persecuted into inarticulate anguish. Knowledge of languages had helped me in my survival.

If it's all about speaking French, then I shall learn French. I refused to change my place of residence because of the threat posed by the French Canadian separatists. Along with many other professionals, I registered for a French course in the closest university to us, Loyola College, which was Catholic.

After my midterm exam my professor wanted to know if I was Jewish.

"Yes," I replied. "Why do you wish to know?"

"Because Jews are smart and they know how to speak many languages!"

That French course gave me the confidence to finally consider furthering my studies. In 1973, I graduated with a B.A. in History. In 1975, I received my M.A. in Jewish Studies. When invited into the doctoral program, I politely declined. I couldn't continue to place that level of stress on my family. My sons were 17, 15, and 11. They needed a mother more than I needed a Ph.D.

For the next eighteen years, I lived in "open hiding." My teaching was a source of satisfaction and success. Our children married and began building their own Jewish homes. I never regretted my silent state. Otherwise I couldn't have embraced my pain and the tasks of building my family, working full time and privately at home, attending university and being active in the community. Although I was silent, I was not isolated. My silent state was a crucial, fertile phase of my growth and the growth of my family. It was the answer to my mother's injunction to "Live."

Upon receiving my M.A. in Jewish Studies from Concordia University in Montreal; June 1975. My son Seth graduated high school that same week.

The greatest challenge confronting me during this time came when my school introduced the Holocaust into the curriculum. I knew I couldn't refuse to teach it. I was forced to tackle the subject, to participate in the memorial assemblies, and to answer the questions posed by my students.

Teaching the Holocaust at first was overpowering. I simply broke down the first few times I tried to prepare the curriculum. Slowly, I trained myself to teach this subject by distancing myself from it as if I wasn't who I was — a survivor. It was extremely difficult to do; nonetheless, keeping my identity hidden was a good thing in retrospect. Otherwise, I could have become the focus, either as a "hero" or a "victim," without doing justice to the many victims and their agony.

I used children's words to reach my fourth-grade class. I taught them using the book of children's drawings and poems, *I Never Saw Another Butterfly.*[4] I told them, "These children were Jewish children living in many places in Europe, including Vienna, Prague, and Berlin. They had homes, parents, brothers and sisters, grandmothers and grandfathers, just like you. Suddenly, overnight, their world was destroyed. They were driven away from their homes, their belongings were taken away, and they were starved. Many died from sicknesses. Fifteen thousand children under the age of fifteen were killed in the concentration camp called Theresienstadt. Only one hundred survived. Each one was an entire world."

Occasionally one of my students would ask, "Morah Leah, did you ever know any of these children who survived?"

I would always answer them, "No." I encouraged my students to share this part of our painful history with their parents and grandparents. Some of them had family members who were survivors, and the exposure in my class initiated a dialogue between them.

One year, the day after I had finished teaching, one of my students came up to my desk. Jeanette had a green ribbon in her blond hair, and she held her pencil tightly with her fingertips at both ends. "Morah Leah, I told my mother about the children."

I waited, as I sensed that she had more to tell me.

"My Bubbie and my mother were in a place like that. And then the Americans came. My mother was a very little girl, she was three years old, and she told me that she used to watch

---

4. *I Never Saw Another Butterfly: Children's Drawings and Poems from Terezin Concentration Camp*, 1942-1944, Schocken Books.

the cats go in and out through the fence. Every day she would tell my Bubbie, 'I wish I could be a cat because then I could go out, too.' My Bubbie told me that when the war was over, she went back to her house. It was empty except for her Shabbos candlesticks. She said the Germans didn't take them because they weren't silver or gold. They were pewter. She lights them now every Friday night."

Before I could respond, Jeanette ran back to her desk and returned with a drawing she had made. On the left side of the page, there was a little girl in a red dress, behind a black fence. The orange spotted cat sat beyond the fence towards the right. A brown train was surrounded by clouds of black-gray smoke. Jeanette had used a pen to draw circles for faces in the train cars. At the very edge of the page was a rainbow and yellow balloons and green grass. "Did you show this picture to your Mommy?" I asked her gently.

"Yes," she nodded. "My mommy said that the rainbow and the balloons are our family."

I looked at my blond-haired, blue-eyed student and was grateful that her place in the picture was on the rainbow side of the page. I was her age when, overnight, my childhood was destroyed. As I patted her on her head, I remembered the feeling of my own hair being woven into braids. My mother would finish with a pat and a kiss on my head.

"I see that you learned a lot from our class. I'm proud of you for sharing this with your Bubbie and your mother. Now you have something to tell your own children when you grow up."

Although I had finished "teaching" the Holocaust, Jeanette's drawing was up on the wall of our classroom for the rest of the year.

When I conducted the memorial candlelighting ceremony, I tried to read my students' faces and to use the opportunity to teach a lesson in faith. As I held the first candle in my hand, I said, "Even though our people have passed through horrible times, *baruch Hashem* we are here to continue our traditions and to remember those who died. The flame is to remember their souls, because the soul is compared to a light. But it also has to be a flame of life for us, so that we always remember to be proud Jews and to live Jewish lives. "

Although Holocaust remembrance week was a yearly nightmare for me, it would pass, and I would return to my silent state of semi-normalcy. I experienced tremendous joy teaching the cycle of the Jewish year. We all looked forward to decorating our classroom for holidays and festivals. For Passover, we conducted a model Seder and I invited the parents to attend. Some parents brought video cameras so they could learn how to conduct a Seder.

I introduced *Kabbalas Shabbos* (greeting the Sabbath) on Fridays. My desk was transformed into a beautiful Sabbath table with white tablecloth, candles, challah, and a *tzedakah* box. We sang Shalom Aleichem, recited *Kiddush* and then the blessing on bread, sang Shabbos songs, and sang Birkat HaMazon.

When Halloween fell on a Saturday night, I invited the children to come either for *Havdalah* (the ceremony marking the end of the Sabbath) or for a *Melaveh Malkah* (a festive meal following the Sabbath). Whatever night it fell on, I encouraged everyone to come in Biblical costumes, with a story to illustrate what character they were.

The Sukkos party was particularly joyful. I received permission from the principal to ask for parental release forms so that the children could come to my home on one of the Chol HaMoed (intermediate) days of the festival. Our sukkah was decorated with colorful ornaments and pictures drawn by the students. As my students crowded inside, I could tell by their faces that they felt they had entered an enchanted world. We made *kiddush* and a "*l'chayim*" and I explained to them why it is that we take four species — Lulav, Etrog, Hadassim, Aravoth — to bless and wave. We then recited the blessing and performed the mitzvah of waving them together. We recited the blessing on cakes and cookies, and the special blessing for dwelling in the sukkah. For some of my students, it was the first time they had learned about these mitzvos.

With the birth of each grandchild, I felt a deeper sense of healing in my heart. The pain of my past would never disappear, as I often wished it somehow magically would. But to see my aspirations for my sons fulfilled in their raising their own children to be proud Jews gave me the strength and reassurance that my decision not to share my past had been a good one. Although I was still plagued by nightmares and headaches, I began more often to feel a tremendous gratitude for the gift of life. My silence was bearing fruit, and the gates of my fortress were securely bolted, or so I thought.

One late afternoon in the autumn of 1993, as I walked home from school, I was recounting in my mind how enthused the parents had been about their children's learning. "Mrs. Kaufman, thank you so much. My son isn't only learning Hebrew and Yiddish — he's learning about Judaism." "Mrs. Kaufman, my daughter wants to go to a Hebrew-speaking camp in Israel..." I joyfully anticipated my students going on to lead full Jewish lives.

When I reached my home, I discovered a message on my answering machine from Gisela Tamler, who was born in my hometown of Herta. She wanted me to help her form a group to educate the public about Transnistria. I quickly returned her phone call and told her I would not be able to participate in her group. I was unprepared for her response.

"Leah, I will not let you rest until you help me. The story about Transnistria belongs to the world. There are not that many of us left to tell it."

Gisela kept her word, but I ignored her phone calls. In order to manage, my survivor self had to be invisible. I had locked her away in my fortress of silence. She dwelled there, in agony and endless suffering, yet I had been able to move forward in my life. The depth of her pain was too overwhelming for me to think about. But Gisela's phone calls haunted me. Did I really have a moral imperative to speak about my past? It was a past that, at best, would be seen through the eyes of a child who was told, "*Maidele, du host a groise fantazie*. Little girl, you have a vivid imagination."

I remembered overhearing conversations among survivors in the teachers' dining room. The older survivors would say, "The children had it easier than us. They were small; they had gentile protectors and foster parents to take care of them. These children are more fortunate because they were too young to remember." I did not take part in those conversations, but the words would echo in my mind.

Now, suddenly, I was being told, "Leah, I won't let you go. Leah, please, you must speak for us. Please, you are the one with an education. You have to help me tell the world about what happened in Transnistria."

"Tell the world." My mother had used those same words. Gisela's relentless pleading reinforced my mother's command.

Around this time, the deniers came to the fore in Canada, those outspoken people whose goal it was to convince the world that the Holocaust had never happened. I realized that no matter what I had to endure, I had to go public. But merely the thought of doing such a thing plunged me into more frequent headaches and more vivid nightmares.

I would wake up from a restless sleep, petrified. There in my recurring dream was Lydia, running as fast as she could away from a blazing fire, which followed her and almost swallowed her up.

There in the darkness, I began to wonder about Lydia, the person I had pretended to be. What was she like? How did I feel at the time about my hidden self? Did I like this girl? Why was she so resourceful? How did I deal with my Jewish self? Was I ever really her? What would have happened to Leah had Lydia remained in the Ukraine? Did I ever have the luxury then, or after my so-called liberation, to think about this life or death question of Jewish survival?

In the 1950s, everyone spoke about survivors and surviving. We were not included in those memories. We were only children. What did we know about suffering? People used to say to us, "Forget about it!" Is it humanly possible to forget our anguished past? In our numb state, we began anew. It was as though part of us was not present in our struggle to survive. But no one offered us a base from which to explain ourselves. Sometimes I wanted to believe, "Perhaps it didn't really happen. Perhaps it was all a bad dream. Did we truly suffer all that much? How much can such a little child remember?"

"Children forget easily," the older survivors said. Did anyone bother to ask us about our memories, our trauma? "Forget it" was a constant comment. Is it possible to forget? Is it possible to be completely disconnected from our home, from the small amount of childhood that we actually did experience? Does it mean that our life began with persecution, with no past, with no family base? Were we never born, never loved? Yet who can penetrate into the world of a child under those circumstances?

I learned from a very young age that every fall is a reminder that when I get up, I must rise higher, do better, accomplish more, realize more of the potential with which Hashem endowed me. As a survivor, I must become a restorer: of myself, of my family, of my community, of the world. I was numb from the brutality of my early formative years. I was terrified that unlocking the memory of my turbulent past might destroy my sanity. How could I speak about the sadism, the hatred, the cruelty that my eyes had seen, without losing my mind?

Wasn't I fulfilling my mother's command by raising Jewish children and teaching the Holocaust to my students, and empowering them to be proud Jews? Why did I have to give personal testimony? What good would it do except to unlock my pain and drive me mad?

"Leah, you must speak for us."

"Live! Remember! Tell the world!"

Gisela's pleas and my mother's command added to my constant inner turmoil. Finally, one day, upon my return from a trip to Memphis after visiting my eldest son Seth, his wife Lisa, and their family, I found my answering machine filled to capacity. It was one message after another from Gisela. "Leah, I won't let you go. Leah, please, you must speak for us." Again I felt tremulous when I dialed her number. "Mrs. Tamler, this is Leah Kaufman. I am willing to meet you, but I will never speak in public, as I have no words to express what I lived through." I did not know that my silence had been an incubation period for an entirely new phase of my life. I did not know how Hashem intended for me to fulfill the last desire of my mother's command, for to do so would require that I unlock the bolts of my silent fortress, and somehow find a way for my hidden, silent self to speak.

Mark and I with our children and
grandchildren at a family get-together
in our home, 2002.

CHAPTER 9

YOU MUST REMEMBER

Three years prior to Gisela's telephone "harassment," a support group of hidden child survivors began in Montreal. I knew nothing about the initial formation of this group. The first time I ever saw the term "child survivor" was in an article in *The Montreal Gazette*. Those words spoke to my heart. Although I was terrified about the prospect of telling anyone about my past, I was curious to know who these hidden children were.

Then, one afternoon in school, one of my coworkers, Thea Slawner, who had survived in Poland by hiding with her parents, approached me. Thea knew I had also survived the war, but she didn't know any details. "Leah, we are having a meeting of people from our community who were hidden children during the war. Why don't you come with me?"

"I can't. I don't want to talk about what happened."

"Leah, everybody there understands each other. No one will doubt your experiences. We all went through it. The meetings are once a month. You can just come and be there; you don't have to say anything. The meetings have a structure. Usually we have a presentation and then we have time to introduce ourselves to the group and share our survival experiences from the war. It is totally private."

It took a few months of coaxing and hours of telephone conversations with the founder of the group, Professor Yehudi Lindeman, a child survivor from Holland who later established the Living Testimonies program at McGill University, to convince me to come to a meeting.

"Leah," he stated emphatically, "the Germans didn't want to just destroy the Jews, they wanted to destroy Jewish memory. Our lives are living testimonials. We memorialize the dead and we transmit memory and conscience to the living. You are not alone. You have a family here, waiting for you to come and join us."

"I can't now. Give me time to think about it."

Yehudi's words stayed with me. *What were the consequences of withholding memory?* I wondered. I was helping to build the community and to educate the next generation of Jewish children. I was trying to live a meaningful life. What difference did it make to the world whether or not I was able to remember and articulate my past? Weren't my memories my private domain, or did they, in fact, because of what I had lived through, belong to Jewish and world history? My silence had been good for me. I did not want to delve into my memories. They haunted me in nightmares at night, and sprang upon me suddenly during the day. I never knew what sound, sight, or circumstance would trigger anxiety within me.

I will recall just one of many examples: During one winter in the early '90s, Montreal was paralyzed by a series of ice storms. Community shelters were created in schools, shuls, and churches all over the city. My friends and neighbors across the street, one of whom was sick, and one who cared for a 92-year-old blind woman, had no electricity. We were among the few houses that had electricity, and after much prodding and convincing, all four neighbors moved into the heated, well-lit shelter of our home. For the next four days, my neighbor and I fed all eight of us from our freezers.

We prepared for Shabbos. The food was in the oven, piping hot. No sooner had we said the blessing over the candles when the lights went out! *Baruch Hashem*, I had prepared for the possibility of a power failure with a lot of memorial candles that were lit everywhere, upstairs and downstairs and in both washrooms. Undaunted, we had a candlelit Shabbos dinner with much song. We then moved into the living room, rolled up the blinds, and watched the silver ice particles whirl against the windowpane. As deadly as the storm was, it was a display of winter majesty.

One of the branches of our young tree in the front yard was hanging at a skewed angle. Being so young and flexible, it survived the ice storm. As I looked at the tree, I became filled with dread. That branch reminded me of myself, clinging to life with destruction all around me. Only I was left. I envied the branch. At least it was still visibly connected to the tree.

Outside, the streets were covered with fallen trees and branches. As I looked through the window, for an instant, I was back in time on the freezing roads of the Death March. From the projection of my memory, the street was covered with piles of frozen corpses, many of them children. I could hear cries for help coming from those who were thrown into the icy Dniester River as families huddled together on the overcrowded barge, crossing to Moghilov, Transnistria.

Although we had no heat, we stayed in our home for the duration of the storm. *Baruch Hashem*, I had enough warm clothing for everyone. We didn't want to evacuate and go to a shelter, because it had too many negative associations with the war.

This was one moment in time, one image of a hanging branch on an ice-covered tree. How could I go and join a group of hidden child survivors who would encourage me to consciously bring back to my mind and heart the events of my shattered and traumatized childhood? How could I bring a description of these brutal events to my lips? I had worked so hard to conceal the fact that I was a survivor. How could I begin to give a voice to that part of me that had lived as a mute for so long?

Yet was remembrance not an integral part of our Judaism? Shabbos was for remembering the Creation. The prayers for all our holidays mention our exodus from Egypt. Our destroyed Temple in Jerusalem is remembered at mealtimes and at all special occasions. Memory has been a central pillar of our continuity as a people. The destruction of our collective memory would only reinforce Hitler's work. My memory was part of a mosaic of tragedy, of mourning and grief. Yet the rebuilding of my life, the joyous raising of my children, and helping thousands of students to be proud Jews bore witness to our eternity. Although my family's branch had broken, I was still connected to our "Tree of Life."

I became cognizant yet again of how fortunate my family was. When so many Jewish communities were totally destroyed, my family has been blessed with a remnant. We have become a thriving tree with many branches.

Although these thoughts made me more receptive to the possibility of attending the group, I was also very anxious about going. I had an unsettling feeling that I was about to embark on another journey. This time, it was not on a train or a ship. It was not sponsored by any organization. It was an inner journey back through time, into the fortress of my memory. There, I would travel through the ravages of my destroyed childhood and begin to face, in a different way, the evil I had seen and experienced. Despite my fear that it could lead to madness, I found within myself the determination to attend the hidden child survivor's group. I did not know where this journey would lead me. But I knew one thing — I could not possibly live with myself if I knew that my silence contributed to Hitler's work. The next time Thea asked me to go with her, I said yes.

It was a cold, snowy evening in January when I went to my first gathering of the hidden child survivors' support group. Although the cold and the rain reflected my state of being, I forced myself to go. As I walked down the hallway to our designated meeting place, I saw that the door to the boardroom of the Cummings building, which hosted so many Jewish organizations, was wide open. I entered quietly and took a seat, hoping to remain unnoticed. As I looked around, I saw some familiar faces, but couldn't quite place them. This evening was devoted to the experience of Hungarian child survivors. It began with a short film, followed by a roundtable discussion. Relieved that I did not immediately have to introduce myself, I settled back into the darkness to watch the documentary. How ironic, I thought, that while I had been sitting on the "luxury" repatriation train, on my way to Dorohoi, the Jews who had survived most of the war years in Hungary were on trains to Auschwitz.

The film was about a hidden child who had survived, and it presented information about the accelerated activity of the murder of the Hungarian Jews at the end of the war. At one point the presenter pointed out that at the beginning of the summer of 1944, in the Birkenau camp, "With each arriving train from Hungary, selections were made, and some men and women from each train were sent to the barracks. But within a few days, twelve thousand Jews were being gassed and cremated every twenty-four hours."[1]

The narrator of the film continued, "We must face the painful and sobering reality that, had the allies bombed the train tracks leading to the death camps, much of this slaughter could have been prevented." In fact, it was such a potentially effective military strategy that the Nazis themselves anticipated that the Allies were planning to bomb the main rail lines that went from Hungary to Auschwitz, Treblinka, and to other camps. But it was not done. On this most incomprehensible fact, Rabbi Haskel Lookstein has written, "The Nazis themselves worried

---

1. Gilbert, p. 675.

about the crippling effect of a raid on the rail lines. In a Jewish Telegraphic Agency Daily News Bulletin report out of Zurich, the pro-Nazi Hungarian government was reported as speeding up deportation from Budapest before the principal rail lines were severed by Allied bombing."[2]

A glance at Holocaust historian Martin Gilbert's description of the rail line network of the death camps and towns serves to heighten the glaring question of: "Why didn't the Allies bomb the train lines?" Of camps to the west of the Bug River, Gilbert says, "Although remote, each site was on a railway line linking it with hundreds of towns and villages whose Jewish communities were now trapped and starving. The first site, at Belzec, had been a labor camp in 1940; the railway there linked it with the whole of Galicia, from Cracow in the west to Lvov in the east, and beyond, and with the whole of the Lublin district. The second site, at Treblinka,...was linked by rail, through both Malkinia junction and Siedlice, with Warsaw and the Warsaw region.

"Auschwitz was not a remote village in eastern Poland, but a large town at a main railway junction, in a region annexed to the German Reich. The railway was part of a main line, with direct links to every capital of Europe, to the Old Reich, to Holland, France, and Belgium, to Italy, and to the Polish railway network."[3]

The film narrarator said, "The main person who repeatedly brought the bombing proposal to the Roosevelt administration was Benjamin Akzin, who later served as dean of the Hebrew University of Jerusalem Faculty of Law. During the war, Akzin was on the staff of the War Refugee Board which, through private funding, managed to save 200,000 Jews and 20,000 non-Jews. The response from the War Department to Akzin's pleas was that the bombing was not 'militarily feasible.' [However, Rafael Medoff, Director of the David S. Wyman Institute for Holocaust Studies, points out that, 'Ironically, beginning in

---

2. Lookstein, p. 196.
3. Gilbert, p. 287.

August, 1944, U.S. bombers repeatedly bombed German syn-thetic oil factories in the Auschwitz complex, including some that were less than five miles from the gas chambers. Dropping a few bombs on the mass-murder machinery was certainly militarily feasible, but the Roosevelt administration considered it politically undesirable.][4] It is not my purpose, my friends, to condemn anyone, I am simply raising a question based on historical evidence: Where was the conscience of man — even those who fought against evil?'"

I was shocked and disturbed by the narrator's presentation, but I couldn't even think about my reaction because suddenly I heard our group leader, Professor Yehudi Lindeman say, "Now I would like to introduce a new member of our group, Leah Kaufman. Some of you might know Leah as a Yiddish-Hebrew teacher, others may know her from the Torah class that she teaches at the Beth Zion Synagogue." I looked around at the people seated at the conference table, people who had come together because they were traumatized, wounded, and tor-tured, yet who had nevertheless rebuilt their lives. I saw doctors, lawyers, teachers, psychologists, and business people from our community. Suddenly I said to them, "Where have you been all these years?" The replies from the group came in unison:

"Where were you?"

"I thought I was all alone."

"So did we."

Little by little, as I attended the monthly meetings, I learned that we were actually part of an international network of hidden child survivors that began emerging in the mid-1980s. One of the earliest research projects on hidden child Holocaust sur-vivors was conducted by psychologist Sarah Moskowitz, who also had begun a support group in Los Angeles. Although I only read a small amount of Moskowitz's writing, I was greatly encouraged by the depth of understanding in her words. In an

---

4. Medoff, Rafael, "The Man Who Wanted to Bomb Auschwitz," *The Jerusalem Post*, online ed. 7 July 2004.

article called "Making Sense of Survival: A Journey with Child Survivors of the Holocaust," she wrote: "Fear pervades the stuff of memory for child survivors, in the sounds of guns, bombs, barking dogs. Entwined with the memory of people kind and courageous enough to hide them is the memory of fear of being abandoned if they fail to please..."[5]

But besides finding myself in Sarah Moskowitz's descriptions of fears and anxieties, it was her understanding of the child survivor's inner drive to create a particularly meaningful life that affirmed my choices: "Although the challenge to live a meaningful life is one we all face, the child survivor may feel a deeper call to not live life trivially. Therefore the major question, 'What am I to do in my life, in light of all that has happened to me, my family, and my people?' has a potentially creative, dynamic social thrust, a thrust so powerful that it can confront the horrendous past and respond with a life that is socially constructive and self-healing."[6] Moskowitz pointed out that there are a disproportionate percentage of child survivors represented in the helping and healing professions. That was certainly true for all of us sitting in the boardroom. It seemed to me that we, the former hidden children, became the rescuers of society.

I was very surprised to discover that some of the members of my group were parents of my former students. After the first meeting, when I got up to leave, a participant I knew from the PTA came over to me with her hand extended. "Morah Leah, I don't know if you remember me, but I am Jeanette's mother. How can I thank you? When you taught the Holocaust the year my daughter was in your class, she came home and told us what you said. My mother and I were in Theresienstadt. I was three years old. I was the little girl who wished she had been a pussy cat. When Jeanette started asking questions, it opened up a dialogue in my family. It was one of my motivations for

---

5. Krell, *Messages and Memories*, p. 11.
6. *Ibid.*, p. 16.

joining this group. Until that time, my daughter knew nothing about my past."

I was grasping her hand while she spoke.

"You did it in a beautiful way. I could tell from the drawing she made in your class and brought home for us to see."

After that first meeting I became a member of the group and was soon on the executive planning committee. With my entry and active participation in the hidden child survivor support group, my self-perception slowly began to change. I was not alone. I had "siblings" who had suffered in similar ways, and who had triumphed in spite of their suffering. They had become educated contributors to the betterment of humanity. They had emerged from hell with the desire and determination to create a better world. As Abraham Foxman, National Director of the Anti-Defamation League of New York City and founder of the International Conferences of Hidden Children, expressed, "We hidden children have a mission, a mission to proclaim and recognize goodness. For the first fifty years after the Holocaust, survivors bore witness to evil, brutality, and bestiality. Now is the time for us, for our generation, to bear witness to goodness. For each one of us is living proof that even in hell, even in that hell called the Holocaust, there was goodness, there was kindness, and there was love and compassion."[7]

Contrary to the dire predictions and fearful expectations of most government officials, medical professionals, psychologists, and educators, who were all certain that our damaged childhoods would doom us to becoming unstable, dysfunctional, socially dependent adults who would burden their host countries with their multiple ills, we excelled!

As psychiatrist Robert Krell, himself a hidden child survivor, has pointed out in his article, "The Challenge of Being a Child Survivor of the Holocaust," "We now know that this group has produced Elie Wiesel, Nobel Prize winning author and activ-

---

7. Krell, p. 72.

ist, the little boy Lulek, the youngest survivor of Buchenwald who [was] Chief Rabbi of Israel, Rabbi Meir Lau,and his brother Naftali Lavie, who became Israel's Consul General to New York."[8]

As we all shared our stories, it became more and more apparent to me that in addition to our trauma and grief, we each had an inner core of strength, stubborn persistence, and determination. I was to learn that once the psychologists created a paradigm for treatment of survivors, in their later research they discovered this wellspring of inner strength and termed it "resilience." It was also the highest form of resistance that we, the former children, could display.

I was in the process of forming a new identity for my survivor-self that I could relate to and be proud of. I was beginning to be able to put some of my horrific experiences into language. Slowly and with trepidation, I began to unlock the memory-vault and to share it with my newfound family. If not for the child survivor groups and my beloved "siblings," I would never have broken my silence. We could communicate with each other with few words. When we spoke within the group, when we cried together, we understood each other's pain. I was no longer alone. I had a family. I had an identity. And, finally, I had a place to mourn.

Each and every one of us is a miracle, a banner raised high, marking G-d's presence in the world. The very fact of our existence, after having overcome so much horror, so much pain, gave me strength. Every fall was a challenge to rise higher, to try harder, to do better, to elevate ourselves and help those around us. Through the darkness of our ordeals, we began to see the light of personal growth and of hope for a better tomorrow.

Beyond the personal benefits that I experienced, being in the group gave me a context for my silence. I was beginning to understand my choice of silence from a much broader perspective. My silence wasn't only a personal attempt to protect

---

8. *Ibid.*, p. 78.

myself from pain and push forward with my life. My silence was a direct response to social attitudes towards survivors. I refused to be part of a stigmatized group. In a departure from the prevailing psychoanalytic norm, Sarah Moskowitz recognized that the silence of child survivors was not only a personal coping mechanism — it was a direct response to stigmatizing attitudes from the public. "But such secrecy, shame, and fear of disclosure cannot be designated as 'their' problems, the problems of survivors. For they are born in reciprocal relationships with us, whose stigmatizing attitudes and behavior set in motion a tragic process. Too often has our fear of contagion, the suspicion that the survivor is a member of a different breed, and the subsequent distancing contributed to the burden of bearing loss in silent isolation."[9]

Through the processing of information and the emotional nurturing we gave each other, my traumatized self was able to begin to shift from its staunch silence. There was a genesis taking place within me. My silent self was beginning to become a "speaking spirit." I had no idea to what extent this was to carry me forward in my life and in the fulfillment of my mother's words.

During one of the meetings of the group, I learned that my headaches, a source of constant pain that doctors had told me were psychosomatic, were in fact typical of child survivors. Although I still shied away from most professional literature, I did read an article called "Severed Ties" written by Klaus D. Hoppe, a German psychologist dedicated to helping survivors heal emotionally, and an expert in German war reparations. Hoppe was ten years old when the Nazis came to power. Although he participated in Nazi youth groups, and later served in the army, he also wrote a play in 1939 about the Jewish persecution. Hoppe did not explain why, but he mentioned that his father was held by the Nazis in solitary confinement until 1945. Hoppe enumerated a list of symptoms that were typical of sur-

---

9. Moskowitz, p. 229.

vivors, but beyond that, he pointed to research among German children that showed that when it comes to their parents' Nazi past, "they have learned to keep it buried."

Hoppe linked the ability to deny human atrocity with an inner numbing of basic humanity. "If one feels nothing, then death is not taking place." When speaking about Holocaust survivors and their persecutors, Hoppe wrote, "There is a common denominator to these otherwise different groups...not only survivors still suffering from the after-effects of gruesome persecution, but also, often, those who served them, arbitrators and then enemies, reveal the same tragic phenomenon of uprootedness. There are severed ties in modern man, who gassed his soul in the ovens of Auschwitz."[10]

I was tormented by the thought that German youth were growing up ignorant of what their parents had done. What were the historical implications of burying the past? Would it take only the short time span of one generation before the Holocaust would be wiped out of German memory? And what about you? Are you not equally guilty? What about Jewish youth; what do they know about the Holocaust?

Although I was already having these disturbing thoughts, when Gisela Tamler first called me, I refused to speak with her or become involved with her project. Our group was private, only for hidden children. I was just beginning to enter my fortress of silence and face my inner "monster" and to recall details that I had repressed for so many years. Gisela's pleading for me to help her go public was asking me to make a quantum leap for which I wasn't ready. Despite my constant refusals, Gisela never took no for an answer. In her memoirs *Before and After*, Gisela writes, "So I heard about a woman from Toronto who is also a Transnistria survivor, from the same concentration camp as we were. I found out her telephone number, I talked to her, and she told me, yes, she's a survivor and she has a group of 150

10. Luel, Steven A. and Marcus, Paul (1984), *Psychoanalytic Reflections on the Holocaust: Selected Essays*, Hoppe, Klaus D., "Severed Ties," p. 95.

people. Among them were people from my hometown, too, and I said, 'Can you please advise me, how do I start it here? I don't know any other survivors. Give me one name.'[11]

"So she gave me a name, Leah Kaufman. I sensed in her voice when we were talking that this is an intellectual and an educated person, without seeing her face to face. And I kept calling her and calling her. I said, 'Leah, look, I don't know anybody who survived who can help me like you. My father was on the same Death March with your family to Transnistria. You cannot allow the memory of those martyrs to be forgotten. You have to tell the world what happened to us. Even the Montreal Holocaust Memorial Center here has no plaque for Transnistria.'"

Now I had the haunting echoes of three distinct voices. Alongside my mother's imperative, "Live! Remember! Tell the world!" I had Yehudi's voice, "Leah, the Germans didn't want to just destroy the Jews, they wanted to destroy Jewish memory." And now, Gisela's plea. But the voice that ultimately brought me to first break my silence was the innocent voice of my eight-year-old granddaughter Talia. She approached me one Passover, took my hand, and quietly said, "Bubbie, tell me your life."

We had been visiting Seth and Lisa and their family in Memphis for the Pesach holiday. Whenever we went to Memphis, we had both Jewish and Southern hospitality at its best.

I didn't know what to say to my granddaughter, so I said, "Just a minute, sweetheart," and went running to my son to discuss her request with him.

"Seth, what should I do? Talia wants to know!"

I was unprepared for his response. With a serious expression, he said, "Mommy, please don't repeat the mistake you made with me. Tell her. Use your own judgment. I trust you."

I went back to sit on the couch with my granddaughter Talia, and held her hand. "You know, Talia," I began, "we can't

---

11. Tamler, Gisela, *Before and After: Surviving The Romanian Holocaust in Transnistria*, p. 115.

understand how G-d runs His world. There are many things that happened to me that are very sad. But look — here we are sitting together, and I want you to know that whatever His reasons, G-d was always making miracles for me, and for many other people. Even though I was alone, I was never all alone, because G-d was always my partner.

"My mother, your great-grandmother, was a midwife and a healer. She helped anyone who came to her, Jew and non-Jew alike. When I was a little girl, I would often be awakened by the banging of the Romanian peasants on the window shutters asking her to come deliver a baby. But one night, when the peasants came to call us it wasn't to help anyone else. It was to warn us to run for our lives because the next day the Jewish residents of my town, Herta, would be killed."

For the next hour I sat with Talia and told her the miracles of my survival on the Death March to Transnistria, how I escaped from the Pechora concentration camp, and how my burst appendix saved my life. Throughout our talk, I watched Talia's face. I could see both sadness and wonder in her eyes.

After I had finished and Talia ran off to play, I kept asking myself, "Did I do the right thing? Did I tell her too much?" My answer came the next day after breakfast when Talia came over to me again and said, "Bubbie, I have to talk to you."

"Okay, honey, here I am. What do you want to tell me?"

"Bubbie, the day you die, it's gonna rain very hard." Talia was adamant and serious.

"Why is it going to rain so hard?"

"Because, Bubbie, all the angels G-d had sent to be your partners are going to cry so hard because they won't be able to watch over you anymore."

I hugged Talia and kissed the top of her head, relieved that she had come through my story with trust and faith. When I returned to Montreal, I was ready to meet with Gisela. I thought that it would be more polite to ask her in person to kindly stop her phone calls.

Gisela Tamler insisted on meeting me in my home. When she walked in and we greeted each other, the strangest feeling came over me. As I held her hands and looked into her face, I felt as though my own mother stood before me. "Leah, we would have been so happy and proud to adopt you; had we only known you were here, you would have been my daughter."

Gisela's life was divided between caring for her husband, who was hospitalized with Alzheimer's, and working to have Transnistria put on the Holocaust map in the Montreal Holocaust Memorial Center.

"Leah," Gisela said emphatically, "you cannot let them destroy our memory. You must help me. Transnistria has to be brought to the public."

"Gisela, give me time to think about what to do."

"Leah, do you know what my librarian received from a man named Ernst Zundel? A pamphlet called 'Did Six Million Really Die?' There are people all over the world who are trying to convince mankind that the Nazis never gassed anyone. The Holocaust deniers are saying that the gas was only for disinfection.[12]

"There are people all over the world who still admire Hitler. In France, Switzerland, Germany, Sweden, England, and the United States, there are professors and teachers who are claiming that the Holocaust never happened. These people are educated, and you are educated. Leah, you must remember, and you must speak for us."

"Gisela, please, give me some time to think."

I was shaken by the implications of the meeting with Gisela. The deniers were very active in Canada, but I hadn't realized the extent of their activity. It seemed to me that Holocaust denial was unique in world history. Did anyone ever try to deny the Crusades? Did any historian ever come forward and declare that the Spanish Inquisition had never happened? It is normal for a murderer to try to cover his tracks. But how is it that peo-

---

12. Prutschi, Manuel, "*Holocaust Denial Today*," p. 2.

ple who were not involved with the genocide of the Holocaust took it upon themselves to claim that the entire thing was a Jewish conspiracy?

Holocaust denial went beyond even the most ruthless "norm" of anti-Semitism. It went beyond the historical hatred and jealously that motivated Jewish persecution and slaughter. Instead of being victims, we are portrayed as perpetrators. The more I learned about their position, the more I realized that the foundation for a new wave of even more dangerous anti-Semitism had been formed. As Manuel Prutschi wrote, "Holocaust denial has brought about the convergence of the radical right and the radical left. Right and left are elements as anathema to one another as fire and water, yet Jews are able to work such miracles even among their enemies."[13]

Was my granddaughter Talia going to be put in a position where, alongside Holocaust history, she would have to read the writings of the "revisionists"? Gisela presented me with a reality I had to confront. My memories belonged to the world's conscience. The security and comfort I had found in my child survivors' group was an embryonic resting place for my spirit. The fortress I had worked so hard to build had to be torn down. The time had come to begin the fulfillment of my mother's last command: "Tell the world!"

Although the last thing I had ever wanted to do was appear in public as a survivor, I formed a committee with Gisela Tamler, Baruch Cohen, a survivor from the labor camps in Transnistria, and Bill Surkis, the director of the Montreal Holocaust Memorial Center. Our purpose was to have Transnistria put on the map at the Holocaust Center, and to educate the public about this forgotten graveyard. We called meetings of all the survivors we knew, and it was decided that we would have a public commemoration with personal testimonials and the unveiling of a Transnistria memorial plaque, donated by Gisela Tamler. The committee decided that I was to be the keynote speaker for the event.

---

13. *Ibid.*, p. 2.

Surrendering to my fate, I thus entered one of the most painful phases of my adult life. Suddenly, I was thrust beyond the personal, into a position of responsibility for memorializing the hundreds of thousands of innocent people who perished in Romania and Transnistria during the war. I had no choice but to face the brutal monster of my lost childhood. I did a lot of research, and in so doing, the fortress I had built between my past and my present was shattered. As I worked, I wept uncontrollably. I felt physically ill, as though I were being beaten.

I could only do this research for limited periods of time, as I couldn't allow myself to break down completely. I was teaching, and I had commitments to fulfill. I medicated myself and tried as much as possible to keep things normal. This was part of my destiny. It was part of the fulfillment of my mother's words. Hashem had given me this challenge, and He would give me the strength and the resources to meet it.

Everything that I had done up to this point in my life enabled me to rise to this challenge. My teaching experience, university studies, Torah class I taught, and involvement with the child survivor groups gave me the skills and confidence necessary. I got information about public speaking, and practiced my presentation over and over again. I was terrified, but determined to go through with it.

Finally, on the 25th of October 1995, after almost a half-century of silence, I stepped up to the podium at the Montreal Holocaust Memorial Center. The rotunda room was packed. More than 250 listeners were in the adjacent room, watching the address on a video screen. I felt as though the souls of the martyrs stood with me as I gave the following keynote address to memorialize those who had perished in what has come to be known as the "Romanian Auschwitz," the Forgotten Cemetery of Transnistria.

Dear Assembled,

Your very presence at this historical commemoration is a true comfort to us, the survivors of Transnistria, and to our families. I have been asking myself why it took so long to testify, and to create a memorial for our loved ones. King Solomon, in Koheles, came to my aide:

"For with much wisdom comes much grief,

and he who increases knowledge increases pain"(1:18).

In these remarks today, I have relied greatly on Elie Wiesel's Foreword and I. C. Butnaru's Preface to I. C. Butnaru's *The Silent Holocaust: Romania and Its Jews*. In certain places I have quoted them directly, while paraphrasing in others.

In order to survive after the survival, I blocked out much of the horrors of my early life. When scholarly books began to appear exposing the atrocities of Transnistria, I was too afraid to face the demons of my childhood. Then the deniers came to the fore, and I decided to break my silence. Along with the other hidden children, I had to become the voice for the hundreds of thousands who were murdered, so very many of them before my childhood eyes.

"When memory is muted, truth is the victim. When the past is silenced, the future is jeopardized. When history is falsified, humanity is impoverished."[14] The Holocaust was not a "causal occurrence" in Romania. It was a premeditated event. It was carried out by Romanians, with unbridled enthusiasm and with total devotion.

In 1939, on the eve of World War II, there were 850,000 Jews in Romania. By 1944, less than one-half remained. Most of the Jews who disappeared from Bessarabia, Bukovina, and Moldova had been brutally murdered. In the quest of a "Final Solution" of the Jewish problem, Hitler was enthusiastically embraced by Ion Antonescu, the Romanian Fuehrer. Ion Antonescu was among Hitler's strongest allies. Permit me to quote a fellow hidden child survivor, Baruch Cohen, who witnessed the pogrom in Bucharest on January 21-23, 1941, where several hundred Jews were butchered

---

14. Butnaru, *Introduction* by Elie Wiesel.

in a slaughterhouse, with unspeakable indignities perpetrated on their hanging bodies:

"I write these words with a pen dipped in blood, with eyes blinded by tears and a heart choked with pain and with throbbing indignation."

For more than fifty years, the silent Holocaust of Romanian Jewry was a forgotten episode in the destruction of European Jews. Today, finally, Transnistria is on the map. And so it was Kristallnacht of Bucuresti, January 21 to January 23, 1941, that signaled the beginning of four years of official measures that destroyed one-half of the Jewish population of Romania. Subsequently, in Lasi, on June 29, 1941, several thousand Jews were murdered and over 2,000 were deported in windowless cattle cars that drove around the countryside for days until all were dead.

Considering the magnitude and malignity of this and other gruesome events, it is difficult to understand the meager attention given to the destruction of Romanian Jews. However, by the end of the war, Romania broke its pact with Germany and joined the allied forces. Ever since then, Romania sought to portray itself as a nation that rescued Jews. This revisionist view has gone virtually unchallenged in Romania and in the rest of the world.

Trian Popovici, mayor of the Romanian town Chernovitz, who heard the voice of his conscience, wrote: "It would have been more humane for us to put the Jews against the wall and shoot them, rather than torture them in cold, calculated fashion with no qualm of remorse in our soul, nor have we any fear of G-d."[15]

We must clarify our understanding that the Holocaust was composed of not one, but two horrors. One was the suffering inflicted on the Jews and other persecuted groups. The other is the fact that thousands of people, men, women, and children of all ranks of society, did the tormenting and

---

15. Butnaru, p. 162.

murdering of Jews, day in and day out, over and over for weeks, for months, for years. These were not unique murderers. They were ordinary citizens, members of a "cultured" society. They were people like us. Before Antonescu's alignment with Hitler, they would have thought of themselves as immune to such savage instincts.

My friends, to all the survivors, Transnistria has remained a place that inspires terror. The very name is branded in letters of blood and fire in the souls of those who escaped and managed to save themselves from that living hell.

Why are we so late in establishing a memorial, the commemoration of which will become a yearly event at this Holocaust Center? A look at the gap in recorded history reveals that historians who teach the Holocaust chose to ignore the fact that so many Romanian Jews were systematically exterminated during the war. And simply because we, the survivors, were and still are so traumatized by our experiences, that we couldn't bring to our lips the pain, the anguish of our suffering. Not to our spouses, not to our beloved children, not to our nearest and dearest friends.

One of the most tragic and bitter aspects of the horror, taking place on the way to and in Transnistria, was the plight of the orphans. The babies and the very little children under age five perished in total abandonment. Those of us who were a little older, with a will to survive, lived a vagabond existence. We were barely clothed in the bitter cold. We were hungry, thirsty, afraid to die, neglected, and oh so very lonely. Every day in the orphanage we awoke to find hallucinating friends, with constant death all around us. According to historian Avigdor Shahan, himself a child survivor, at one time, there were 10,000 orphans in Transnistria.

Many of us who survived took on a temporary Christian identity and became cheap labor for the Ukrainian population. But we felt grateful and very lucky for the hope of survival. The Holocaust shattered and damaged every aspect of our lives. But most of all, the shattering of the self was the deepest form of damage, a damage almost beyond repair. The feeling of nothingness is not foreign to me, but during this darkest period of my life, my so-called life was reduced to a bare existence, to dust. Nonetheless, I became acutely aware that even the horrendously dreadful existence was far better than death. As long as one lived, one hoped to survive, and above all, to remember and to tell the world.

In response to my Romanian tormentors, I paraphrase Branisteanu, in his preface to Matatias Carp's book, *Sarmas*:

You have robbed me of all my innocent games of childhood. You have deprived me of the wonderful, comforting love and nurturing that my murdered parents and siblings longed to give me. You have robbed me of the possibility to properly mourn my beloved parents and my six brothers and sisters.

You have poured salt and bitterness into the sweet cup of my childhood and my youth. You set malicious calumny and mockery in my way as a Jewish child. Nevertheless, you have not succeeded to cut me off from my path and from my beloved people, Israel. I have reached my goal. But I have reached it struggling bitterly, deprived of joy. In the end, I have no right, and no power to forgive. All retribution and punishment belong to Hashem.

Whenever I see a picture of a prison, there I see Romania, my so-called homeland. Whenever I see or read of persecution, along with the persecuted, I too, breathe the air of my childhood memories. I stand before you on this memorial day, the former nine-and-a-half-year-old child who was destined for death.

Thank G-d, my tormentors have failed. I am a proud Jew, married, with three married sons and thirteen grandchildren [as of this writing twenty-two]. I graduated from the Montreal Hebrew-Yiddish Teachers Seminary, of Catholic Loyola University with a B.A. in History, and from Concordia University with a Masters in Jewish Studies. For the past forty-five years I have, through my teaching, imbued thousands of Jewish chil-

On the steps of the Canadian Parliament with Mark.

dren with pride in their heritage. I have taught and continue to teach our holy Torah to countless adults. I have gained recognition for my educational work from the Beth Zion Synagogue of Cote St. Luc and from the Jewish Cultural Community of Montreal.

I am a very proud daughter of a very ancient people.

AM YISRAEL CHAI!

I stood there, looking into the faces of my listeners, and I knew that no matter what my personal suffering had been, together we were contributing to world history because finally Transnistria had been given its place on the Holocaust map. This moment was the pinnacle in the process of my transformation. I had taken the leap into the public arena. Suddenly, I was surrounded by people who lined up to speak to me. I was prepared with packets of photocopied information about Transnistria.

"Leah, it was excellent."

"Leah, we are so proud of you."

"Mrs. Kaufman, please, you must come to my school."

From that time on, I was bombarded with requests to testify. The commemoration became an annual event at the Montreal Holocaust Memorial Center. Gisela and I were interviewed by Mark Abley, a reporter for *The Montreal Gazette*, and one Sunday morning we found ourselves on the front page. Regardless of the demands of my teaching schedule, it was very hard for me to say no to anyone who asked me to speak, as I understood the urgent need for public education.

As my survivor self entered the public arena, my life was coming full circle in other areas. Two years after our first commemoration, I retired from teaching to devote myself exclusively to speaking about the horrors of Transnistria and Romania during the war. On November 18th, 1998, the Zachor committee, along with B'nai Brith, Canadian Jewish Congress, Canadian Holocaust Remembrance Association, Canadian Friends of Simon Wiesenthal Centre, and the Canadian Society for Yad Vashem, invited fifty Holocaust survivors to be honored by the Canadian Parliament. I was one of those honored.

The purpose of the event was to commemorate the approaching fiftieth anniversary of the Universal Declaration of Human Rights, and to acknowledge the outstanding contributions that Holocaust survivors had made to Canadian life. Under strict security, we were gathered in the Parliament Building on Parliament Hill in Ottawa, Ontario, the capital city of Canada. We were chosen to represent all Canadian survivors at this special ceremony. Herb Gray was functioning as acting Prime Minister, as John Chretien was overseas. We were treated royally, given a tour of the building, and provided with kosher food as well as yarmulkes for the men.

When we entered the Parliament, in the

Certificate presented by the Canadian Parliament.

House of Commons, the members of the three main political parties rose separately to greet us. When we were called up individually, we were presented with a citation of excellence for our contributions to Canadian life, and renewed Canadian citizenship. During breakfast, when I was sitting at the table with the other survivors, suddenly a fellow named Jack jumped up, looked at me, and said, "SS Sturgis!"

"What about the SS Sturgis? That's the ship I came over on."

"It brought me to Canada in the winter of 1948," he said, as he stood up and stared at me with a glint of recognition. "You remember those fist fights when the other passengers called us dirty Jews?"

"How could I forget? The ship's crew had to separate everyone."

We beamed at each other, overcome with joy.

When the opportunity arose, I approached the Minister of Foreign affairs, Mr. Lloyd Axworthy. He was a very tall man, and had donned a *kippa* in honor of the occasion. He had to bend down so I could speak to him. "Mr. Axworthy, before you let us into Canada, the slogan was 'None is too many!' You were afraid to bring the children in because you thought we were damaged for life. I want you to know that I was never on welfare, never on unemployment, and I paid very high taxes because of my qualifications in my profession. For all of that, I am still very grateful because I was able to become educated and to rebuild my life in Canada, a country I will always love."

Mr. Axworthy paused as he surveyed the table of survivors before him. Bending down again, he said softly into my ear, "We are all humbled before you, Mrs. Kaufman."

CHAPTER 10

TELL THE WORLD

t was a clear, sunny day in July of 2004. I stood between the library archives and the education buildings at Yad Vashem, the Israel Holocaust Center, and looked out at the nearby forest, the blue sky, and the Judean hills. The distinctive beige Jerusalem sandstone of the buildings was framed by the panoramic view of our land. I had come here early to think, and to review my notes. Within the hour, I would be standing at a podium in the large auditorium, addressing a group of 250 students who had come to Israel to learn more about being Jewish. My husband Mark went to photocopy the letter response forms that we hand out, and to set up the tape recorder there.

Standing between these two buildings, I stood literally between our past and our future. In the archives, among the thousands of recorded histories, was my testimony about the death march to Transnistria. That is our tragic yet miraculous past. Each time I speak to students, I strive to communicate the transcendent spirit that rests within each of us, that enables

Our three sons and daughters-in-law join Mark and me to celebrate our 50th wedding anniversary at the Reich Hotel in Jerusalem, June 2004. R-L: Chaviva, Rachel, Lisa, me, Mark, Seth, Baruch, and Yossi.

us to make the noble choice no matter what the circumstances facing us may be. That ability to choose is our future, both as individuals and as a nation.

So much had transpired since that keynote address at the Montreal Holocaust Memorial Center in 1995, which had been both an end and a beginning for me. It was the official end of my silent years, and the beginning of my active testimony. Much to my reluctance and amazement, I was drawn into the arena of public speaking. My testimonies about the Death March to Transnistria were in the archives of McGill and Yale Universities as well as the Speilberg Foundation. Once the Montreal Holocaust Memorial Center discovered me, I was called upon very often to testify. I had only one stipulation: to speak primarily to young people. During those years I spoke almost weekly to both Jewish and non-Jewish groups.

At this time, my main goals were to inform and educate the public about the Holocaust in Romania and to create awareness about Transnistria, that "Kingdom of Death," where "...not one community was spared. All were decimated...in thousands and thousands of ways. There was the terror, the threats, the nocturnal death marches, the sealed wagons, the starvation, the plagues, the humiliations, the public executions, the fires... The orders came from on high, from Marshal Antonescu himself ...Romanians, Germans, and Ukrainians outdid one another in cruelty. Everywhere it was the same. In the towns as in the villages, summer as in winter, being Jewish meant subjection to torment and torture."[1] I wanted my presentations to be a living memory for the martyrs, and I wanted to warn the young about the dangers of hate and indifference.

In 1999, we fulfilled our dream of moving to Eretz Yisrael — the Land of Israel. Prior to that time, I had retired from teaching in order to be able to respond to the many requests to speak. It was a difficult decision to leave our home, close friends, and community in Côte St. Luc, Montreal. Yet the love for Eretz Yisrael that had been planted in my childhood filled me with longing to live there. As I watched the contents of fifty-two years of my life being dismantled and packed, I was both sad and anxious. I had no idea where this step would lead and how I would continue to "tell the world" from our new home in Israel.

Gazing at the landscape from the terrace of Yad Vashem helped me to focus my mind, but my heart was laden with the plight of the young, and with anxiety and grief about the state of things in the world and in the Land of Israel in particular.

We had moved to Eretz Yisrael on the eve of the new intifada. I was devastated to see scenes of the Holocaust repeated in our land. The violence and brutality against us, the polarization of secular and religious, and the assimilation among the youth weighed heavily on my mind and heart. A recent study

---

1. Elie Wiesel, foreword to Radu Ionid, *The Holocaust in Romania: The Destruction of Jews and Gypsies Under the Antonescu Regime, 1940-1944.*

conducted by the Israel Democracy Institute showed that 35% of Israeli secular youth do not want to live in Israel.[2] What were we going to have to live through before we would reach the peace for which we all hoped and prayed?

The world at large was shaken by the destruction wrought on September 11, 2001, and the constant threat of terrorism. The problems among the young, the inner alienation from the human ability to love, to communicate, to reach out, and to relate to people, were all reflected in the alarming increase of drug use, violence, divorce, and other social ills. The international rise of anti-Semitism and the recent campaign to deny the Romanian Holocaust filled me with an even greater necessity to speak out.

How could I begin to address the current issues that were pressing on my heart? News reports were filled with incidents of anti-Semitism. France, with a population of six million Muslims, was the leader: There had been over five hundred threats or incidents in the last six months. But France was not alone. In his testimony before the Commission on Security and Cooperation in Europe, Alfred H. Moses, the former United States Ambassador to Romania, cited as targets Budapest, the Ukraine, Belgium, Denmark, Berlin, and Greece. Physical and verbal assaults, synagogue bombings, cemetery desecrations, and threats were rampant. Pictures appeared in the papers depicting international demonstrations with people holding placards with Jewish stars equated with swastikas, side by side!

As former Ambassador Moses stated, "The historical anti-Semitism of Europe has been given new life by voices on both the political right and the left...With anti-Semitism now at its greatest peak since the most tragic of all human episodes, the Holocaust, let us be mindful of this history. Let us speak out.

---

2. Harel, Israel, "We Are All in the Same Boat," Ha'aretz, May 27, 2004, courtesy of Am Echad.

Let us use our influence, let us remember the price of inaction or denial; and let us act now."[3]

I could sense the winds of prewar Germany blowing across the world. History was repeating itself in the vicious and virulent contemporary form of Muslim anti-Semitism. I had found an excerpt from the Spandu prison diary of Albert Speer, one of Hitler's closest confidants. On November 18, 1947, Speer wrote, "I recall how [Hitler] would have films shown in the Reich Chancellory about London burning, about the sea of fire over Warsaw, about exploding convoys, and the kind of ravenous joy that would then seize him every time. But I never saw him so beside himself as when, in a delirium, he pictured New York going down in flames. He described how the skyscrapers would be transformed into gigantic burning torches, how they would collapse in confusion, how the bursting city's reflection would stand against the dark sky."[4] What kind of a tomorrow could a young person today anticipate? How could a tender, young heart hope to help create a better life, a better world?

Since my arrival in Israel, I have been privileged to speak to thousands of young people from diverse populations from all over the world. The more I addressed young, unaffiliated Jewish audiences, the more I became aware of a crying need for them to learn about their heritage and their history. It was my youngest son, Yossie, who shared my concern for our future generations. As soon as we moved to Israel, Yossie opened many new and challenging doors for me as he was working for Heritage House, a Jewish youth outreach organization.

One day, Yossie received a phone call from Rabbi Naftali Schiff, the director of Aish HaTorah in England. "Yossie, I need a speaker for my summer fellowship group. I need a Holocaust survivor."

---

3. Moses, Alfred, Testimony for Parliamentary Forum: Combating Anti-Semitism in the OSCE Region, Commission on Security and Cooperation in Europe, December 10, 2002 http://www.csce.gov/witness.

4.Wistrich, Robert S. "Muslim Anti-Semitism, A Clear and Present Danger," AJC Publication.

"Fine, I'll ask my mother."

"Yossie, stop joking with me! I need a speaker as soon as possible."

"Rabbi Schiff, I'm not joking. My mother is a survivor from Transnistria, and she spoke very often in Montreal before my parents moved to Israel. She is particularly interested in addressing groups of young people. She was a teacher for fifty years."

"Okay, how do I reach her?"

That was the beginning, in the year 2000, of my relationship with Rabbi Schiff and the thousands of young people who benefit from the wide range of programs that Aish HaTorah offers. Since then, Aish HaTorah brought me to England twice, where I was privileged to address thousands of young people in Jewish schools and universities across the country. Yossie was also the one who opened the door for me to Yad Vashem and to Hebrew University, which led to "Birthright," a philanthropically sponsored program of tours to Israel for Jewish youth around the world. It was Yossie who inspired writer Sheina Medwed to interview me and to write "Bubbie, Tell Me Your Life," and include it in her anthology of stories. Now, as we were working together on my memoirs, between the speaking and my "writing assignments," I had almost daily confrontations with my past.

I was among those children whom the Holocaust sought to destroy and consume but somehow did not. That "somehow" is my story. Growing up in hell and surviving, I've often asked myself, *Why, why did I survive, when so many millions of children did not?* After years of guilt, pain, and shame, I discovered the *raison d'etre* for my being here. We who were in the midst of the inferno and had survived must serve as witnesses to the horror that had ripped apart our lives, and to the miracles, bravery, and kindnesses that preserved us. The deepest ideals and most immediate concerns of the Jewish people must be ever present at the core of my life. I who survived must teach and defend the traditions, hopes, and visions that the Nazis wanted to eradicate forever.

I could see from the reactions of my audiences that they were seeking something, something that could fill the void of emptiness and fear that they carried and suffered from in their daily lives. What was this amorphous thing that was defined by its absence? No amount of money, materialism, sensation, media stimulation, wanderlust, or "artificial" religion could fill the empty hole of longing for a more meaningful, value-filled life.

For my Jewish audiences, I began to realize that for some, the lack of a real Torah-based Jewish education was a tragedy that created an ongoing destruction of their lives. Without an anchor to the past, that indispensable joining with our past that forms the fundamentals of universal self-worth our children so desperately seek, our young people are like lost ships on the sea of life. At best, they float around and around until, hopefully, they happen upon a relatively safe harbor. At worst, they are tossed up and dragged down like the remains of ancient driftwood. Some land on foreign islands far, far away, never to return.

It was my encounter with the girls who were visiting from the Eitz Chaim Bais Yaakov, the Jewish religious school of Toronto, that had caused me to reexamine my priorities. When I entered the rotunda room of the Montreal Holocaust Memorial Center, the young women stood up and did not sit down until I did. I sat in the center of the hall and I asked them to gather close to me. They sat on the floor, surrounding me in a semicircle. We began with a song, "*Kol ha'olam kulo gesher tzar me'od — v'ha'ikar lo l'facheid klal.* The whole world is a narrow bridge — But the main thing is not to be afraid." Watching their earnest faces moved me deeply, as I saw the faces of the murdered children and who they might have become had they lived. I thanked Hashem for this moment. After I finished, the girls asked me many carefully thought-out questions, and they gave me their written responses which left me speechless and extremely proud.

Ashreinu, mah tov chelkeinu...How happy are we, how goodly is our portion...

How fortunate we are indeed to have such magnificent daughters of our people. When I concluded, these beautiful girls stood up in silence. Some came over to hug me and to cry on my shoulder and to thank me for caring enough to share and to strengthen their *emunah*. Despite living in a religious world and attending a school that is an extension of their home, nonetheless there was still room for strengthening their faith. As I was the only religious survivor to testify, the Eitz Chaim School in Toronto would contact me in my home every year, to ascertain that I was available to address them.

Upon making *aliyah* in 1999, my priority and my focus expanded. I wanted to tell the world our history, but I also wanted to respond to the needs of the youth. Strengthening Jewish identity, emphasizing Jewish continuity, contributing to the future of humanity became my goals for each and every encounter.

A knowledge of our history is essential to Jewish identity and survival. When we sever our ties to the past, we place ourselves in danger. Even our enemies are aware of this eternal truth. One Passover, Palestinian Legislator Selah Temari was a security prisoner in an Israeli jail. Temari, who had begun to study Jewish history to search for the key to our survival, saw his jail warden eating bread. "...He asked the jailer how he could eat bread on Pesach. The jailer answered, 'Do you really expect me not to eat bread because of something that happened over 3,000 years ago?' In the course of the sleepless night that followed, Temari relates, he decided that not only could the Palestinians win a state, they could one day evict the Jews. Without an attachment to the past and the land, he concluded, the Jews could be worn down." [5] The greatest weapon we have against our enemies is to become living links between our history and our future. We must learn and embrace who we are.

As a nation, we are experiencing the birth pangs of our redemption. The response of the world to terrorism in Israel

---

5. Rosenblum, Jonathan, "Remembering the Past to Preserve the Future," *The Jerusalem Post*, April 2, 2004, courtesy of Am Echad.

has created a shift in the paradigm of our identity. Even those who are far away from their Jewish identity, and far away from any association with the State of Israel, are being made to feel uncomfortable in their professional and social circles, as Muslim anti-Semitism becomes, more and more, a socially acceptable political position.

As a result, from the full spectrum of our people we need now to be strengthened, we need to join hands. Whether it is to intensify our commitment, or to investigate our Jewish identity, we must take action. Hitler showed us that we are, for better or worse, one people. From our yeshivos, synagogues, and mansions that are built on foreign soil, to the houses of learning and Jerusalem apartments overlooking the Kosel, to the caravan homes established on the rocky desert soil, we must learn that hatred and divisiveness are not, and will never be, answers. Not for Israel, not for our nation, not for the world.

When I speak to our youth, I speak about commitment. Last year, on Tishah B'Av 2003, I addressed a group of students at Jewel, a Jewish women's educational network. This time, they got more than a lecture — they had "show and tell"!

On the Ninth of Av, 2003, I was scheduled to speak first at Jewel in the Ramat Eshkol neighborhood of Jerusalem, and then go to a hotel in downtown Jerusalem to address one hundred B'nei Akiva participants from England. It was an extremely hot day. I had arranged for a taxi to take us from our home in Beitar to Ramat Eshkol to speak at 9 a.m. and then pick us up at 10:30 to go to the B'nei Akiva group for an 11-12 o'clock presentation. Mark, my gracious recording technician, came with me as usual.

As is my habit from my teaching career, we arrived at Jewel early. It was before 8:30 in the morning, and we waited outside on the patio in the shade. Suddenly, I felt faint and asked for a drink. Mark reached for the water bottle, but by the time he turned to hand it to me, I was passing out! He caught me and lay me down on the sidewalk. The counselors and the girls arrived to see that their speaker had fainted. They immediately called an ambulance.

By the time the ambulance arrived, I had regained consciousness. The medics checked me and gave me lots of grape juice to drink. They then said, "Come, we are taking you to the hospital."

At this point I regained my composure and responded, "I came here this morning to Jewel to speak to the girls, to deliver a message from the hell called Transnistria, to speak about the miracle of my survival and of hashgachah pratis (Divine Providence), not to go to the hospital. I intend to accomplish what I came here for."

"Lady, what's the matter with you? You must be checked by a doctor," they insisted. "Come, let's go."

"Thank you for your care and concern, but I am here to speak to the girls."

The urging of the attendants made no impression on me. In despair, they finally said, "Geveret (lady), we take no responsibility for you whatsoever. You will have to sign a waiver stating that the decision to stay here is yours and yours alone. We are not responsible for the consequences."

Baruch Hashem, the worried young women received a show and tell lesson never to be forgotten: When you set out to accomplish an important assignment, especially when the future of our young people is at stake, don't let anything stop you. I delivered my presentation much to everyone's surprise, including my own. Then the taxi came on time and took us to the B'nei Akiva group from England, where I spoke again to one hundred young boys and girls. The taxi showed up on time, and took us home to Beitar.

Not until I lay down on my own bed did I begin to comprehend the lesson to be learned in what had happened to me that day, Tishah B'Av, 5763 (2003) in Yerushalayim Ir Hakodesh. Our Sages tell us that if you have the will, nothing can stop you. When you work very hard to achieve a goal, you will find much more than what you hoped to accomplish. With a positive attitude, you will realize that you have begun to aspire anew towards a new goal.

"Leah, it's time."

My husband's voice reminded me that it was time to walk to the Yad Vashem auditorium. I entered and stood at the podium, watching the young people take their seats. They had come from colleges and universities all over America, Canada, and England. Some of them had a Jewish education, while others had none. I had one hour to speak to them. The auditorium was filled to capacity, and my heart was filled with love and urgency I began addressing my students with the following words.

"You and I have something very special in common. I am of the last generation of survivors of the manmade hell called Transnistria. You are of the last generation to hear direct testimony from a survivor. With both of us being the last of our kind, we share a higher level of responsibility towards the future. Who will bear witness after the living witnesses are no longer here?

When I come to Yad Vashem, it is a double comfort to me. Firstly, here is the only place where I can remember and mourn my family who perished on the Death March to Transnistria. Today I am going to share with you that part of my story. Yet it is not my purpose to dwell on destruction and death. There is a second part to my story, that of rebirth and rebuilding a Jewish life and a Jewish family. If my story ended with the building of my own family, I would be forever grateful.

But as destiny has it, my story does not end there. Because in the winter of 1941, when I was a nine-year-old child on the Death March, clutching my mother's hand as we trudged over the frozen earth, my mother, of blessed memory, would say to me over and over: '*Du muzt lebn, du muzt gedenken, du muzt dertzeiln der velt vos die Rumanier hobn tzu undz geton* — You must live, you must remember, you must tell the world what the Romanians did to us.'

Thus, the third part to my story includes you, you who are sitting here today, who have come to learn more about and deepen your connection to Judaism and to your Jewish heritage. You are the third part of my story because you are the future of our people and the future builders of the world. How can a person look at the world today and not shudder? How can a person look at the world today and not feel anguish and despair? Yet I, who am a living spark from the inferno of the Shoah (Holocaust), am here to tell you today that we must never give in to the pit of despair. Despair leads to apathy, to indifference, and to inaction, and these are worse than death.

Even in the tragedy of 9/11, I can find positive aspects. This might seem incredulous to you, but the eyes of a survivor see things differently than the rest of the world. Those who were left bereft of relatives and friends know the date on which it happened, they know where it happened, they have a monument and a place to mourn, and the United States went to war for them.

As for myself, I have no dates for the deaths of my parents and siblings, nor are there any burial sites. Chances are, dogs devoured them. There is no monument where I can mourn my family. I have been left mourning my lost childhood, and the loss of their nurturing, all my life. I do not have even one photograph of my family in my possession.

One morning a few months ago, I received a phone call. When I said hello and heard the voice on the other end, I felt a chill of recognition. The accent was distinctly Romanian. A team of researchers from Romanian National Television wanted to come to interview me in my home. They are making a documentary film on the Holocaust and they wanted to hear my testimony about the Death March.

When I was a nine-year-old child wandering alone in the forests of Transnistria, did I ever dare to imagine that the grandchildren of my tormentors would someday come to record my testimony of that evil and horrendous time? Yet my mother's words girded me for this task. It was as though she anticipated that at some time in the future, the deniers would want to eradicate the Holocaust from world conscience and world memory. She was not alone in her valid concern.

On April 15, 1945, General Dwight D. Eisenhower, while he was recording the devastation in Europe, wrote a letter to General George C. Marshall. In it he said, 'The things I saw beggar description...The visual evidence and the verbal testimony of starvation, cruelty, and bestiality were...overpowering...I made the visit deliberately in order to be in a position to give first-hand evidence of these things if ever, in the future, here develops a tendency to charge these allegations merely to "propaganda."'[6]

This was a prophetic intuition for our time. Finally, sixty years later, the Romanians are making a recorded history of what truly happened. Let's hope it will make inroads into the mind of the general population, for their form of Holocaust denial is uniquely insidious. This form of denial, named by scholars as 'selective negationism,' is today, in Romania, a school of thought.

The Romanian form of Holocaust denial is called 'selective negationism.' In other words, Romania doesn't deny that a Holocaust happened. It denies that it ever happened in Romania. As Michael Shafir reports in his article, 'Selective Negationism of the Holocaust in East-Central Europe: The Case of Romania' ('ATAC', No. 19/2002): '...nowhere in post-communist East-Central Europe — to the best knowledge of this author — is selective negationism as blatant as in Romania. According to its champions, [it is] not only wartime leader Marshal Ion Antonescu who is innocent of any crimes against the Jews, but even the Iron Guard has never touched a Jewish hair. The Romanian champions of selective negationism are not (as one might have expected) semi-educated marginals. Two of the most emblematic figures among them are university professors, one a historian specializing in modern Romanian history [Gheorghe Butzatu] and the other [Ion Coja] teaching Romanian linguistics at the University of Bucharest.'

---

6. General Dwight D. Eisenhower to General George C. Marshall, 15 April 1945, Box 80, "Marshall, George (6)" DDE to Marshall, Eisenhower Library. As seen in the United States Holocaust Memorial Museum.

Butzatu was a deputy chairman of the Greater Romanian Party, deputy chairman of the Romanian Senate, and chairman of the Marshal Antonescu Foundation. Coja had been active in various ultra-nationalistic parties and had almost been a presidential candidate in 1996. The Holocaust had been reduced to a debatable issue. There were even symposiums that these people have chaired where they presented invented testimonies of support from Jewish leadership at the time of the war.[7]

Anti-Semitic beliefs are still deeply rooted in the Romanian population. The fall of communism in 1989 initiated the beginning of the revitalization of the Christian orthodoxy associated with the Greek Orthodox Church. Concurrent to this, Romania has been witness to the reemergence of ultra-nationalistic movements and Nazi organizations dedicated to the memorial portrayal of Marshal Antonescu as a martyr and hero. Although he was executed as a war criminal in the early summer of 1946, many statues of Antonescu were erected, and at least thirty streets were named after him.

The Jewish community in Romania, which once hosted 850,000 members, lost half of its population during the Holocaust. Another 350,000 Jews emigrated during the 1950s and 1960s. The Jewish community in Romania today, with only about 800 young people aged 15-35, is now a remnant of 7,000-9,000 people, most of whom are elderly, and who need financial assistance to survive. Despite this low-income factor, 'the results of a nationwide published survey conducted in October 2002, demonstrate that the majority of Romania's population believes that Romanian Jews are in better financial shape than the rest of the population,' and should adopt the model of the Jewish businessman 'in order to improve the poor Romanian economic situation.'[8]

---

7. Shafir, Michael, "Selective Negationism of the Holocaust in East-Central Europe: The Case of Romania" ('ATAC', No. 19/2002): wwwrfel.org.

8. Katz, Marco Maximilian, "Anti-Semitism in Romania," 2002 Report, The Center for Monitoring and Combating Anti-Semitism in Romania.

Although the actual numbers of anti-Semitic incidents have been low, certain segments of the population of Romanian youth are showing signs of anti-Semitism and xenophobia in their culture. A February 2000 article from *The National*, a Romanian newspaper, describes violence and xenophobic literature to be part of the weekend football culture, with visual displays of swastikas and other anti-Semitic slogans. It was reported that one gallery display had a sign that said, 'Hungarians, Gypsies, Albanians...Got any Jews?'

The newspaper article went on to state that, 'These young people who come from underprivileged environments and who are inclined to violence only lack a real leader in order to become what they only claim to be. The slogans are already in their brains. The display of anti-Semitic, racist, or xenophobic symbols on the stadiums is ignored by the authorities, even though such manifestations are illegal.'[9]

The establishment of a Democratic government in Romania, and the attempt to pass Emergency Ordinance no. 31, which would have been the first active legislation against anti-Semitism and xenophobia, still did not prevent the Romanian authorities from making further statements denying the Holocaust. In June of 2003, a communiqué issued by the Romanian government claimed: '...the position of the Romanian government: encouragement of research regarding the Holocaust in Europe while emphasizing the fact that within the borders of Romania, there was no Holocaust between 1940-1945.'

In response to this and numerous other Romanian attempts to exempt themselves from the annals of evil, Avner Shalev, chairman of the Directorate of Yad Vashem, with the support of the United States Holocaust Memorial Museum and many other concerned organizations, wrote to the president of Romania. They proposed the establishment of a 'commission of historians

9. Romania Jewish Community Website, "Hungarians, Gypsies, Albanians...Got Any Jews?" From the National and the Cotidianul newspapers, February 27, 2000, www.romanianjewish.org/en/antisemitism.

so that together we can investigate the historical truth and publish the facts regarding Holocaust-related events in Romania.'[10]

The government, which wants to become part of NATO and the European Union, did respond positively to this request and has established an international commission, headed by Professor Elie Wiesel and co-chaired by Dr. Radu Ioanid, Associate Director of the International Programs Division at the United States Holocaust Memorial Museum. The government has agreed to provide unconditional access to its archives, to accept the report of the scholarly commission, to publish the findings, to make the information available through the school systems, media, and other avenues of public education. To this date, they have removed one of the statues of Antonescu and have prevented four other municipalities from erecting new monuments.

After the Romanian documentary crew had interviewed me and left, I must admit to you that I felt a mixture of triumph and sadness. How ironic it is, I thought, that the Romanians are coming to me to close this tragic circle, and that I was asked to help them record this brutal part of history for the world. Let us hope that the commission will achieve its goals, and that the cancerous hatred of others will be removed from their country and from the world.

But we must concern ourselves with yet another circle. As my seminary teacher, *Lehrer* Shtern, used to say, let us imagine the entire Jewish nation contained within one circle. At the center of the circle is G-d and our Torah. Where are we, as a nation today? Where does the world put us and where do we put ourselves? Historically, when we have tried to break out of the circle, the nations of the world have thrust us, brutally, back inside.

The waves of violence that are crashing through the world now are the Divine wake-up calls for us to examine and clarify our priorities. When I read the admonitory parts of the book of Devarim, when I read the book of Eichah, I see bus bombings and Transnistria before my eyes. When the Arabs lynched

---

10. *Ibid.*, p. 9.

two of our soldiers in Jericho, I saw my friends butchered on the snow-covered fields of Transnistria. When the Twin Towers crumbled on 9/11, I saw the death camps blazing. When world opinion was predominantly opposed to Israel building a security fence against terrorism, I saw the world's indifference to the annihilation of the Jews in Europe. Is there a place in this world that is an island of sanity, sanctity, and security that is [far] away from the waves of violence, terror, and hatred that are currently crashing over the world?

Our Sages tell us that, '...The suffering of the children affected the *Shechinah* (Divine Presence) itself. When the *Sanhedrin* (Great Council of Judges) was exiled, the *Shechinah* did not go into exile with them; when the priestly watches were exiled, the *Shechinah* did not go into exile with them. But when the infants were exiled, the Shechinah went into exile with them.'[12]

As a nation, at this time in our history, are we not all, to some extent, like orphaned children? Who among us has not been touched by fear, by loss, by confused choices? Are we not walking on the path of humanity, asking ourselves what is going wrong? Why is there so much violence and horror exploding now in our world?

Yet, ultimately, all an individual has in his or her hands is the ability to choose how he will respond to his life circumstances. And so, in the midst of my suffering and despair, I chose faith, I chose G-d, I chose goodness, and I chose life. In the worst times of loneliness, when I was starving, freezing, covered with lice and filthy rags, walking barefoot in the winter forest of Transnistria, I felt Divinely guided in my choices. I believed in the G-d that my parents and older siblings had taught me to believe in. And as I clung to Him, I was somehow able to hold on to the image of the Divine within my soul, and to look for that spark of Divine goodness within others, even my persecutors.

I never hated or envied my enemies. I befriended a Ukrainian girl my age and taught her, thus providing food for

---

11. *London Jewish Tribune*, March 25, 2004.

my family. When I was in hiding, posing as a Ukrainian child working in a café, I saved crusts of bread from the plates of the *SS Einzatzgruppen* to feed to my friends in hiding. Years later, when I was free, and I saw a group of starving, ragged Nazi prisoners, I threw them the food I had in my hands. The nobility of my parents' upbringing would not allow my soul to rejoice in their misery. I felt only pity for the spirit of subhuman degradation that the choice of evil brings upon man, for the Nazis were more lowly than animals, who kill only when they need food. When we live up to the nobility of the Divine within our own souls, nothing can stop us from achieving our destinies — as individuals, as a people, and as an international community committed to democracy and goodness.

Thus, in the midst of my suffering, I came to learn that we are never alone. We are never lost, if only we do not lose ourselves. The vision of a world of goodness is not beyond our reach, if only we would reach into our hearts and spirits and commit to living more meaningful lives. Commitment to a goal transforms, and can enable us to go far, far beyond our self-conceived limitations.

When it came to authentic Judaism, the Nazis themselves knew the difference. Although they were determined to exterminate the entire Jewish race, they were occasionally subject to bribes, as long as the deal involved the more assimilated Jews from Western Europe. It was the religious Jews of Eastern Europe who posed the greatest threat to their vision. The Nazis knew that all it took was one *tzaddik*, one dedicated great rabbi, to escape across the ocean, and from this one person could come the rebuilding of the genuine Jewish world.

As Rabbi Gershon Weiss relates in his book *The Holocaust and Jewish Destiny*, 'The Nazis' aim was to uproot what they termed the "poisonous weed" of Jewish religious values. Correctly they perceived that the pious Jews of Eastern Europe were the chief carriers of those values. Thus, while willing to

---

12. *Me'am Lo'ez, Midrash Rabbah, Eichah*, The Book of Lamentations, p. 102.

cut deals under some circumstances to save the lives of the more assimilated Jews of Western Europe, they were never ready to allow the more Jewishly oriented "Yidden" of Eastern Europe to escape, lest the seeds of Judaism be replanted. A memorandum from the Third Reich's Office of Internal Security states this explicitly: "The immigration of Jews from Eastern Europe means the continuation of live Judaism. From the ranks of these Jews — due to their recognition of authentic Judaism — come most of the rabbis and teachers of Talmud, who are very much in demand by Jewish organizations, especially in the United States. They will constantly work to rejuvenate the Jewish spirit, to achieve a renaissance of Jewish civilization in any land to which they emigrate." (signed, I. A. Eckhardt).'[13]

I have learned to accept and to be grateful that my family has a remnant. I have learned to see the cup as half full and not half empty. As I look back at my tormented childhood and youth, I am ever so grateful to Hashem for all the good that came my way; for all the angels in human form to guide me, to become my role models, and for the ability to chose the proper path, the sum total of who I am.

When I was marked with a Yellow Star, and driven on the Death March, it was only because I was a Jew. Along with my life, the Nazis wanted to rob me of my faith, of the core of my inner dignity, of the noble values and morality of my childhood home. Thank G-d, the Nazis didn't succeed. I was determined, at the young age of nine and a half, that life without knowing who I [was] would have been unbearable.

During my struggle for survival, I was like a seed in the dark ground: cold, lonely, decomposing. I was in the process of total decay. In fact, if not for Heavenly intervention, I would have perished in the dark world of Transnistria.

Hashem's miraculous Hand plucked me out of the darkness, decay, and despair. After seven years of struggle to survive after survival, being brought to Canada, to the teachers' seminary, rays of light and hope engulfed my very being. This is where and when I began the process of rebirth. Graduating the Hebrew-Yiddish Teachers' Seminary empowered me to understand that the yellow star was a distinction that enabled me to choose to live a noble and meaningful life.

When I finally began teaching, I was given the means and shown the way to give back to Hashem. Every student I encountered became my free will offering to my people, to perpetuate the golden chain of Jewish continuity. And so, I endeavored to imbue all of my students with Jewish pride, Jewish values, kindness, and love for Jews and for the goodness in humanity.

I had to succeed not because I suffered, but in spite of the brutality that was inflicted on me. It is all a question of attitude…I had no choice. I had to rise above my lost childhood, by choosing to be worthy of my painful travails. I had to find within myself the capacity to rise above my cruel fate. I had to carve out success from each and every opportunity given to me. Thus I was paving the way for the Jewish home I was to establish as well as living a life of commitment to my family and to my community. The Yellow Star then became a badge of honor, of defiance, strength, and courage.

It took almost half a century of silence to prepare for this unique task of passing on the memory of survival, the remembrance of what a very advanced society did to us, a nation of innocent men, women, and children. We were a defenseless part of humanity, declared to be inhuman, and suitable only for total destruction.

Most of the time, resistance was impossible for moral reasons. Was it right to kill an SS German when, as a consequence, hundreds of our Jewish brethren would be executed in reprisals? Despair and hopelessness overpowered our so-called existence. Death was the only realistic redeemer of the victims on a Death March. All of Europe became a prison for us. There was nowhere to run. Every Jew and every community was abandoned without leadership, as the leaders were murdered. We had to face the

---

13. Weiss, Gershon, *The Holocaust and Jewish Destiny,* Introduction, p. XV,.

enemy in total isolation, as most of the free world looked on and did nothing. The backbone of our resistance was in choosing to remain human, despite our inhuman circumstances.

Nevertheless, we must know for a certainty that to respond to hatred with hatred is not the answer. It is not easy for me to go back to that terrible time and to share with you both the experiences that I had and the lessons that I learned from them. I do it for your sake, for the sake of Jewish continuity, and for humanity. I will not give you a message filled with hatred or bitterness. I want you never, never to hate, because hatred causes discordance between people. The other becomes the enemy, and before you know it, it facilitates murder. When someone says they hate you, believe them, and stay away from them. Hatred is a very contagious, disastrous disease. Don't even say, 'I hate to eat' something. Try to take that word out of your vocabulary. It's very, very important.

Our world is again being filled with hatred. Now they hate Israel because we have a home, and we have the moral right and ability to defend ourselves. Our enemies don't like that. They like it better when we cannot defend ourselves, or when, like in the Gulf War, we didn't strike back. When Israel does what any country would do in response to, G-d forbid, terrorist attacks, we are portrayed by the media as persecutors. But this abnormal response is G-d's way of reminding us that anti-Semitism is a Divine mandate. Its roots are ancient. The faces of the oppressors change with history, but somehow time bears witness to both our oppression and our eternality.

Hitler wanted to be able to tell the next generations of Germans, 'Once upon a time, there was a Jewish nation. I made sure to destroy them, to wipe them off the face of the earth.' How many people today would also like to tell that story?

But the question we are facing now is not about the Germans. It is about what you will be able to tell your grandchildren in twenty years' time. Will they become educated, proud Jews, flaming torches of the transmission of our eternal law, or will ignorance reduce them to ashes through addiction to the technological media that is burning out the minds of our youth?

I have spoken with you today not because I want you to believe that the world is evil. I want you to see that, despite evil, there are basic sparks of goodness in the world. It is up to us to build our lives in ways that recognize and embrace the goodness in people. The Torah is the universal blueprint of nobility for the world. If we allow ourselves to focus on hate and violence, we destroy the spark of G-dliness and nobility within ourselves.

If I had indulged in hatred and schemes of revenge, I would never have joined the worldwide community of those who want to build and restore humanity to its honorable achievements. At any given moment in time, all we have are the circumstances we find ourselves in, and our ability to choose how to respond to them. When, through the exercise of our intellect, we use our free will to make the noble choice, we become more human and we build a better world.

I am not proud to be a survivor. I am not proud to be a victim. I didn't choose to be a survivor, nor a victim. It was imposed on me. But you, my friends, can choose. You do not have to be victims. Not of your culture, not of your desires, and not of materialism or ignorance. You can, as the Torah says, *u'vacharta b'chaim*, choose life.

Now I must read to you the words of Elie Wiesel, from his 'Hidden Memories' speech, when he spoke, in 1991, to over one thousand child survivors in New York: 'For years and years, you and I have asked ourselves certain questions. Among them, the most important one: Why the children? Why has an entire regime, if not an entire people with some exceptions, mobilized its national energies and resources in hunting down Jewish children? Why were they the first to be marked and singled out, the first to suffer, the first to perish? Of all the crimes conceived in fanaticism, in hatred, the war against the Jewish children, I believe, will remain as the worst, the most vicious, the most implacable, in recorded history.

'My friends, as I prepared myself to meet with you...I went back into our collective memory and tried to find out who was the first hidden child in Jewish history. You may be surprised to learn his name: Moses.

'You see, there are precedents. You remember the first hidden baby was Moses. Moses, too, was abandoned by his parents simply because he was in danger, as were all other Jewish male children then. Moses was abandoned in order to save him. And one day, a gentile woman, a princess,...Batyah, the daughter of Pharaoh, went for a walk at the Nile River and heard a child weep. From the child's tears she understood, according to the Bible, that he was a Jewish child.

'Like our tormentors of antiquity we know now that Hitler's Germany made the Jewish child its principal target. In condemning our people to death, it sought to deprive us, as a people, of our right to a future and of our childhood memories. In forcing hunger and despair upon Jewish children, Hitler's Germany sought to eliminate laughter and joy from our entire lives.' [14]

And so I implore you, after you hear me, to become witnesses of the Shoah, now, and once we are gone. I implore you to pledge yourselves to live full, committed lives. To raise families where your children can be happy and laughter can be heard. For what brings more happiness than a child, a baby? Remember, the first Jewish child was called Yitzchak, which means 'laughter,' because he filled the home of Avraham and Sarah with laughter. I implore you to build communities wherein your children have a place to discover their proud heritage. The greatest gift a child receives is a thorough Jewish education with care, love, and devotion, for their own development, and for the future.

You owe it to the little children who, each and every one of them, perished alone in such a brutal fashion. We can't think of a million and a half. We have to think of one by one, one by one. As Wiesel continues in relation to the murdered children, 'How many Nobel Laureates were there among them? Some of them might have developed cures for cancer...Others might have written poems and composed music of such force that they would have sensitized multitudes to the evil of indifference and war. In allowing a million and more Jewish children to die, humankind inflicted suffering and punishment on itself as well.' Let us not allow ourselves to be unknowing victims. Let us fill ourselves with knowledge of our glorious yet painful history and only then will we be able to fulfill the commandment that every Jew has, *zachor v'al tishkach*, remember and never forget.

And here, Dr. Robert Krell, a hidden child survivor from Holland, appeals to us:

'Collect, collate, learn the stories of eyewitnesses. They must be told and re-told, if not to convince others of the unassailable truth, to serve as our collective memory that it should not happen again, to express our universality and humanism through Judaism. To search for another identity is a waste of precious time. There is nothing good and decent in any religion that you will not find by living as a Jew. Ensure that our children will know as much and more, much more than we do. Not primarily of the Holocaust but of our history...

'Some people have nothing better to do these days but to look after their bodies or their possessions or accumulate more money, without a sense of family or culture, without a sense of history or tradition. "I'm working so hard for my children. I'm doing this for my children," but they're depriving children of the most precious gift a parent can give them: Time.

'We cannot live a thousand lives but we must try to live one Jewish life completely and very, very well with our head up high.'[15] I want you to know that with all my suffering and my pain, if, G-d forbid, I had to go through it again, I would never want to be anything else but a Jew. I feel so sorry for the young people today who have to come to terms with their grandparents' participation in the Holocaust. Can you imagine what it must be like to discover those kinds of roots? And think of you. The further back you go, the prouder you will be.

14. Krell, p. 41.

When you're a person that has empathy you have empathy for whoever suffers. I remember the Kurds in '91 running away from Saddam Hussein. I was at home with pneumonia. I was crying as if it was I running away in the rain, barefoot. They were I and I was them. When I studied the Inquisition or the Crusades I had nightmares about it. Bosnia affected me deeply, deeply. And I'm horrified at how slow the world is in reacting to pain, to suffering.

About a month ago, I received a call from Aish HaTorah in England with the good news that they had a letter of approbation for me from the Rosh Yeshivah, R' Noach Weinberg, Shlita. A few days later, the next call from England left me in shock: Late Friday evening, June 18th, the Aish HaTorah outreach center in Hendon, England, was attacked by arsonists. *Baruch Hashem*, no one was hurt, although three fire engines were needed to get the blaze under control. The following morning, when Rabbi Naftali Schiff arrived for the nine o'clock Shabbos services, he was greeted by a police barricade. The officers allowed him into the charred and blackened synagogue, to lift the torn Torah scrolls off the floor.

In an address given by Rabbi Schiff at a gathering of solidarity, he described his response that Shabbos morning: 'The initial thoughts, through tears and trembling, were of my grandmother, who escaped from Germany in the 1930s, and of my other grandmother's family, who perished in the fiery hell of Auschwitz. Then, I literally got up from the floor, with the Torah scroll still in my hands, and was filled with a very different sensation. A feeling of strength, of determination, of pride, of resolution surged through me. Perhaps what these evil people did not know about us is that the Jewish response to adversity is to grow from it. To emerge stronger as a result. To stand taller and prouder than ever.

'That Torah scroll I was holding was ripped [at] next week's portion. The tear was right next to the curses of Bilaam, a man

---

15. *Ibid.*, p. 29.

who came 2,500 years ago to curse the Jewish people, but from his curse there came only blessing. "*Ma tovu ohalecha Yaakov, mishkenosecha, Yisrael* — How goodly are your tents, Jacob, your dwelling places, O Israel" (*Bamidbar* 24:5).

'The buildings of our people are dedicated to goodness, to kindness, to tolerance, to charity, to family, to understanding, to knowledge, to the building of a better world. That is what our building was and is dedicated to achieving.

'The exact same column of the Torah scroll also contains the verse, "A people that dwells alone" (*Bamidbar* 23:9). The only way to tackle anti-Semitism at its root is to remind ourselves what we stand for as individuals and as a people, inculcate it and teach it to the world. We gave the world monotheism, love your neighbor, charity, equality before the law, and being happy with your lot. We live in a world in which many of our own community are ignorant of and apathetic towards any of these or any other Jewish values.

'Let us today make a commitment to learn these lessons ourselves. Teach them to our children, and transform the Jewish people into what it can be for us and for all of mankind. Until we do this, there will be hatred, malice, and selfishness both in our community and beyond.'[16]

As I read Rabbi Schiff's words, I thought to myself, how can we accomplish this? How can we rebuild from the ashes of the past, and unfortunately, from the anti-Semitic fires of current attacks? We are the target of elements from both within and without, that are intent on destroying us. The words exposed from the ripped Torah scroll are our answer: '*Ma tovu ohalecha Yaakov, mishkenosecha Yisrael* — How goodly are your tents, Jacob, your dwelling places, O Israel.'

Our Sages tell us that when Bilaam saw the modesty, respect, and love embodied in the Jewish people, instead of cursing them, he exclaimed, 'Deserving is this people that the Divine Presence rest upon it!'[17] Bilaam saw the homes where, because of modesty and noble character, the Divine presence rests. He saw the houses of prayer, where prayers from sincere hearts can avert harsh decrees and bring blessing to our nation. Bilaam saw our houses of study where, 'Like gardens planted by the river are gathered the students of the academies in assemblies, their faces aglow with the light of the Torah... an external dwelling place for His *Shechinah* (Divine Presence) — will the Israelites also exist forever.'[18]

My mother commanded me: 'Live! Remember! Tell the world!' The first level of fulfillment of her words meant that I had to survive. After surviving, I then had to force myself to enter the crucible of my memory to become a living witness for the history of our people. Finally, I had to fortify myself so that I would be able to give voice to the horrors I had witnessed.

But I am sure that my mother, of blessed memory, did not mean for me to only tell the world about man's capacity for evil. That was not her purpose or goal. Rather, it was to tell about the evil so that we, who are commanded to strive for nobility, would be even more devoted and determined to fulfill our purpose which I entrust you with today: Live a Jewish life, remember your history, teach it to your children.

In order to accomplish this, we need houses of study, houses of prayer, and to build Jewish homes. For education alone is not enough. The Jewish home is our eternal victory. Building healthy families is our salvation. The family is the cornerstone of the transmission of faith, values, and history. It is the place where people are formed to learn to bring goodness and kindness into the world.

It is within the walls of the home where people, especially young people, first learn to govern their physicality by the ruling power of their intellect and soul. The home is an oasis of energy

---

16. Schiff, Naftali, "A Fire That Destroys, A Fire That Builds," Aish.com/jewish issuesjewishsociety, June 24, 2004.

17. *Me'am Lo'ez*, p.199, *Bamidbar*. 24:2,3, reference to *Bava Basra*, Chapter 3, Rashi.

18. *Me'am Loez*, p. 204.

flowing with love and creativity. It is the place where the inde-
structibility of the human spirit is born, nurtured, and blossoms.

When I stand before my audiences, the souls of thousands
of children whose lives were brutally cut short in Transnistria
stand with me. Yet with them also stand my parents, brothers,
and sisters, whose love and nurturing formed my spirit and
gave me my wellspring of inner light and faith to go on.

My seminary teachers who nurtured me and spurred me on
are with me always. Their dedication bound me to my people.
Their love empowered me with hope and perseverance. Although
they perished, the home that I carried within my heart was never
destroyed. It blossomed forth in my teaching, in my own home,
and the homes of my sons, their wives, and children.

As the last of our kind, we share something else in common. We are remnants. I am the remnant of my family, and the
remnant of an entire world in Europe that ceased to be. You are
the remnants of an ongoing silent Holocaust of assimilation. But
the enemies of assimilation are not the Nazis, the Romanian
gendarmes, or the Ukrainian soldiers. The enemies today are
lack of education, apathy, and indifference to our past.

But we will never escape from the lessons of history. We
will never become 'a nation like other nations.' Our destiny as
a people who live a G-dly life through the precepts of the Torah
awaits us. When we accept our Divine mandate, the banner of
nobility will once again be the emblem of the Jewish people.
The curses of our enemies will become blessings and we will
move forward in our role as a model for the world as 'a kingdom
of priests, and a holy nation.'

As I accompanied my mother on her midnight healing journeys, so too, the spirit of her nobility and goodness has accompanied me throughout my life. This legacy that I carry with
me does not begin and end with us. As my mother, of blessed
memory, took care of Jew and non-Jew alike, she taught us
that kindness and respect for humanity was the foremost ingre-
dient of noble character. The merit of her kindness saved me.

It is her legacy of righteousness that I have been privileged to bequeath to the world."

Epilogue

"Dear Leah"

pon my return from a recent trip to England, I shared the following about my speaking experience:

It's amazing: when I am standing in front of the audience, I don't exist.

Somehow we become one. Their future is my future. Their continuity is my continuity. I stand there glued to my place, and the words just come. The audiences are inspiring, frightening, and awesome. We join together in a bond that goes beyond any one of our individual selves. I feel as though Hashem, my family, and those children who perished so mercilessly stand right there beside me.

Here are excerpts, chosen from among thousands of response letters from an audience that consists of an international student body:

"I believe you have reached all of us in sharing such a difficult and personal story. You have done what the history books and documentaries never could; you have given us the ability to understand the Holocaust on a level which allows us to personally relate to it. Thank you for surviving and encouraging hope. Thank you for sharing such difficult experiences. Your history is all of ours." Josh Z. Bonder Birthright, Canada

"Your dignified account is life-affirming, G-d-affirming, and Judaism-affirming. The only improvement I can think of suggesting is to tell it more often to more people." L.W.

"Your talk filled every part of my soul with hope and inspiration...on so many levels filling me with information, love, hope for my growth as a Jew...Your story has the added dimension of pride in your Judaism and the message of the importance of the continuation of Jewish belief...Thank you from the bottom of my heart." Adam Logatto, University of Birmingham

"Every once in a while I hear a speaker who makes me look at myself and question my behavior and ask myself, 'What can I do to be a better person?' Thank you for being such a person. You have inspired me to go searching for ideas as to how I can contribute more to the Jewish community." Justin Chorin, London

"Your story...makes a fire burn inside me. I begin to want to fight with my words, my money, to save our people from a repetition of the Holocaust. How can we live...and pretend that everything is fine, like the Jews of Europe thought before the Holocaust? Your life is important to our survival as a people, and to future Jewish contribution to humanity." Jacob Weinstein, Cornell University

"Listening to you has been an honor. I am the last generation to have the opportunity of hearing the truth directly from not just a survivor, but an angel who survived to remind us of what is important, who we are, and where we came from. I hope I can be a messenger." P.W., Salford

"Thank you for coming. Your talk certainly impacted me. In your speech I was greatly affected when you said how your sister Devorah cried herself to death — that is my name, and hearing that made me realize that I could have been that child." D.H., Oxford University

"Soul-wrenching and inspirational. You have fulfilled your mother's wish more than can be expressed." Caroline Cross, London

"Hate and genocide continues to rear its ugly head. [sic.] It is so important for people like you to deliver your message to the world so that it may be passed on to generations to come. May our prayers for peace be answered." Rebecca Hoffberg, post-graduate student, LSE Human Rights Program

"No matter how hard it gets, you gave me the inspiration and strength to keep on believing and, most important, to pass on our gift which is the Torah and the pride of being Jewish." Daniel Kahan, Salford University

"To me, your talk was not merely a 'talk,' it was an enlightenment into my soul." Neil Taylor, Liverpool Hope University

"As a British Indian Muslim who grew up in Saudi Arabia, and went to an English boarding school, I had heard so many divergent sides of this terrible chapter in our world's history. Your talk cut straight to my heart, and I want to thank you for the honor of listening to you...I believe that your work will ensure that we will never forget, and never go back. Thank you once again." Shireen Ali, London School of Economics

"It was more than just something cultural. It was challenging. Leah is challenging in such a quiet, beautiful way. After she spoke, I asked her, 'What should we all be learning from the Holocaust?' Right away she said, 'You tell me.' I was shocked because I expected her to give me her own opinion, but she brought me right into a direct confrontation with my own existence. In this present moment, what did the Holocaust mean to my life? I knew that an authentic response meant that my relationship with my own Jewish identity was at stake." Kim Benjamin, seminary student, Jerusalem

"Your speech tonight has rekindled the flame inside of me to remember and never forget our history, the history of our people. I thank G-d that you are here today, to educate and spread the love you have for all of us. I am utterly amazed and inspired by your life, your resilience and your ability to enlighten, teach, and love those around you. Thank you again." Leah Manning, Hebrew University

"Having witnessed you deliver speeches to thousands of Birthright Israel participants who have made their way to Israel from Canada over the last five years, I can attest to the tremendous impact that your story has had on so many lives. I have learned from the participants who have had the privilege of hearing from you that your story is not only compelling due to your astounding survival in the face of unimaginable horror, but because of the triumphant way in which you have chosen to build with your life.

"In today's modern world of quick-fixes, fast food, and heavy emphasis on materialism, the search for meaning is taking on a fresh significance in the lives of young people. Your story addresses this significance by demonstrating a life of dedication that speaks volumes about the notion of living a meaningful life. I am therefore so pleased to hear about the publishing of your book so that your message can continue to be accurately spread beyond those who have heard it from you personally, as well as those who undoubtedly heard it passed along from them.

"I wish you all the best in your future endeavors, and I look forward to the next opportunity of witnessing evidence of the profound impact of your message." Justin Korda, Canada Israel Experience

BIBLIOGRAPHY

Ancel, Jean, *Transnistria, The Rumanian Mass Murder Campaigns, Volume One, History and Document Summaries,* (2003) Jerusalem, Israel, The Goldstein-Goren Diaspora Research Center, Tel Aviv University

Ancel, Jean, *Tolodot Hashoah Romania* (2002), Yad Vashem, Jerusalem

Artscroll *Chumash, The Stone Edition* (1993), general editors, Rabbi Nosson Scherman/Rabbi Meir Zlotowitz, Mesorah Publications, New York

Bachrach, Yifat "Romania: The Journey to Truth," *Yad Vashem Quarterly,* Vol. 32, p. 8 Winter, 2004

Ben-Chaim, Tzvia, Personal interview about her family history, and the Theresienstadt Concentration Camp, Har Nof, Jerusalem, 2004

Bokser, Howard, "Witness To War," Reprinted from *McGill News,* Fall 1995 Issue, Living Testimonies Website, http://ww2. mcgill.ca/alumni/news/f95/2.htm

Butnaru, I. C. *The Silent Holocaust: Romania and Its Jews (Contributions to the Study of World History)* (1992), Forward by Eli Wiesel, Greenwood Publishing Group, New York

Carmelly, Felicia, *Shattered! 50 Years of Silence, History and Voices of The Tragedy in Rumania and Transnistria,* (undated) Scarborough, Ontario, Canada, Abbeyfield Publishers

Carmelly, *The Nizkor Project,* www.nizkor.org

Charter of the French Language, English Section, courtesy of The Quebec Office of The French Language, Government of Quebec, 2002

Dalia Ofer, "The Holocaust in Transnistria, A Special Case of Genocide" pp. 133-154, Sharpe, M.e. Inc. New York

Dobroszycki, Lucjan (Ed.) & Gurock, Jeffrey S. (Ed.) *The Holocaust In the Soviet Union: Studies and Sources on the Destruction of the Jews in Nazi- Occupied Territories of the U.S.S.R. 1941-1945* (1993)

Eisenhower, General Dwight D., letter to General George C. Marshall 15 April 1945, Box 80, "Marshall, George (6)" DDE to Marshall, Eisenhower Library. As seen in the United States Holocaust Memorial Museum

Fisher, Julius S., *Transnistria, The Forgotten Cemetery* (1969), Thomas Yoseloff Publisher, Cranbury, New Jersey

Fishman, Gele, Personal Interview on the Hebrew Yiddish Teachers Seminary August 2003, Riverdale, New York

Gilbert, Martin *The Holocaust, The Jewish Tragedy*, (1986) Fontana/Collins, Great Britain

Harel, Israel, "We Are All In The Same Boat," *Ha'aretz*, May 27, 2004, Courtesy of Am Echad, Jewish Media Resources shafran@amechad.com.

Hilberg, Raul (1985), *Destruction of the European Jews*, Holmes & Meier Publishers, Inc. Chicago

Ioanid, Radu, *The Holocaust In Rumania: The Destruction of Jews and Gypsies Under the Antonescu Regime, 1940-1944,* (2000), Ivan R. Dee, Inc. Chicago. Published in association with The United States Holocaust Memorial Museum.

I Never Saw Another Butterfly: Children's Drawings and Poems from Terezin Concentration Camp, 1942-1944 (1978), Schocken Books, New York

Katz, Marco Maximilian, "Anti-Semitism in Romania," 2002 Report, The Center For Monitoring and Combating Anti-Semitism in Romania, www.antisemitism.ro

Kosinski, Jerzy, *The Painted Bird* (1965, 1976), Grove Atlantic Inc., NY, NY

Krell, Robert (Ed.), *Messages and Memories: Reflections on Child Survivors of the Holocaust* (1999), Memory Press Vancouver, BC

Lindeman, Yehudi, *Living Testimonies* at McGill University, the Department of English and the faculties of Arts and Graduate Studies and Research, http://ww2.mcgill.ca/alumni/news/f95/2.htm

Lookstein, Haskel, *Were We Our Brother's Keepers? The Public Response of American Jews to the Holocaust 1938-1944*, (1985), Vintage Books, Random House, New York

Luel, Steven A, and Marcus, Paul, *Psychoanalytic Reflections on the Holocaust: Selected Essays*, Hoppe (1984), Klaus D., "Severed Ties" pp. 94-111, Holocaust Awareness Institute Center For Judaic Studies, University of Denver, and Ktav Publishing House, Inc. New York

Magriso, Yitzchak, *MeAm Loez* (1764), Constantinople Book Fourteen, Final Wanderings, Translated by Dr. Tzvi Faier, Edited and with Notes by Rabbi Aryeh Kaplan (1991) Moznaim Publishing Corporation, New York/Jerusalem

Martz, Fraidie *Open Your Hearts, The Story of the Jewish War Orphans in Canada* (1966), Vehicule Press Montreal, Quebec, Canada

Medoff, Rafael, "The Man Who Wanted To Bomb Auschwitz," *Jerusalem Post*, Online edition, July 7, 2004 http://www.jpost.com/

Medwed, Sheina (1998) "Bubbie, Tell Me Your Life," in *A Mother's Favorite Stories*, Mesorah/Artscroll, pp. 241-252, Brooklyn, New York

Moses, Alfred, *Testimony for Parliamentary Forum: Combating anti-Semitism in the OSCE Region*, Commission on Security and Cooperation in Europe, December 10, 2002 http://www.csce.gov/witness.

Moskovitz, Sarah *Love Despite Hate: Child Survivors of the Holocaust and Their Adult Lives* (1983). Schocken Books, New York

Prutschi, Manuel, *Holocaust Denial Today*, http://www.nizkor.org/ftp.cgi/orgs/canadian/canadian-jewish-congress/holo-caust-denial-today

Romania Jewish Community Website, "Hungarians Gipsies, Albanians...Got Any Jews?" From the *National* and the *Cotidianul* newspapers, February 27, 2000, www.romanian-jewish.org/en/antisemitism

Rosenblum, Jonathan, "Remembering the Past to Preserve the Future," *Jerusalem Post*, April, 2, 2004

The Black Hole of Jewish Identity, *London Jewish Tribune*, 25 March, 2004 courtesy of Am Echad) shafran@amechad.com

Safran, Rabbi Alexander, *Resisting The Storm, Rumania, 1940-1947* (1987), Memoirs, Yad Vashem, Daf Noy Press, Jerusalem

Schiff, Naftali, "A Fire That Destroys, A Fire That Builds," Aish.com/jewishissuesjewishsociety, June 24, 2004

Shachan, Avigdor *Burning Ice: The Ghettos of Transistria* (1996) Translated by Dr. Shmuel Himelstein, East European Monographics Number 447 USA, Columbia University Press

Shafir, Michael, "Selective Negationism of the Holocaust in East-Central Europe: The Case of Romania" ('ATAC,' No. 19/2002) : www.rfel.org

Tamler, Gisela, *Before and After, Surviving The Romanian Holocaust* (2003), The Canadian Institute For Jewish Research, Canada

Weiss, Rabbi Gershon, *The Holocaust and Jewish Destiny* (1999), Targum Press, Michigan

Wikipedia, The Free Encyclopedia, http://en.wikpedia.org./wiki/ Front de Liberation du Quebec

Williamson, David (2001), Audiotape interview with Leah Kaufman, Jerusalem, Israel

Wistrich, Robert S., "Muslim Anti-Semitism, A Clear and Present Danger," "Islamic Fascism": Ominous Parallels in Light of September 11, AJC Publication, wwwajc.org

Yerushalmi, Rabbi Shmuel, (1986) *Me'am Loez, The Book of Eicha*, Translated and adapted by Rabbi Eliyahu Touger Moznaim Publishing Corporation Publishing, New York, Jerusalem

Videos:

Transnistria Plaque Dedication, Montreal Holocaust Memorial Center, October 29, 1995

"A Hell Called Transnistria," Yad Vashem Archives